Psychology of Language

A Critical Introduction

MICHAEL A. FORRESTER

SAGE Publications
London • Thousand Oaks • New Delhi

SAGE Publications Ltd
6 Bonhill Street
London EC2A 4PU

SAGE Publications Inc
2455 Teller Road
Thousand Oaks, California 91320

SAGE Publications India Pvt Ltd
32, M-Block Market
Greater Kailash – I
New Delhi 110 048

British Library Cataloguing in Publication data

A catalogue record for this book is available from the British Library.

ISBN 0 8039 7990 8
ISBN 0 8039 7991 6 (pbk)

Library of Congress catalog record available

Typeset by Mayhew Typesetting, Rhayader, Powys
Printed in Great Britain by The Cromwell Press Ltd,
Broughton Gifford, Melksham, Wiltshire

Contents

Acknowledgements   viii

1 Introduction   1
The study of language in different disciplines   3
Influences on the emergence of psycholinguistics   5
A cognitive account of language processing   12
The aim of this book: extending the scope of the psychology of
language   15

2 Language Structure and the Significance of Recursion   18
Cognitive representations of grammar   19
Psychology and language: the relationship between theory,
data and explanation   25
The cognition-dominant view   26
    Cognitive science and methodological solipsism   28
The language-dominant view   32
Summary   36

3 Semantics: The Concept of Meaning   38
Semiotic definitions of meaning   39
Philosophical underpinnings of psychological theories of
meaning   40
Five approaches to indirect meaning   42
    Meaning as reference   42
    Meaning as logical form   43
    Meaning as context and use   45
    Meaning as conceptual structure   47
    Meaning as culture   48
    Post-script to an overview of theories of indirect meaning   48
Implicature and the co-operative principle   50
Speech act theory   52
Pragmatics   54
Summary comments on the nature of meaning   56

4 Deixis: The Interface between Language and Social Interaction   58
Deixis   59
Deictic comprehension and conceptualising the deictic centre   61

Person deixis   63
Place, space deixis   64
Time deixis   66
Discourse deixis   68
Social honorifics   70
The acquisition of deictic terms   74
Deixis and the conversational context   76

5 **Conversational Analysis and Accountability in Everyday Talk**   78
Prospects for the study of non-verbal behaviour   81
Visible activity in talk: the significance of non-verbal
behaviour in communication   82
    Visible activity in talk: gesture   82
    Visible activity in talk: proxemics   83
    Visible activity in talk: gaze   85
    Visible activity in talk: touch and body contact   86
    Visible activity in talk: posture and body orientation   87
    Visible activity in talk: facial expression   88
Summarising the distinctions between non-verbal behaviour
and non-verbal communication   90
Methodology in language research   91

6 **Processes and Procedures in Conversational Interaction**   95
Mechanisms and procedures within conversation: adjacency
pairs   98
Closing sequences: how to end a conversation   101
Turn-taking and interruption   103
Topic selection, narrative and topic change in conversation   105
The role of the hearer in conversation   108
The predictability and projectibility of talk: affordances in
conversation   109
Concluding comments   112

7 **Power Relations in Language**   115
Power in conversational contexts   115
Power and role relations in language   119
Talk and text: expressing power in different discursive domains   123
Power relations in language: texts, discourses and ideology   125
Concluding comments   129

8 **Sign-Systems and Social Semiotics**   131
Signification process and sign-system production   134
Ideology and social semiotics   136
Peircean semiotics   138
Applied social semiotics: photography   140
Applied social semiotics: interface design   142

Applied social semiotics: film 145
Concluding comments 149

9 The Role of the Reader in Text Interpretation 150
Psychological approaches to the study of reading 150
Eye-movements and reading processes 152
Psychological models of reading 154
  'Bottom-up' models 155
  'Top-down' models 156
  Interactive or schema-theoretic models 158
  Summary of cognitive approaches to reading 160
Reading as a skill and strategies of reading 160
Critical theory and reading 161
Concluding comments 164

10 Writing and the Construction of Narrative Text 166
Investigating writing by studying the development of writing
skills 169
Cognitive models of writing 172
Narrative and writing 174
Hypertext, hypermedia and the author–reader relationship 176
Concluding comments 182

**11 Postmodern Psychology and Language: Discourse Analysis and
Social Psychology** 184
Postmodernism and postmodern psychology 185
Discourse analysis and social psychology: language as social
action 188
The social context of memory: a primary site of dispute
between cognitive psychologists and discourse analysts 191
Prospects for a postmodern psychology of language 192

References 197

Index 211

Acknowledgements

Grateful acknowledgement is given to the following for permission to reproduce quotations and figures: to Cambridge University Press for the Levinson extract on page 62; to Elsevier Science for figure 4.1 on page 65; Macmillan Press for the Tagg extract on page 140; ©Apple Computer Inc. 1990. Used with permission. Apple® and the Apple logo are registered trademarks of Apple Computer Inc. All Rights Reserved; for the figure on page 144; MIT Press for the Stitch extract on page 30; Prentice-Hall for the Sinha quote on page 27; Manchester University Press for the extract on page 146, and Blackwell Publishers for the figure and extract on page 133. I would also like to thank Steve Bell for permission to reproduce the cartoon on page 195, David Reason for his contribution to Chapter 8, and Silvia Sbaraini for innumerable helpful comments.

1

Introduction

It is difficult to imagine what life would be like without language. Even if we could visualise such a state of affairs, our imaginations and thoughts would themselves depend upon the language we are brought up with. For most of us, we think in the language we learn as children, and in some curious way it could be said that our thoughts are not truly 'our own'. In other words, although each of us has a unique way of putting together the sounds we know in order to carry out the innumerable activities which depend on the use of language, we need to remind ourselves that the forms, structures, rules and parameters of that language exist before we are born. Using language in everyday contexts is, for most of us, similar to using our bodies – we don't think about it unless we have to – and we rarely remember how we learned to do so in the first place. However, if we wish to understand human psychology, then the study of mental life and human action would be incomplete, if not impossible, without a knowledge of the relationship between language and psychological processes. One aim of this book is to provide a broad view of the study of language, with particular emphasis on identifying important relationships between language and human psychological processes.

Our everyday understanding and use of the word 'language' can lead to a certain amount of confusion where our concern is with the psychology of language. When we say that somebody has a very distinct body language, we are probably referring to the fact that he/she uses particular arm or facial gestures when talking to us. Again, where we describe somebody as a good communicator, we are likely thinking of the way he/she speaks. The word 'language' derives from the Latin *lingua*, meaning tongue, and Harris (1989) reminds us that 'it was the invention of writing that made speech *speech* and language *language*' (p. 99). This quote should help remind us that there are a number of important differences between the words 'language' and 'communication'. Consider examples of how the words are defined in the *Oxford English Dictionary*,

> *language*: a system of human communication using words, written and spoken, and particular ways of combining them; any such system employed by a community, nation, etc.

> *communication*: the transmission or exchange of information; making or maintaining of social contact, conveying or exchanging information; succeeding in evoking understanding.

There is considerable difference between the systematic, structural and rule-governed phenomenon called language and a quite different behaviour altogether, communicating (talk, speech, sound, gesture, and so on). Communicating can clearly take many forms (textual, audio, visual, kinaesthetic), and it will be important in the following chapters not to lose sight of key distinctions between communication and language. The latter can be subsumed within the former, as in one commonly used definition of communication theory, 'the branch of knowledge which deals with language *and other means* of conveying or exchanging information' (OED – my italics). At the same time language can find expression in a variety of 'de-contextualised' forms (loosened from the constraints of immediate participative contexts), where it is not always clear what the originating communicator intended to convey. One only has to consider the difficulties philologists of ancient Egyptian or Armenian have in interpreting obscure texts, or the continuing criticism and debate over interpretations of James Joyce's *Ulysses* or *Finnegans Wake*.

This book aims to cover in detail three forms of communication which have particular significance for a psychology of language: self-communication (or thinking); talk – where the emphasis is upon everyday conversation; and text, including the study of reading and writing. Throughout, what will be of central significance is understanding how the many and diverse areas of language study contribute to a psychology of language concerned with communication processes. There is clearly more than one 'system of communication' or form of language available to us when we are attempting to 'evoke an understanding', i.e. communicate, and we will be considering the many forms such systems can take.

Understanding how language bears upon communicative processes, broadly conceived, requires that we move beyond the commonly observed boundaries of the psycholinguistics textbook. There are important historical and institutional reasons why psycholinguistics has tended to emphasise certain aspects of language (particularly the formal-structural ones) at the expense of others. During the late 1960s and 1970s, the bringing together of descriptive linguistics with the experimental methodology of psychology resulted in a creative and mutually beneficial antidote to the rather stilted conservatism of late behaviourism. However, the emergence of psycho-linguistics glossed over or ignored many areas of language, some of which should be of considerable interest to the psychology student. Such topics as conversational analysis, social semiotics, deixis, power relations in talk, narrative analysis, and so on, can be found in domains which border psychology (e.g. sociology). Often, however, relevant approaches to the study of language are found in more distant disciplines (e.g. literary criticism). Part of the reason for this is that post-war psychology was particularly sensitive to the accusation that it was not a proper scientific discipline, and thus it tended to avoid disciplines which employed non-scientific methods of academic inquiry. We will go on to discuss the relationship between methodology and the study of language in due course.

For the present, and at some risk of oversimplification, an overview of those disciplines which study language (and their related sub-branches) would help inform what is to follow.

The study of language in different disciplines

Given the central significance of language as a human activity, there are many academic disciplines which have an interest in the study of language, and for several different reasons. Speech therapists study language because they want to know how best to assist people who display some difficulty in communicating; computer scientists study language because they wish to build artificial intelligence systems that can communicate with us; neuroscientists study language because they want to understand those parts of the brain with a causal/physical role in language comprehension and production. And of course, within the humanities, the study of language is interdependent with our cultural outlook, in addition to its primary aim as part of a humanities education: i.e. critical analysis through textual comparison (in whatever form).

One way to gain an overview of the primary subject areas with an interest in language is to consider the variety of disciplines found within the four faculty areas commonly found in institutes of higher education (see Figure 1.1). The first thing to note is that at least one subject area within each faculty has the word 'linguistics' attached to it (except of course in humanities, where linguistics itself is to be found), reflecting the considerable influence linguistics has had on emerging sub-disciplines such as sociolinguistics, computational linguistics and psycholinguistics. Linguistics is generally defined as the scientific study of language, and linguists are primarily concerned with the description and explanation of the formal structure of language. We will go on to consider how historical developments within linguistics have influenced the three themes of this book – thinking, talk and text.

Within the social sciences, language studies are to be found in social anthropology, the social psychology of language and sociolinguistics. Social anthropologists are interested in understanding how different cultures use language in order to classify and categorise their experience of the world, and a sub-branch of the discipline is known as linguistic anthropology (Hickerson, 1980). Sociolinguists examine the association between language and society. Their primary concern is with the social function of language and they examine how factors such as gender, environment, social class, upbringing, and so on, influence the way we use language. Social psychologists study the ways in which individuals are influenced by, and in turn influence, their membership of different groups. For them, questions about language have to be answered with respect to issues such as personal and social identity, social categorisation and power relations between people.

Information technology, and in particular the various branches of

Social science

Sociolinguistics
Social psychology of language
Social anthropology

Humanities

English studies/
Literary criticism
Linguistics
Philosophy of language

Information technology

Computational linguistics
Artificial intelligence
Hypermedia/hypertext

Natural science

Psycholinguistics
Neuroscience

Figure 1.1   *Subject areas which study language*

computer science, also have a growing interest in language. Computational linguistics is concerned with the description and explanation of formal languages (natural and purely symbolic languages). Trask (1993) notes that the term now covers a very broad range of activities, all involving computers. These include machine translation of natural language texts, computer searching of texts and the construction of large concordances of literary works. One example of this is what is now known as hypermedia and hypertext. This area examines the possibilities and problems associated with having an infinitely large number of texts (including video and sound-clip 'texts') available on computer which can be linked together in a multitude of different ways. Within computer science, the field known as artificial intelligence (AI) has had the greatest interest in the study of language. Attempting to construct intelligent systems which could communicate called for modelling of knowledge processes and procedures, including human thinking. Researches in AI were particularly influenced by the developments in linguistics which followed the publication of Noam Chomsky's (1957) work on grammar. Providing a mathematically precise way in which to describe and formalise language created considerable enthusiasm within the research community which continues to the present.

The post-Chomskian revolution in linguistics also gave rise to the emergence of psycholinguistics. By bringing together the methodological approach of experimental psychology and the descriptive formalism made available by Chomsky's proposals about the nature of grammar, a whole new range of topics were opened up for study. Psycholinguistics continues to have considerable interest in how people understand words and sentences, their knowledge of sentence construction, their comprehension of metaphors and numerous other topics. We will go on to look at the historical development of psycholinguistics in more detail below. For now, we can note an increasing interest in study of language from other areas of the natural sciences. Neuroscientists and neuropsychologists, for example, attempt to map out those areas of the brain which underpin language processing. Given the central hypothesis of neuroscience, i.e. the brain is the source of behaviour, research which identified areas of the brain responsible for language contributed significantly to the emergence of neuropsychology as a distinct research field. Technological advances in the area are interdependent with the progress of theory and method, and the more recent enthusiasm for the study of language processing is due in part to the development of brain scan procedures (such as CT and PET[1]). This makes it possible to study in detail brain activity during language comprehension and production.

It hardly needs to be said that within the humanities there are many areas where the study of language has a long tradition. Aristotle and Plato discussed and debated sentence structure, propositions and the nature of metaphor. Theology and religious studies contain many instances where influential writers and commentators turn their attention to the nature of language. Throughout history, different cultures have sought to understand the relationship between myth, ideas and language as cultural anthropology and psychoanalytic studies have demonstrated. Many key religious propositions have a pronounced reliance on beliefs about the divine nature of language. And of course, debate and controversy regarding the importance of language can be found in many contemporary fields within the humanities (e.g. certain schools of philosophy propose that a philosophical critique of *any* kind, is first and foremost a critique of language).

Language as the object of study is, of course, central to English and other languages as academic subjects. English studies and literary criticism rest upon a detailed and continuing critical commentary on language and the texts which make up its subject matter. Literary criticism in particular has had considerable influence on ideas surrounding authorship, the role of the reader in text comprehension, narrative models, the social conventions which bear upon the act of writing, and so on. Such studies also have a significant bearing on cultural developments more generally, for example where academic debates and commentary over postmodernism, deconstruction and post-structuralism find expression in our everyday experience of language – attention to criteria underpinning the language of 'political correctness'.

Influences on the emergence of psycholinguistics

There is little doubt, however, that the formal study of language within the humanities is primarily the domain of linguistics. One way to better understand the significance of linguistics for the psychology of language is through a consideration of its primary historical developments. This is summarised in Figure 1.2. This figure can be used as a kind of navigational

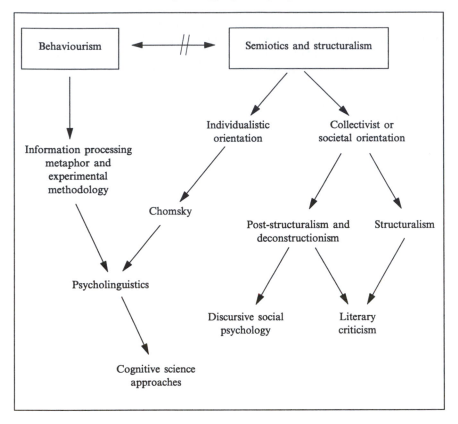

Figure 1.2 *Different theoretical strands in the psychology of language*

aid in our efforts at identifying the underlying influences on any given approach to the study of language. One thing which should be clear by this point is that one of the greatest difficulties for the student of language is understanding why there are so many different approaches in the first place. Another difficulty, particularly for the psychology of language student, is understanding why a neuropsychologist's approach to the study of language seems to be nothing like that of the developmental psycholinguist (somebody studying the acquisition of language in children). Again the psychologist interested in understanding how people comprehend extended texts will use theories and methods quite distinct from the conversational analyst who wants to know how people manage their conversational interchanges (everyday talk). These are some of the issues which this book seeks to address; for the present, it is important to gain some familiarity with the theoretical ideas which inform contemporary psycholinguistics, as well as understanding why some topics remain somewhat marginalised.

Psychology had originally emerged as a discipline which to some extent crossed the divide between science and the humanities. However, by the

1940s it was clear that without a firm commitment to scientific principles, there would be little progression and development. The study of behaviour or behaviourism provided a means whereby the appropriate methods and procedure of science could be applied to the study of human beings and their activities. The goal was the development of *nomothetic* theories of generalised human behaviour, rather than *idiographic* explanations of the behaviours of specific individuals. In fact, the concern with the establishment of the discipline as a science, combined with the scepticism about earlier ideas regarding the nature of the mind (e.g. what was known as introspection), gave rise to the view that 'mentalistic' questions (e.g. what it might mean to have an internal image in your head) were viewed as very suspect. If a psychologist at that time was to use the word 'mind', he/she would have been considered as either improperly trained or maybe even a little demented. Behaviourism was the dominant theme up until the late 1960s.

A behaviourist approach to language was primarily concerned with function. The kind of question a behaviourist would ask would be: what is being accomplished with the use of particular words in specific circumstances? The answers to such questions were to be sought in the relationship between the responses 'called out' by exposure to the particular stimulus involved. The essential nature of this approach is summarised by Skinner (1957) in his book *Verbal Behavior*. A popular account of this view of language would propose that, as children, over time we learn to respond (make a sound) in an appropriate way, because any noise attempts we make which sound anything like real words are reinforced, i.e. we gain a pleasurable reward through the positive responses others direct to us on hearing these noises. Commentators have noted that there are certain correspondences between this approach and the 'taxonomic' developments within descriptive linguistics during the 1940s and 1950s. Sturrock (1986), discussing behaviourism, reminds us that 'language was a certain kind of physical event in the world, a response to stimuli from the environment, and its structures, accordingly, were all on the surface, being the sum total of all known grammatical practices' (pp. 7–8).

However (and see Figure 1.2), in contrast to the behaviourist approach to language, from the 1920s onwards, in both Europe and the United States, as a central part of the movement that became known as structuralism, linguists began to move their attention away from the description of different languages, which had dominated their activities throughout the nineteenth and early twentieth century, towards a *theory of language*. Ferdinand de Saussure, who is often looked on as the patron of structuralism, was interested in uncovering the structural nature of language, in other words he was seeking to articulate what was *constant* in all languages. Structuralism, as a definition, is used both as a description of an influential intellectual movement and as a specific set of ideas which can be utilised in a diverse number of disciplines (e.g. history, literary criticism, philosophy). The definition of a language offered by a Saussurean structuralist would be that it is a system formed of linguistic signs. And semiotics, as the science of signs, would include language as one of many different possible sign-systems (see Sturrock, 1986, for a valuable introduction to structuralism).

A structuralist would point out that there are at least two ways to study language, a diachronic approach, which involves the study of the evolution of language over time, and a synchronic approach, which involves a static structural analysis – an examination of linguistic facts in a single system. Structuralism is really concerned with the synchronic view. The earlier work by descriptive linguists and linguistic anthropologists had provided sufficient evidence for the formulation of a synchronic 'theory of language'. Saussure was fundamentally concerned with the semiotic analysis of language as a sign-system, and one of the first important distinctions he formulated was between *langue* (language) and *parole* (the speech or written event). The first is an abstract theoretical system, the second the actual concrete event. The first is system, the second practice. But you cannot have one without the other, and what is critical in understanding *the process and principles of signification* is the production and comprehension of recognisable signs.

Every word is a sign, and the sign has both a *phonetic* or *acoustic* element (if you like, a sound aspect, but note written signs would not necessarily have to be sounded out or pronounced) and a *meaning* element. Saussure used the term 'signifier' for the first and 'signified' for the second, but he was always at great pains to stress that in recognising or producing a sign, the elements are indissoluble. It is also very important to recognise that the term 'signified', or the meaning element, has nothing to do with what philosophers of language call the 'referent'. When you ask a child what the word 'cow' means, and you are lucky enough to be out in the countryside at the time, then she will quite understandably point to one nearby. However, a structuralist would remind you that although the word (sign) 'cow' may have many different signifiers (cow in English, *vache* in French, *kuh* in German), this does not mean that it has a common signified. The signified of 'cow' is to be found in the collective consciousness of the English-speaking community, the signified of *vache* in the collective consciousness of the French speaking community, and so on. And none of these signifieds is to be found standing in a field. This is not an easy idea to keep a hold of, as we are particularly susceptible to confusing signified with real objects in the world (their referents). Such correspondence might be possible if language consisted of only nouns and verbs, but you only have to think of the difficulties of pointing to a 'perhaps' or an 'although' to see why the comprehension of signs is not as simple as it might first appear.

Saussure took as his originating object of semiological enquiry the word. He went to considerable lengths to show that the recognition and status of any sign, as sign, was only with reference to the whole system of which it was one element or part. In contrast, the influential linguist Chomsky took the sentence to be the key structural aspect of language. For Saussure, signification processes were essentially collective; linguistic structures and their meaning pre-existed any specific individual, and 'signifieds' (the conceptual element of this abstract sign-system) were part of the human collective consciousness. For Chomsky, meanings were individual competencies, part of any human being's genetic inheritance. He argued that children had to be genetically endowed with the ability to comprehend and produce language. Significantly for psychology, he also wrote a thorough, and damning, critique of Skinner's book *Verbal Behavior* (Chomsky, 1959), and during the same period provided a mathematically rigorous outline of language competence which, he argued, could explain the inherent creativity of children's language abilities (Chomsky, 1957).

Two quite distinct accounts of language emerged from structuralism. One emphasised the role of society and has an essentially collectivist orientation (social semiotics). The other, and one which had considerably more influence on psychology during the 1960s and 1970s, was distinctly individualistic (leading to the emergence of a distinct psycholinguistics). There were other important factors which bear upon the emergence of psycholinguistics. Experimental work within what had been known as 'verbal learning' (now memory research) implicated the existence of more than one kind of memory, which was simply anathema to the behaviourist approach, which eschewed any serious consideration of mental states (Postman, 1961). At the same time, psychologists were beginning to borrow metaphors and ideas from information theory and were proposing theories of human information processing (Lindsay & Norman, 1972). And although this new cognitive psychology inherited the operational methodology of behaviourism, it had a much closer kinship to Chomsky's proposal that language competence should be considered as the internal manipulation of symbols.

The coming together of Chomsky's theories of grammatical competence with the experimental procedures and methods of experimental psychology produced an enthusiastic flurry of new studies into language comprehension (see Garnham, 1985, for a review). There is little doubt that the birth of psycholinguistics as a new branch of the discipline is interdependent with the publication of Chomsky's (1957) book *Syntactic Structures*. We will go on to consider Chomsky's ideas in more detail in the next chapter; for now it is important to recognise that cognitive psychologists hold to the principle that human cognition is essentially concerned with the internal manipulation of symbols (mental states, propositions, and so on). Arguably, many post-Chomskian linguists share the same views, and both these disciplines have a significant influence on what is now known as cognitive science. Cognitive science is a collocation of different subjects (artificial intelligence, cognitive psychology, linguistics, neuropsychology and the neurosciences, philosophy and social anthropology) which all share a commitment to understanding symbol-manipulating systems, human and artificial. The research programme has been described as a formally complete understanding of the nature of human mental processes [where the fundamental premise] is that human behaviour is rule governed and generative. That is to say, algorithmic rules intervene between different stages in coding processes in order to permit goal-directed problem solving. (Sinha, 1988, p. 115)

Returning to Figure 1.2, in parallel to the developments within psychology, during the 1960s and 1970s structuralism and semiotics were having a significant influence on disciplines outside psychology. In social anthropology, the work of Lévi-Strauss (1963) illustrated how a structural analysis could be applied to the study of myth and folklore. In history, structural analysis was employed by Braudel and became known as structural historiography. Rather than concentrating on events, a structuralist historian looks for 'the system within which events happened and by reference to which their historical value may be assessed' (Sturrock, 1986, p. 59). Within philosophy structuralist and post-structuralist ideas and theories have come to dominate 'Continental' philosophy (Descombes, 1986). And within cultural criticism, debates surrounding post-structuralist and 'deconstructionist' ideas have generated considerable interest in the media and the quality press.

Some of the reason for this interest stems from the radical nature of the propositions being discussed. Post-structuralists such as Derrida (1977) argued that Saussure, although providing the necessary tools for the structural analysis of language, did not take the programme far enough. Derrida, as a philosopher of language, took the view that the Saussurean critique and analysis of language provided the means to dispel some long-cherished and 'idealist' views about the nature of thought and language. Derrida's accusation was that Western philosophy since Plato and Aristotle presupposed the existence of a realm of 'meaning' underpinning language. For Derrida, this is simply wrong; nobody can step outside language and somehow attain a pre-semiotic intuition. One essential point of the deconstructionist view is that no 'sign' exists somehow on its own, and every 'signified' has the potential for being another's signifier. The upshot of this kind of view is that meanings cannot be somehow easily 'contained' within texts, given that they depend in part on an ever-receding interconnected 'field of unlimited semiosis'.

In parallel with these developments, within literary criticism post-structuralists such as Roland Barthes and Julia Kristeva were calling into question long-cherished notions about authorship and the role of the reader. In a well-celebrated essay 'The Death of the Author' (Barthes, 1977), the traditional view that the originating author is the ultimate authority on the text is critically analysed or 'deconstructed'. As Selden (1985) notes:

[Barthes's] author is stripped of all metaphysical status and reduced to a location (a cross-road) where language, that infinite storehouse of citations, repetitions, echoes and references, crosses and re-crosses. The reader is thus free to enter the text from any direction; there is no correct route. The death of the author is already inherent in structuralism, which treats individual utterances (paroles) as the products of impersonal systems (langues) . . . [readers] are free to connect the text with systems of meaning and ignore the author's intention. (p. 75)

The intricacies and complexities of the debate between structuralists and 'deconstructionists' deserve considerably more space than can be allowed in a book on the psychology of language. Suffice it to say that the study of language within literary criticism (reading, writing, text analysis, comprehension) adopts methods and procedures quite different from those found in experimental psycholinguistics, as we well go on to consider in Chapter 9.

Post-structuralism as a movement is not concerned solely with the study of language. Architecture, art, media and film studies, social anthropology, sociology and cultural studies have all been influenced by changing conceptions of originality, authorship, responsibility, accountability, thinking, the nature of literary texts, and so on. We should not be surprised, given the close affinity between sociology and social psychology, that a specific 'discursive' social psychology has emerged. Discursive social psychology has adopted key ideas and methods from discourse analysis (linguistics) and ethmethodology (sociology) and integrated these in a social psychological approach which focuses upon the 'discursive' nature of action and cognition. For discourse analysis language

exists as a domain of social action, of communication and culture, whose relations to an external world of event, and to an internal world of cognitions, are a function of the social and communicative actions that talk is designed for. (Edwards, Potter & Middleton, 1992, p. 442)

Certainly the agenda within this sub-branch of psychology is different from the concerns of psycholinguists. There have been some noteworthy debates over the nature of the relationship between language and memory (Baddeley, 1992). Some philosophers of the social sciences argue that the orientation of the discursive social psychologists and other social constructionists will have a pervasive and radical influence on psychology as a discipline (Harré, 1993). Leaving aside such prophecies for the moment, our brief history of the study of language has only touched on the influence of sociolinguistics and social semiotics. Essentially sociolinguists search for general patterns in the relationship between language and society. For example, they will examine linguistic variation within different speech communities and attempt to identify the social factors which explain specific trends. In a useful introduction to the subject Holmes (1992) suggests that these common trends can be seen as sociolinguistic universals, e.g. the observation that as the social power and status between people increases you tend to find an increase in linguistic forms expressing negative politeness.

Social semiotics can be described as a contemporary critique of semiotics, and has developed from the position that the social dimensions of semiotic systems are so intrinsic to their nature and function that systems cannot be studied in isolation. Hodge and Kress (1988), for example, argue that the orientation developed in semiotics (largely of an abstract and 'independent' form – i.e. as the study of sign-system structure) appeared to ignore the very thing it was said to study – the social basis of sign-systems. Although Saussure affirmed the social over the individual, he did so only as an abstract, somewhat immobilised, version of social reality. This order itself is open to potential threats by the particular actions of individuals and groups, and social semioticians consider that the study of language, as an examination of signification processes, is interdependent with an analysis of culture, politics and ideology. There is a recognisable affinity between feminist social psychologists and discourse analysts and the theoretical approach of contemporary social semiotics.

A cognitive account of language processing

This short, and deliberately selective, overview of historical developments in the study of language will help provide a background frame for placing the topics and themes of this book. Throughout the following chapters, orienting comments and reminders should assist the reader in understanding why one or other approach appears either similar to, or quite distinct from, another. Given the considerable diversity of this field, unless the reader can occasionally refer back to the underlying theoretical orientation of any given approach (and its historical antecedents), it will remain difficult to gain a coherent global picture of the psychology of language. We have seen already how language can be treated as an object of study, as the study of human behaviour, and as a method of examining the relationship between language and thought. All such views (and more) are to be found in the psychology of language.

Another difficulty the psychology of language student faces is with terminology. Linguistics as the scientific description of language has a whole variety of terms and definitions which serve to identify the basic elements and objects of inquiry. At this point it would be useful to provide a summary description of the areas of language study which have received the most attention within psycholinguistics. Figure 1.3 outlines the principal fields, as described by Greene (1986).

Lexical processing: The study of lexical processing rests on the fundamental assumption that each of us has within our heads some kind of dictionary or 'mental lexicon'. Within linguistics the term 'lexicon' describes that complete list of words which make up any natural language. Traditionally the lexicon has been seen as 'the repository of miscellaneous facts forming no part of any generalisation' (Trask, 1993). Within psycholinguistics lexical processing has focused on word recognition and there have been well over a thousand studies of word recognition over the last ten to fifteen years. Considerable effort, for example, has been spent on identifying the relationships between the 'visual lexicon' and cognitive letter detection

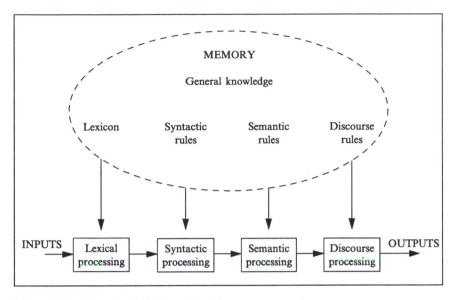

Figure 1.3 *Greene's (1986) model of language processing*

processes. There is also extensive research within neuropsychology which employs the word recognition paradigm in studies of brain damage and related disorders. Given the already well-documented texts on this topic (Garnham, 1985; Taylor & Taylor, 1990) and the problems of including all aspects of language in a text of this nature, this is an area which will not be covered in any great depth in the following chapters.

Syntax and syntactic processing: Syntax is the analysis of sentence structure, the rules and procedures whereby individual words go together to form sentences. In Chapter 2 we will consider how significant the study of syntactic processing has been for psycholinguistics, particularly with respect to the models of mind and cognition which underpin theories of syntactic processing.

Semantics and semantic processing: This part of the study of language is concerned with what words and sentences might mean. Understanding the nature of meaning has been a central problem for the philosophy of language for many years. Psycholinguists are interested in the 'rules of meaning' which people appear to employ when they make sense of the language they hear and read. The study of semantics has close ties with developments within formal logic, and for many researchers in artificial intelligence and computational linguistics formalising rules of meaning remains an important goal of their work.

Discourse processing: Within linguistics, discourse analysis has traditionally meant the application of methods developed in research on syntax and semantics to the study of extended texts. In contrast, some psycholinguists use the term 'discourse processing' to refer to how people comprehend text, whereas social psychologists use 'discourse analysis' to refer to study of everyday language behaviour. This is a good example of the care we must take in identifying not just what a definition might mean, but who happens to be using it. In the Greene (1986) model in Figure 1.3, she uses the term to refer to the rules which we appear to use when understanding text (i.e. our comprehension of the structural devices in texts which help us understand how a story develops and so on).

Judith Greene's (1986) model (Figure 1.3) serves as a useful illustration of how one school of psycholinguistics would approach the study of language. When we read or hear language, we first have to be able to recognise the individual letters and words which make up the basic elements (lexical processing). This is said to depend on the lexicon, a store-house of words which we have built up throughout our lives and exists somewhere in our memory as general knowledge (as do all four of the above components). Next, we are able to recognise how these words are put together in meaningful chunks, according to the rules of the language that we happen to understand. We could not utter intelligible sentences if we did not (intuitively) know the rules for grammar. But of course, it is not enough to know the rules of sentence structure, if we don't know what this sentence or utterance is meant to convey. The often quoted example 'Colourless green ideas sleep furiously' was employed so as to remind us that structure can be recognised, without anything meaningful being communicated (people tend to say that this strange expression is a grammatical sentence even though it is meaningless). There has to be an element of semantic processing, therefore, and meaning must be structured and obey particular rules and conventions. Finally, larger chunks of meaning as 'discourse' are processed, and thereby we can understand and construct extended texts.

In this cognitive 'linear stage model' approach to language, there are a number of missing topics which are of considerable interest to psychologists. How people interact during everyday conversation, how language is used to carry out particular speech acts, the use of specific words in order to indicate social status, are all topics which call for an approach to the study of language which goes beyond the boundaries of a cognitive orientation. A contemporary psychology of language will include key topics such as conversational analysis and pragmatics. Again, we can summarise these briefly:

Conversational analysis: As the name suggests, conversational analysis is an approach which examines the structural elements of conversation, including turn-taking procedures, use of intonation patterns, interruption strategies and methods of opening or closing a conversation. It derives from an approach within sociology known as ethnomethodology, which takes as its starting point the investigation of participants' own methods, techniques and forms of rationale for interpreting and producing their social worlds. In contrast to the 'deductive' approach found in experimental psycholinguistics, the methodology employed is largely 'inductive', i.e. it concentrates on identifying rules and regularities through an examination of a large body of naturally occurring examples.

Pragmatics: The sixth, broadly defined area of language study is pragmatics. Some commentators have described pragmatics as the study of every phenomenon within language, except for formal syntactic analysis (i.e. everything beyond the level of the sentence – see Levinson, 1983), and, as such, this would include conversational analysis. Within psycholinguistics, the study of pragmatics has focused principally on intentionality, speech acts and issues of co-operation and communication (e.g. Grice, 1975). In later chapters we will go on to consider the extent to which both pragmatics and conversational analysis have become central topics in a psychology of language.

The aim of this book: extending the scope of the psychology of language

So far, this introduction has accomplished two things. The first is in providing a brief historical overview of some of the key influences which bear upon the contemporary study of the psychology of language. In considering this, it has been clear not only that there are many distinct and equally interesting approaches to language, but also that it is increasingly difficult to provide an overview conceptual framework for one distinctly psychological approach to the study of language. The study of language within psychology has at least four distinct divisions. There is the primarily cognitive approach of psycholinguistics, which includes research which studies the relationships between memory, attention and problem solving with language processes (and this would include the extensive work on reading). Alongside this, the 'neuroscience'-inspired orientation of neuropsychology has a particular interest in language, one which shares many of the theories, methods and concerns with the cognitive psychologists. There is also a distinct social psychology of language, which, although sharing theoretical and methodological allegiances with cognitive psychologists (particularly methodological), also incorporates ideas from sociology and communication studies. More recently, a 'discursive' social psychology has emerged, and, as we noted above, its interest in the study of language is informed as much by disciplines outside psychology as it is by other themes within the discipline.

The second aim of this introduction has been to provide some background to what is to be accomplished in the following chapters. In service of the previously noted aim of working to clarify distinctions between language as a formal object of inquiry and the study of communication, the aim of this book is to outline a psychology of language which places at centre-stage the importance of communication in a broad sense of the term. To fulfil this goal, we will begin by considering the relationship between language and thinking, with the proviso that thinking is ultimately a form of 'self-communication' (at least some of the time). Thus, the early part of the book will move from 'in the head' formulations of language and thought which have tended to emphasise the importance of syntax and semantics (Chapters 2 and 3), outwards through 'the interface with the social', by studying what are known as deictic terms,[2] and on to considerations of everyday talk (language in practice).

The second theme, talk, begins in Chapter 4 by picking up on key aspects of social interaction implicated in certain studies of deixis (Oshima-Takane, 1988), thus introducing conversational analysis (CA). First, the ethno-methodological basis of the CA approach is outlined and key principles explained (e.g. intersubjectivity). Rather than going into details at this point, however, the importance of the approach is highlighted by comparing and contrasting CA with the achievements and limitations of what has traditionally been known as non-verbal behaviour. Too often, non-verbal behaviour has been confused with non-verbal communication, and CA studies of telephone conversations encourage a reconsideration of the significance of what is popularly known as 'body language'. Chapter 6 will summarise the primary details of the CA approach, covering such topics as the 'local management system', adjacency pairing, openings and closing sections in talk, and so on. Here, examples are used throughout so as to convey the significance of the principal phenomena, for example by considering research which has shown that children as young as two years are oriented towards structure and predictability in talk.

Moving towards the end of the talk theme, Chapter 7 will serve as an important extension of the previous chapter (by outlining criticisms of the CA approach) and a link to the final theme of the book (text) – power and ideology. The focus in this chapter is on the role of power relations in talk and how (as Goffman has proposed) talk can be considered as a micro-sociological context where participants act with regard to the institutional forces which bear upon everyday interaction. The role of power relations in talk is (towards the end of this chapter) compared with expressions of power as instituted in language (where considered as a formal object). Here, the feminist critique within text linguistics serves as an important avenue for moving on to the third theme of the book – text.

The final theme of the book begins by outlining the dangers of pre-supposing a simple and generalist notion of communication when we treat text (sentences) in much the same way as talk (speech or utterances), and vice versa. Building upon recent work within the philosophy of language, reasons why a psychology of language would benefit by clarifying the distinguishing features of talk and text are outlined. This is then followed by a chapter on semiotics and a consideration of the extent to which structuralist and post-structuralist ideas can inform the study of text in the psychology of language. The study of reading and writing is then considered (Chapters 9 and 10), concluding with an analysis of what has become known as a postmodernist psychology of language: discourse analysis.

This concluding chapter begins by highlighting aspects of the previous chapters which indicate the 'postmodernist' turn within the study of language (e.g. the deconstructionist critique and 'political correctness' in Chapter 7; post-structuralist theories of reading in Chapter 9). Then, as a way of drawing together the three themes of the book (thinking, talk and text) the emergence of discourse analysis in social psychology is considered in some detail. Primarily this serves as a 'test-case' for considering whether the psychology of language (as a sub-discipline) now encompasses more than what would traditionally be conceived as 'psycholinguistics'. The implications of this perspective for other areas of psychological inquiry are outlined in the concluding comments.

Notes

1. CT is better known as computer axial tomography and PET as positron emission tomography. See Posner, Peterson, Fox and Raichle (1988) for an example of the use of such techniques in neuropsychological research.

2. Deictic terms are all those examples of language which tie the comprehension of an utterance to the interaction context of the speaker and hearer (such as *this* and *that* or *here* and *there*).

2

Language Structure and the Significance of Recursion

You have only to stop for a second and consider the nature of language to recognise that it has structure. As children we learned in the first few years of life that we couldn't just arrange the sounds we made in any old fashion; they had to follow a certain order. There were 'sound-rules' to comply with, ways of saying things in the correct fashion. As adults we know that it is simply impossible to communicate any thought independently of language,[1] and it has been suggested that when we give attention to the medium, we are giving attention to the substance of our thoughts. But, the age-old question of which comes first, thought or language, remains as controversial as ever. Certainly some structuralists would argue that if we talk of language as if it somehow serves to convey 'thought', thus assuming the existence of some 'beyond' of language to which we are given access, then this is simply misleading (Sturrock, 1986). In this chapter we will see that much of psycholinguistics and cognitive psychology rests on the assumption that there is indeed a level of cognition underpinning language. Whether this is innately specified, symbolic or diffuse, serial or parallel in operation, and so on, are the kinds of questions that make up the agenda of contemporary cognitive science. Before going on to consider why the study of language structure serves to inform these debates, we need to understand the specifics of the approach to language comprehension which owes its existence to Chomsky.

There were two developments which together helped inaugurate the new field within psychology which become known as psycholinguistics. The first was the distinctively individualistic interpretation of structuralism outlined in Chomsky's writings. Within structuralism, signification (sign-system) processes were viewed as essentially collective. Linguistic structures and their meaning pre-existed any particular individual and were part of the human collective consciousness. Chomsky, partly in response to the behaviourist orientation of American descriptive linguistics, which he saw as very limited, was convinced that the 'grammatical competence' we seemed to possess, almost as an intuitive skill, had to be genetically endowed and was a fundamental part of an individual's mind.

The second development, which occurred in parallel with Chomsky publishing his ideas on formal grammar, was the shift in emphasis within psychology from the study of behaviour to the study of mind. A new 'cognitive psychology' was becoming the dominant framework, and, in contrast to the previous climate of suspicion for topics 'mentalistic', research paradigms were emerging which employed the operational methodology of behaviourism to study internal cognitive life. The cognitive processes associated with language comprehension and production were obvious candidates, and understanding issues such as grammatical competence were high on the agenda.

But what exactly are we talking about when we refer to 'grammatical competence'? Simply the ability to recognise that sentences or utterances such as *Rachel is tired of working so hard all the time* or *Angela looked closely into Jonathan's eyes* are grammatical, while *Of is hard so Rachel working time the* and *Eyes Jonathan's closely Angela looked into is not* are ungrammatical (at least for English-speaking people). The famous example employed by Chomsky to make this point, 'Colourless green ideas sleep furiously', is normally recognised as grammatical, even though it is meaningless. A common definition of the word 'grammar' might be *a system for organising individual words into larger units* (usually called sentences). More technically, however, a grammar is essentially a theory, and as with any other theory, it is an attempt to explain some aspect of the phenomenal world. Here the natural phenomenon is the knowledge of a language that is possessed by every native speaker of that language. Dale (1976) suggests that grammars are theories in at least two senses:

1 They represent a linguist's best attempt to summarise and characterise the language of a speaker.
2 They are an attempt to describe the organisation of language in the mind of the speaker.

For the psychology of language, the second sense is of more interest than the first, although their interdependence should be clear. Understanding grammatical competence will depend in part on an understanding of syntax. Syntax is the analysis of sentence structure, the rules and procedures whereby individual words go together to form sentences, and, as a method of linguistic analysis, it is indispensable to psycholinguistics. For individualistic structuralists like Chomsky, knowledge of grammatical competence is going to be closely tied to conceptions of the mind and thinking.

Cognitive representations of grammar

Already, in trying to summarise even the basic framework for introducing ideas in this field, technical terms are inescapable. In order to guard against an understandable resistance to engaging with what might appear to be unnecessary detail, this section begins by outlining, as clearly as possible, the essential ideas within Chomsky's theory. Let us start with the issue of grammatical competence and our apparently intuitive ability to recognise when a sentence is grammatical, and when it is not. Remember, syntactic theory is relevant in a cognitive sense because the main task of any syntactic theory within psycholinguistics is 'to model the system that enables us to know which sentences are part of our language . . . and which are noise' (Stillings et al., 1987, p. 242). In other words, speakers know the patterns of their language, and the argument is that these patterns are represented as a set of rules that define what is a permissible sentence, and what is not. This account can provide us with one explanation for the inherent creativity of language, an issue which seriously undermined a strictly behaviourist account of language.

Chomsky's (1957) theory of syntax rests essentially on the assumption that the mind is some kind of recursive computational entity. To *recur* commonly means describing a situation where something comes back or comes around again. The process of recursion is where an algorithm or procedure which involves reference to itself (re)occurs in a repetitive fashion. Many programming operations in computers involve procedures (sections of code) which 'call themselves' when activated. This is a paradoxical, yet very important, idea for understanding theories of syntax. Recursion is the main reason why people have argued that the human mind has the capacity to recognise and produce an infinite number of sentences, even though our brains are clearly finite entities. In order to gain some idea why this proposal is significant we can try the following exercise:[2]

First, imagine a very minimal abstract language that consists of only two symbols (A and B) and one simple rule, and of course some system for processing or comprehending language. The system has to be able to recognise these symbols and have the ability to substitute one string for another if need be (arguably a fairly basic set of abilities). The rule states that whenever the system (human, artificial, or whatever) 'sees' or recognises the symbol A, then it has to substitute the A symbol with an AB string (i.e. the A and the B beside each other). The basic elements, rules and activity are shown in Figure 2.1(a).

It is important before continuing to recognise the importance of the recursive nature of this re-application rule or algorithm. On the second application, the system simply sees the A at the end of what resulted after the first application (BA), and AGAIN applied the rule, this time resulting in a string that had a new BA, this time placed alongside the first B, left over, if you like, from the first application (now to BBA). And so it continues.

Now, this simple system will reject as ungrammatical any 'sentence' which takes a form such as ABAB. Such a combination of elements could not be a 'real' sentence, could not have been 'generated' from within the system. In Figure 2.1(b) we can simply turn what we have in Figure 2.1(a) through 45 degrees, and represent the outcome of this recursive procedure hierarchically.

So, the ability to be able to 'compute' symbols in a recursive way makes it possible to conceive of a system which can 'generate' an infinite number

A simple abstract language containing

    1 Two symbols – A and B
    2 A rule

Symbols	=	A	or	B
Rule	is when you 'see'	A $\longrightarrow$ apply string BA		

Original state = A

so,

1st application of rule	substitute	A $\longrightarrow$ BA
2nd application of rule	"	A $\longrightarrow$ BBA
3rd application of rule	"	A $\longrightarrow$ BBBA
4th application of rule	"	A $\longrightarrow$ BBBBA
.		
.		
.		
10th application of rule	"	A $\longrightarrow$ BBBBBBBBBA
nth application of rule	"	A $\longrightarrow$ B^{n}A

(a) Basic constituents

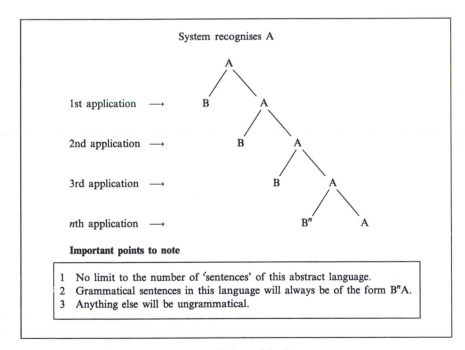

Important points to note

1 No limit to the number of 'sentences' of this abstract language.
2 Grammatical sentences in this language will always be of the form B^{n}A.
3 Anything else will be ungrammatical.

(b) The minimalist system represented hierarchically

Figure 2.1 *Recursion as a computational process*

Sentence (S)	⟶	Noun phrase (NP) + tense + verb phrase (VP)

Noun phrase (NP)	⟶	Article (art.) + adjective (adj.) + noun (N)
Tense	⟶	Tense marker (past)
Verb phrase (VP)	⟶	Verb (V) + noun phrase (NP)
Noun phrase (NP)	⟶	Article (art.) + adjective (adj.) + noun (N)

(phrase marking before lexical insertion, i.e. putting in the actual words)

Noun phrase (NP)	⟶	Article (the) + adjective (small) + noun (child)
Tense	⟶	Tense marker (past)
Verb phrase (VP)	⟶	Verb (is crushing) + noun phrase
Noun phrase (NP)	⟶	Article (the) + adjective (sweet) + noun (flower)

(phrase marking after lexical insertion)

Represented hierarchically as:

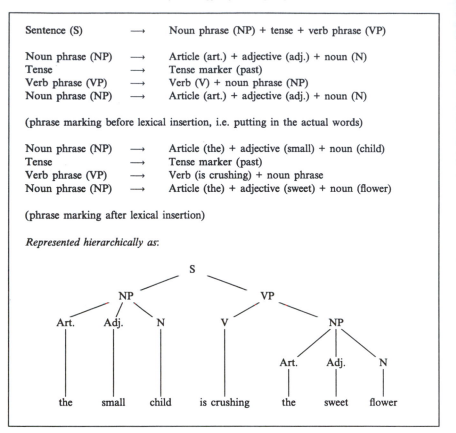

Figure 2.2   *Sentences as 'rewrite rules' in a recursive system*

of sentences. It was for this reason that Chomsky's theory was originally entitled a theory of 'transformational generative grammar'. Consider what happens when we represent sentences, and the elements which make them up, as components in a system which applies rules recursively, as in Figure 2.2. Now, instead of As and Bs, you have sentences (Ss) and the parts that make them up (noun phrases – NP; verb phrases – VP). As in the previous diagram, the system applies recursive 'rewrite' rules (when you see S, then substitute with NP and VP and so on). The system is the mind and the significance of Chomsky's proposal is that the mind must be some kind of 'recursion' engine.

The hierarchical representation above is what you find peppered throughout linguistic textbooks. Open one up and you will find it replete with hierarchical 'trees' of this nature. Such representations are known as 'phrase structure' trees, and phrase marking is represented by the form of the structure (i.e. without reference to the actual sentence which we have at the bottom of the diagram). The latter has popularly been known as the 'surface structure' of the sentence, a distinction Chomsky emphasised when

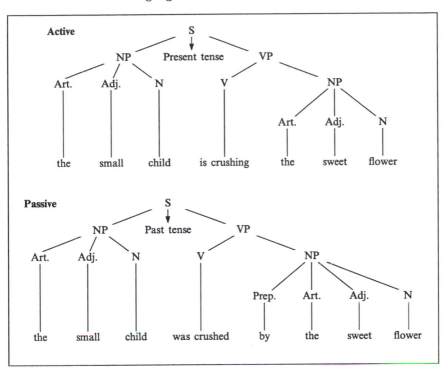

Figure 2.3   *A simple transformation from the 'active' to the 'passive'*

talking about grammatical competence, i.e. between 'surface structure' and 'deep structure'. The 'deep structure' is represented by all those parts of the Figure 2.2 sentence above the actual words. To understand what Chomsky meant when he talked of 'transformational rules', consider the differences between the two phrase structure trees in Figure 2.3. The sentence has changed from being in the present (active) to the past (passive) tense. Leaving aside the slight difficulties we might have imagining a small child being crushed by a sweet flower, the important point to grasp is that such transformations are essential elements of any given language, and that our ability to generate, as if 'intuitively', distinctions between, for example, 'active' and 'passive' forms of a sentence is something we inherit. Remember, this was one of the important differences between 'collectivist' and 'individualistic' orientations in structural linguistics (see Figure 1.2, p. 6). Chomksy's aim was to discover the universal features which under- pinned the communicative power of human language. He was particularly concerned to show that it was simply impossible to explain the acquisition of language through a simplistic notion of imitation. In the spontaneous language of a five- or six-year-old child, one can find numerous examples where utterances seem to have been 'transformed' in appropriate ways representing the past-tense rule (adding -ed to verbs, *talked* for *talk*), or rules for plurals, negative and so on. Developmental psycholinguists have debated this ability at length, sometimes referring to it as the 'learnability problem' – a young child simply couldn't just generalise these complex rules from only listening to the speech he/she hears around him/her. There simply isn't enough time (the child simply would not hear enough examples) to do so.[3] Many researchers are compelled to accept the proposition that somehow this ability must be genetically endowed, an innate predisposition. This 'innateness' hypothesis has been summarised by Garnham (1985) as follows:

> The features of language that children must acquire from the speech around them are the unique features of their language, and they include the transformations of that language. . . . Children do not have to learn those features of the deep structure that are universal. (p. 89)

The surface structure is what you hear or read, in the exact serial order it occurs, and the corresponding 'deep structure' encapsulates or represents the grammatical relationships from which a sentence is derived. Any grammar that claims to assign to each sentence that it 'generates' both a deep structure and a surface structure, and to systematically relate the two, is said to be a transformational grammar. In Chomsky's original theory there were many key transformations and transformational rules, elements of which were said to be universal features (common to all languages). Chomsky's cognitive model is summarised in Figure 2.4.

It is important to remember that this theory is about competence, not performance (competence as our ability to 'automatically' recognise whether a sentence is grammatical or not). This is a proposal about the nature of grammatical competence as it comes to be represented in the individuals mind. The competence–performance distinction has its parallels in the *langue–parole* differentiation proposed by Saussure. The first in either pair is always an abstract theoretical structure, the second actual language behaviour, speech or text. And a key assumption underpinning Chomsky's model, as we noted, was that the mind has to be some sort of computational engine. Without the recursive nature of 'phrase structure' rewrite rules, the possibility of recognising an infinite number of grammatical sentences was unrealisable. Towards the end of this chapter we will consider some of the problems that have arisen with respect to the Chomskian paradigm, but there is no doubt that this model has had considerable influence within psycholinguistics, and it represents a key example of the relationship between a model of the mind (in this case recursion) and language processing.

Before continuing, however, it may help the reader to step back a little and consider the association between underlying theoretical assumptions and whatever particular model we are concerned with. All too often we fail to see the way in which a particular theory is both informed, and constrained by, the constructs which permeate its philosophical underpinnings.

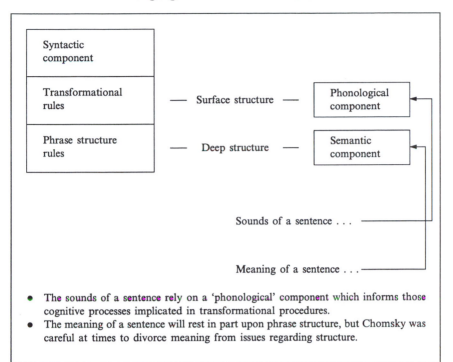

- The sounds of a sentence rely on a 'phonological' component which informs those cognitive processes implicated in transformational procedures.
- The meaning of a sentence will rest in part upon phrase structure, but Chomsky was careful at times to divorce meaning from issues regarding structure.

Figure 2.4   *Relations between deep structure and surface structure (Chomsky, 1965)*

Psychology and language: the relationship between theory, data and explanation

In a useful commentary on the developmental psychologist Vygotsky, Williams (1989) draws attention to the relation between methodology and psychological theory, which is pertinent here. As he puts it:

> The formation of a theory is a twofold process: The theory begins with some object of study, or unit of analysis; for example a reflex, an introspectible subjective state, a behavior, a cognitive capacity or whatever. It then develops a general explanatory principle; for example, appeal to conditioning, introspection, flow chart model, and so defines itself from the perspective of the logic of this philosophical tradition. This view of the relation between psychological theories and philosophical perspectives underscores the importance of developing a critical awareness of the presuppositions that support the content of a particular theory. (p. 111)

Developing an awareness of the relationship between underlying theoretical assumptions and particular models in the study of language is not very easy. The models are of such complexity in themselves that trying to identify what kinds of assumptions about 'mind' lie beneath them is an additional level of complexity we would often rather avoid. However, precisely because there are so many diverse approaches to language, having some idea of what kinds of theoretical assumptions they share can often help us understand the orientation of a specific approach. Arguably, there are two general approaches to the *mind–language* relationship found in the psychology of language:

- *Cognition-dominant:* Concepts, cognitive states and categorisation processes generally constrain and support thinking and language.
- *Language-dominant:* Language constrains and facilitates thought. Our language determines the order of our experience and the world.

We have already looked in some detail at a 'cognition-dominant' view in Chomsky's proposals. Without the underlying assumption that the mind is a 'recursive' computational system, language competence would not be possible (in the way described). In contrast, a language-dominant view emphasises the primacy of language – as a set of social practices that pre-exists any individual life. Philosophers of language such as Wittgenstein have had considerable influence on the development of this orientation, arguing that it is only on the basis of language practice (Wittgenstein's 'language games') that we can make any justifiable inferences about cognition or conceptual processes at all.

The cognition-dominant view

By far the greater number of models in the psychology of language have favoured the 'cognition first' view. This should be of no great surprise given the importance regarding ideas about individuation, thinking and ego-identity pervasive in Western thought and culture over the last three centuries. Prior to Descartes, it is fair to say that issues of identify, the self, thinking and language were closely tied up with theology and the importance of the relationship between the 'soul' and the divine (God). What was important about Descartes, reflected in that often misunderstood phrase 'I think, therefore I am', was his articulation of the relationship between self (I), or intuition or identity, and judgement (the emphasis in the quote is on the word 'therefore', which presupposed the ability to draw a conclusion, to judge and to categorise). As Sinha (1988) points out, it was the creation of a space between intuition and judgement that helped initiate the 'methodological individualism' central to the human sciences, and 'secured the foundations of the tradition in Western philosophy . . . within which empiricism and rationalism contested the claims of experience and inheritance' (p. 6).

For Kant, however, Descartes's ideas did not adequately account for the problem of internal representation or mental images. Rather than judgement being derived from intuition, he turned the problem on its head and proposed that the conditions of the possibility of representation derived from the nature and operations of judgement. There had to be a *cogito* in the first place before any notion of experience could come into play – judgement and sensation were synonomous. Representation becomes a psychological (not an epistemological) problem and Kant can certainly be seen as the founding father of 'mental representation' as it is understood in cognitive psychology and cognitive science. Why this is important for our understanding of the study of language is summarised succinctly by Sinha (1988), where he reminds us:

> Although Kant was not a philosopher of language, his investigations profoundly influenced the development of theories of language. Firstly, his separation of representation from language and discourse implied that language itself could no longer be seen as a transparent tool for the revelation of both nature and reason, but must rather be studied as an object of investigation in its own right. Language . . . was henceforth subject to the higher claims of empirical investigation. (p. 12)

The Cartesian (after Descartes) and Kantian influence on psycholinguistics remains significant. Again, it might help to identify why by tracing the form this influence takes, as in Figure 2.5. On the one hand (top of Figure 2.5), we have a view of language and cognition that has a clear commitment to individual cognition, the cognition-dominant orientation. In contrast, a social-constructionist approach would argue that the criterion for asserting this or that view of individual cognition ultimately rests on social practices (conventions of one sort or another), i.e. the language-dominant orientation. We can go through the steps of each level of the contrasting frameworks.

Starting with the cognitivist view, it is the 'existential status' accruing to the existence of propositional attitudes which supports the view that concepts underlie language in the first place. A propositional attitude is said to describe the relationship between an intentional stance and mental states. The fundamental assumption is that mental states are essentially representational, and thus psychological concepts are 'objects' of intentional stances. So, in order for mental states to exist at all they have to be the end product of a *cogito* which permits the existence of critical judgement in the first place. Thus the starting point is the assumption of the existence of propositional attitudes, and the status of individuation is assured by the foundational criteria of a *cogito* or an epistemic subject.

We find concepts and categorisation processes at the next level. The extensive work of Rips, Shoben and Smith (1978) and Rosch (1975) and her colleagues provides evidence that people appear to possess prototype concepts and categories. And one such set of concepts will be those underpinning identity, self, personality and all those essential categories and ideas which are said to underpin our comprehension and use of language. These conceptual processes are also 'rule-governed' in the sense that the processes and procedures involved in cognition can be described formally. This idea is so important for cognitive psychology and experimental psycholinguistics that we need at this point to take a slight detour and explain another key assumption underlying cognitive science: a commitment to methodological solipsism.

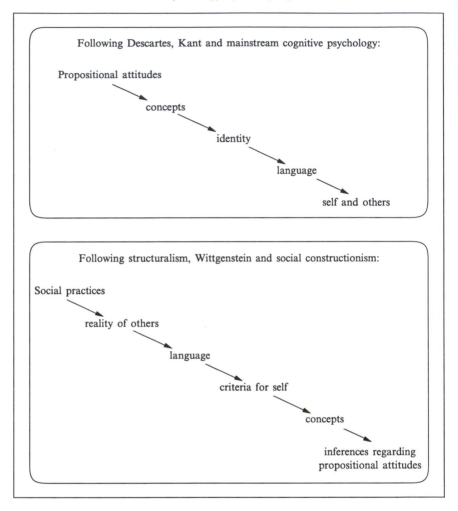

Figure 2.5 *Cognition, categorisation and language*

Cognitive science and methodological solipsism

The word 'solipsism' comes from the Latin *solus*, meaning alone. It can be defined as the theory that self-existence is the only existence, a form of absolute egoism. The reason why it is important for cognitive psychology, and experimental psycholinguistics, is that although there is plenty of scientific evidence that we do indeed experience a 'cognitive life', it is much more difficult to show how that cognitive life or cognitive system directly interacts with the outside world. This is the case both with the relationship between stimuli from the environment and the internal workings of the human cognitive information processing system, and between our cognitive systems and the responses and actions we carry out on the environment. Figure 2.6 summarises methodological solipsism as a principle.

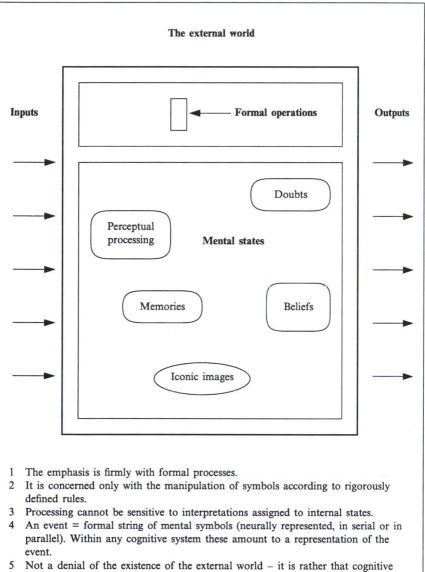

1 The emphasis is firmly with formal processes.
2 It is concerned only with the manipulation of symbols according to rigorously
   defined rules.
3 Processing cannot be sensitive to interpretations assigned to internal states.
4 An event = formal string of mental symbols (neurally represented, in serial or in
   parallel). Within any cognitive system these amount to a representation of the
   event.
5 Not a denial of the existence of the external world – it is rather that cognitive
   science is as yet unable to comment on how cognition relates to it.
6 The autonomy principle (see inset).

Figure 2.6 *Methodological solipsism in cognitive science*

The autonomy principle (after Stitch, 1983)

A popular way of explaining what cognitive scientists call the autonomy principle is by telling a science-fiction story about kidnap and
deception. First, you have to imagine that some malevolent person
has succeeded in building a 'robot' which is in fact, an exact replica
of you (and you happen to be a cognitive psychologist). Next, one
night when you are asleep, this person kidnaps you and you are
replaced with the robot replica. Now, this replica is so perfect that it
is totally exactly the same as you. So much so, that the replica has no
consciousness that it is not really *you* at all. And, although the story
really ends there (not much of a narrative I know), as a cognitive
psychologist you are asked to consider the state of the replica's
psychology.

Consider, the replica is an exact physical copy and will always
behave in exactly the same way as the *real* you would behave, if
you were in the same circumstances. And if the replica is exactly the
same physically, and you (as a cognitive psychologist) were interested
in understanding the replica, then there is no need for you to pay
attention to anything at all concerned with the physical body (irrelevant really to a cognitive psychologist). Furthermore, the replica's
psychology must be exactly the same as the cognitive psychologist
him/herself. As Stillings et al. (1987) put it, 'this is what methodological solipsism comes to . . . for the purposes of cognitive science,
an organism's information-processing states can be characterised
without reference to their meaning or their connection to the external
world' (p. 337).

Information comes to us from the environment through the myriad of
ways the cells of our bodies react to stimulation (light stimulating cells in
our retina; touch stimulating cells on our skin and so on). Correspondingly,
when we wish to act on the environment, we either react spontaneously
(e.g. a reflex action) or seek to carry out an intentional action (I am going
to raise my arm so as to reach something on my bookshelf) and
'automatically' find our body reacting in accordance with our wishes (most
of the time). However, the precise way in which the input (stimuli) and the
output (responses) actually interact with our cognitive system remains
unknown for a great number of activities. This is not to say that such work
is not continuing, and is doing so at some considerable pace (e.g. work on
the visual system by Livingston & Hubel, 1988, and Marr, 1982), only that
for the present cognitive psychologists await the research findings of
neurobiologists and neurophysiologists.

Continuing with Figure 2.6, it also remains unclear how exactly our neurophysiology interacts with our cognitive systems. In the recent past considerable work has been carried out by neuropsychologists who have been slowly and painstakingly piecing together many parts of this very complex jigsaw (Luria, 1973; Petrides & Milner, 1982; Roland, 1984). Many important insights have been gained by examining the relationships between our cognitive systems and the environment through careful study of people who, for one reason or another, have experienced some neurological dysfunction. By analysis of what we know occurs when things are not operating as we would expect, we might gain some insight into how the relationship between cognition and neurophysiology works in the first place.

However, it has to be recognised that there is still a long way to go, and thus we need to understand and remember the rationale underlying the orientation a cognitive psychologist has. In other words, given that there is a good deal of sound scientific evidence that there is a cognitive system, and, of course, our everyday experience of possessing a rich 'internal' cognitive life, we do not have to await all the fine detail of how this system interacts precisely with the environment, but can proceed with our scientific investigations of the system as an internal formal abstract entity. This is a very important idea to understand. Cognitive psychologists rely on data from experiments which are complex in the sense that it is only on the basis of a careful analysis of the results that we can build up a picture of how the internal workings of our cognitive system operate. Moreover, we have to have models of what this system might look like in the first place for conducting experiments at all. Thus model building is a very important part of cognitive psychology (and what has become known as cognitive science).

So, the term 'methodological solipsism' reflects: (a) that we are dealing with the study of an internal formal abstract entity – our own cognitive system; and (b) methodologically, while we wait for the final story of how this system interacts precisely with the environment, we will proceed by employing the full range of scientific procedures and processes utilised when studying any formal system.

Some commentators have argued that it is the shared commitment to methodological solipsism which is the defining, and unifying, construct within cognitive science. Disciplines as diverse as neuropsychology and the philosophy of language can recognise that although they may be approaching issues from very different perspectives, nevertheless they can recognise the commonality in the presuppositions which inform their theory building. Many linguists, and without doubt computational linguists, have no difficulty in articulating reasons for the emphasis on rigour and formal process. Numerous aspects of descriptive linguistics focus on the analysis of that abstract side of the *langue–parole* formulation, and they are content to side-step the issue of whether there is a core set of cognitive concepts and categories underpinning language understanding.

To conclude our outline of the cognition-dominant view of the relationship between mind (thinking) and language, many contemporary versions of how language maps onto underlying cognitive constructs remain in sympathy with the 'conduit' or information transmission model of Shannon & Weaver (1949). The idea that language is the medium for communication between people is so pervasive in our culture that we may find it difficult to consider the proposal that the 'idea' itself can be viewed as a cultural product (i.e. the outcome of language practices, not the cause). We think of language as a way of conveying ideas, and the ideas (concepts, constructs) are 'in our heads'. And because our everyday experience of the ideas we have is often of fleeting, vague, ill-defined, half-articulated sensations and thoughts, it seems perfectly reasonable to talk about the language system somehow 'packaging up' the ideas and sending them (through speech and writing) to others. These others then unpack the system (in reading text and listening to speech) and then 'get the message', cognise the ideas, recognise the propositions, and so on. This is often referred to as the 'conduit' metaphor (Lakoff & Johnson, 1980). Returning to the top half of Figure 2.5, language, finally, provides the system within which categories of self and other (e.g. through the pronoun system) are defined and clarified. Within this cognition-dominant orientation, social psychologists of language will study those variables said to influence self-categorisation and identity through a detailed analysis of the use of language in context.

The language-dominant view

We can now move to the language-dominant view within the psychology of language. Here, the source of the criteria underlying the analysis of language starts from, and is embedded within, particular social, cultural and institutional practices. So, if one treats language as a formal object for analysis, then the rationale for proceeding in this way rests upon certain assumptions regarding what it is to be objective, analytical, precise, and so on. These assumptions are themselves interdependent with the language you use, the practices you ascribe to, the historical precedents provided by prior research, i.e. the procedures deemed appropriate in the particular cultural context you are in. Analysing language as a formal system should be conducted with due concern with, and respect for, reflexive critical inquiry.

Throughout the later half of the twentieth century, philosophy (particularly European philosophy) has been particularly concerned with the problematic status surrounding notions of truth and identity, which is beginning to exert some influence upon contemporary psychology (e.g. Feldman & Bruner, 1989; Kvale, 1992). Although at times this orientation may look like an extreme form of behaviourism, it does not rely on a 'stimulus–response' metaphor, nor is it predicated on the social-discursive practices of the experimental laboratory (Lachman, Lachman & Butterfield, 1979). A social-constructionist orientation to language takes as axiomatic the significance of social practice and semiotic systems (any sign-system used for communicative purposes). The comprehension of any communicative phenomena must rest upon sets of social practices and 'forms of life' without which representational processes would remain unrealisable. The most significant of these social practices is language, which of course would not exist without the reality of self and other.

Adopting this view and playing the Robinson Crusoe-fantasy game, the significance of the relationship between language and thought can be foregrounded. Somebody asks you to imagine what you would think if you had been left as an infant on a desert island. Would you think? If you did, would you think in words or images? What would your dreams be like? Would you 'communicate' with animals using signs? Would you speak? Leaving aside the remarkable ability we have to place ourselves in such 'imaginary contexts', clearly such questions are simply unanswerable, and in fact we could never 'step outside' language in order to ascertain the status of this or that 'truth'. However, playing such a fantasy game does highlight the continuing controversy over which comes first, language or thought (Brown, 1986).

A language-dominant view of cognition owes part of its allegiance to existential philosophy. This philosophical outlook rejects the Cartesian–Kantian view of eternal or absolute truth in favour of an orientation which focuses on our 'being-in-the-world', where an understanding of our existence should not entail turning away from our everyday experience. At the same time, there is the recognition that any answers or glimpses of understanding will be inherently paradoxical: on the one hand, our experience is that we 'live' in bodies which are quite categorically 'real', but yet, on the other hand, our very recognition or comprehension of self, body and 'other' is interdependent with our use of language (conceived here very broadly as encompassing all sign-systems). Moreover, language itself 'produces' versions and visions of reality as codes and conventions embedded within particular cultural contexts. Existential philosophy

> stresses that we are not neutral observers [in the world] but rather, situated participants in an ongoing, open-ended, socio-historical drama. It claims that truth comes into being in our concrete co-existence with others and cannot be severed from language and history. (Langer, 1989, p. 19)

Language as social practice exists before any of us are born and thus, although it might be argued that we share some kind of 'pre-reflective bond'[4] with others (Merleau-Ponty, 1962), in our everyday lives we are participants in the shaping of our world, including the multiplicity of discourses (re)produced and extended in a continuous and negotiated dynamic construction of 'reality'. DeBarnadi (1994) reminds us that the argument that language shapes its speakers more than its speakers shape language is one that repeatedly recurs within the study of language. Sapir (1921) and Whorf (1956) were strong proponents of the view that language shapes world view: i.e. if you want to learn about my culture, then learn my language first. Anybody who has tried to learn a second language to

any considerable depth[5] will recognise that learning the idiom involves
attaining a deep understanding of the social practices which underlie the
use of any particular expression in a specific context: a formal grammatical
translation of one sentence into another will not get you far enough.

So, and to return to our diagram in the lower part of Figure 2.5, we are
born into a culture with its own particular set of social practices, everyday
activities, institutions and conventions which form the presuppositional
framework underpinning language practices. The 'reality of others' is
interdependent with our inculcation into the language community, in fact
our very recognition or awareness of 'self' and 'other' is embedded in the
use of language. This problematic nature of this view is an issue often side-
stepped by developmental psychologists where they are concerned to
understand the earliest forms of intentional behaviour. Dore (1979), for
example, employs a communication model to explain the infant's early
attempts to 'bridge the gap' between him/herself and his/her mother.
However, as Freud recognised, the whole notion of separateness in the first
place (why identity?) is linked to language practice and use. Why should
the very young infant have any notion of separateness at all, and if he/she
has, how are we to access such an understanding?

For example, consider a young child around one year old, out of her
mother's sight and helping herself to some jam in the larder (assuming she
can reach it of course!). Having helped herself for a while she comes back
into the living room, and, with jam all over her face, hears her mother say
to her, 'Oh, so you've been at the jam then have you!!' From this infant's
point of view, there is no reason to believe that she *didn't* know that her
mother was unaware she was helping herself to the jam in the first place.
Thus, it might be argued that it is through the use of language itself that
separateness (and identity) is being created and shaped in the first place
(oh, so YOU've been at the jam, have YOU).

Such an example can only give a flavour of the view developed by
psychoanalysts such as Lacan (1977) who propose that it is only through
language that the child begins to attain any notion of self and other at all.
Enculturation into language also implies an entry into the 'Symbolic order'
– that aspect of language which both facilitates and constrains our
developing sense of ego and identity. Even our dreams and unconscious
desires are infused with the signs and signifiers of the culture we are
brought up in – we cannot recognise a word, object, sign, visual image,
except through the prism of our language.

Sociologists have also emphasised the pervasive nature of language and
its interdependence with thinking. Throughout the 1960s and 1970s,
although social psychologists of language were increasingly influenced by
the cognition-dominant paradigm (e.g. Giles, 1979; Robinson, 1978),
sociologists and sociolinguists continued to focus on language as social
activity. In later chapters we will go on to examine the influence that
ethnomethodology had on such developments. For now we can note that
social theorists such as Berger and Luckman (1967), in their emphasis on

the social construction of reality, point to the foundational role of language as social practice. The power and pervasiveness of language activity is paramount:

> Language originates in and has its primary reference to everyday life; it refers above all to the reality I experience in wide-awake consciousness, which is dominated by the pragmatic motive (that is, the cluster of meanings directly pertaining to present or future actions) and which I share with others in a taken-for-granted manner . . . as a sign system language has the quality of objectivity. I encounter language as a facticity external to myself and it is coercive in its effect on me. Language forces me into its patterns. (p. 53)

The relation between language and self can be considered as the next level of concern (Figure 2.5). In his insightful analysis of the roles and rituals people display in different contexts, Goffman (1981) focused on how everyday conversational contexts can be considered as 'micro-sociological' contexts. In other words, in face-to-face interaction with each other we produce and re-enact conventional codes of behaviour, rules and procedures which are not so much determined by institutional forces in the wider society as (re)produced with reference to such 'outside' forces. In fact, notions of self and identity are so closely tied up with such practices that Goffman might have claimed that the self is much more akin to a subset of predispositions or expectations tied to specific role scenarios. Commenting on this aspect of Goffman's theory, Collins (1988) notes:

> We are compelled to have an individual self, not because we actually have one but because social interaction requires us to act as if we do. . . . The self is only real as a symbol, a linguistic concept that we use to account for what we and other people do. It is an ideology of everyday life, used to attribute causality and moral responsibility in our society, just as in societies with a denser (e.g. tribal) structure, moral responsibility is not placed within the individual but attributed to spirits or gods. (p. 50)

Moreover, if the self is an 'ideology of everyday life', then arguments and proposals surrounding the existence of concepts and categorisation processes cannot be considered separately from language use. The question of linguistic relativity has a bearing on this issue as many people hold to the position that language structures the way we think, such that people who speak quite different languages (i.e. particularly languages where the rules and regularities at the level of grammar and syntax are very different) actually think in quite different ways. Brown (1986) comments that often this view of language is asserting not simply that cognitive structures covary with language structures, but that the language structure shapes and limits cognitive capacities.

At this point we can simply clarify what the implications of a language-dominant view are for the study of concepts and categorisation processes. A language-dominant view is not trying to say that there is no such thing as a 'cognitive life' (certainly our everyday experience might make a strong version of such a view untenable). Rather, it is a question of theoretical emphasis within the psychology of language and a call for more critical reflection regarding the status and authority accruing to the existence of cognitive structures, concepts, and so on. So, where we are concerned with examining investigations of concepts or propositional attitudes (Fodor, 1983; Rosch, 1975), if we ignore the particular social-discursive context which surrounds asking somebody to take part in a psychology experiment or whatever, then we will fail to see the extent to which the 'evidence' produced is interdependent with the task, the context, the underlying theory and philosophical position taken, in other words the whole set of social activities which underpin the nature of carrying out tasks associated with conventions of scientific practice.

According to the language-dominant view, the existence of propositional attitudes cannot simply be assumed and considered as the philosophical starting position. Rather, what needs to be asked is under what conditions can we justifiably infer that this cognitive behaviour, model, rational process, or whatever, rests upon the individual possessing propositional attitudes? And the word 'justifiably' awakens our attention to the set of accountable practices which surround the drawing of a warrantable conclusion: a set of socially ascribed criteria which is foregrounded by a set of conventions or codes.

Summary

Understanding the significance of Chomsky's conception of grammatical competence for psycholinguistics is not an easy or a particularly accessible task. The nature of language as structure can strike the unacquainted as both technically complex and sometimes irrelevant. Our everyday familiarity with language as practice (talking, reading and writing) can make questions such as what is the relationship between language and thought seem akin to asking what is the relationship between walking and sitting down. Language as a 'form of life' in which we are prime participants can often make us resistant to examining what this particular human activity actually involves. However, it can be argued that once we have taken the initial plunge, then we find ourselves considering the most fundamental human activity: critical for any understanding of psychology.

This chapter began by considering the importance of Chomsky's ideas for the birth of psycholinguistics and in particular his conception of the role of the mind as a 'recursive engine'. Certainly this has been one of the most elegant mathematical explanations of how the infinite generative power of language can be derived from the limitations of a finite system (i.e. the brain). We should not lose sight, however, of the principal reasons why transformational grammar has had such an influence on cognitive psychology and cognitive science. First, it was an exceptionally welcome antidote to behaviourist accounts of language (e.g. Skinner, 1957), which simply couldn't accommodate the inherent creativity of language. Second, it was precise, formal and abstract, in the sense that the formalism could be utilised by any rule-governed system. This was particularly important for the later contributions that artificial intelligence would play within cognitive science. Third, it permitted a whole new range of addressable questions for psychologists of language, given that they now had a formal theory to use alongside the methodological rigour inherited from behaviourism. Fourth, it was a uniquely individualistic formulation of the structuralist conception of *langue–parole*. Rather than *langue* existing in the collective consciousness of the culture, it was to be found in the innate capacities of the individual mind. Mentalism was certainly once more on the agenda for psychologists. And fifth, transformational grammar helped establish methodological solipsism as research methodology. There is no doubt that without Chomsky a distinct experimental psycholinguistics would not have emerged, or if it had, it would have looked quite different.

The relationship between theory, data and explanation is sometimes overlooked in psychology textbooks, and this next point we looked at in some detail, as well as clarifying precisely what is meant by methodological solipsism. However, the history of experimental psycholinguistics can be better understood by comparing and contrasting two primary views of the study of language: the cognition-dominant view and the language-dominant orientation. This helps articulate why on occasion the study of specific topics within research areas (e.g. language acquisition) can look very different, i.e. dependent upon the orientation the researcher has adopted. Without an understanding of the world view that a particular theory holds to, it is much more difficult to ascertain why there is considerable diversity in the study of language.

Notes

1. Leaving aside for now whether such displays as non-verbal glances and so on are language in the formal sense – certainly to be recognised at all they have to be recognised as 'signs' and thus fulfil the criteria of being a language.

2. This example rests upon the detailed description provided by Stillings et al. (1987) in their discussion of transformational grammar.

3. Although see Howe (1993) for a theoretical account of language acquisition which does not rely on the innateness assumption.

4. Being alive at a minimal level entails that we share with others some kind of intuitive pre-linguistic empathy simply due to the very facticity of our existence.

5. Particularly where there is little 'cultural overlap', say English–Japanese rather than Italian–French.

3

Semantics: The Concept of Meaning

One of the problems with syntactic approaches to the study of language is the precise role of semantics or meaning in the models proposed. On occasion critics of Chomsky have ridiculed the theory of transformational grammar as being largely irrelevant with respect to what words and sentences actually mean in context (Grice, 1957). However, it needs to be remembered that the Chomskian tradition in linguistics and psycholinguistics does not evade the question of meaning (see Figure 2.4, p. 25), and it is often recognised that transformational grammars and other such formalisms, although providing insights into the form or structure of language, are not appropriate analytical tools for studying meaning. Saussure and Chomsky, as structuralists, are concerned primarily with language as an abstract structure: language use in context (what utterances mean for communicators) is another issue altogether. In this chapter a number of approaches to the study of meaning are considered. In doing so, I will develop the argument that the study of meaning in psychology and psycholinguistics may be better understood within the broader framework of pragmatics.

When many people discuss the nature of 'meaning' it is very often where somebody has said something, or written something, that somebody else doesn't understand. What did she mean when she said that? What does this diagram mean? Does this sign on the wall mean something? The question of meaning arises whenever there is a gap or break in communication – the recognition that somebody has tried to communicate something but this 'something' is not clear. For the most part we consider meaning as transparent: meaning is something we generally take for granted.

Leaving aside for the present the distinction between meaning in conversations (talk) and meaning in texts (sentences), many psycholinguists equate the study of meaning with the study of *word* meaning (e.g. Greene, 1986; Taylor & Taylor, 1990). Here, the idea is that words refer to things in the world, and we use words to build sentences – chunks of communication with can encapsulate meanings of varying levels of complexity. This view might be summarised by

SYMBOL (word) = THING

In contrast to this view, semioticians argue that the problem cannot be as simple as that, given, for example, that there is no referent or thing which is

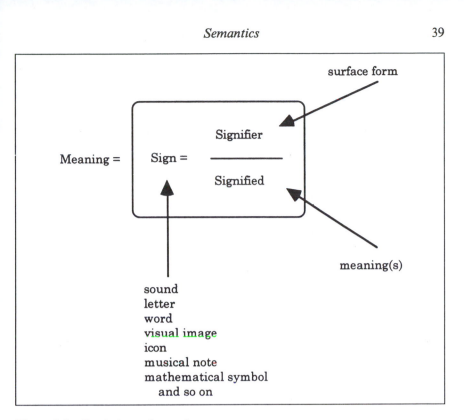

Figure 3.1 *Semiotics and meaning*

associated with the word 'happiness' or 'perhaps'. For semioticians, the nature of meaning is tied up with the notion of the sign.

Semiotic definitions of meaning

Semiotics as the scientific study of sign-systems is concerned with the nature of meaning or the process of signification. All languages (verbal, non-verbal, iconic, visual) are sign-systems. Frawley (1992), in his analysis of theories of meaning, restricts the definition of semiotics to the discipline that studies all meaningful signal exchange. All meaningful signal exchange includes culture as sets of rules for acceptable behaviour, talk, text, the visual media and literature and art as conventionalised aesthetic meaning. So, the study of Meaning[1] is the study of signification processes, where the essential element is the sign (see Figure 3.1).

Any semiotic theory of meaning is critically concerned with the nature of the sign and associated signification processes. However, the Meaning of any sign is an indissoluble association between signifier and signified. For example, if we consider the process of signification encapsulated in our everyday use of traffic lights, the *sign* for the occasion where traffic is instructed to stop can be described as in Figure 3.2.

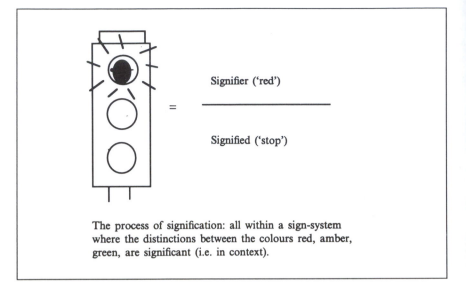

The process of signification: all within a sign-system where the distinctions between the colours red, amber, green, are significant (i.e. in context).

Figure 3.2   *The semiotics of traffic lights*

The importance of recognising the arbitrary nature of signs is crucial, a point we will go on to to consider in more detail in Chapter 8. For now, Frawley (1992) provides us with a succinct semiotic definition of meaning:

> To say that something has meaning is to say that it is a *sign*, a composite unit consisting of a relation between an overt signal, called the *signifier*, and the information that this overt signal evokes, called the *signified*. The signifier, signified and <u>the relation</u> make up the sign. (p. 5; my emphasis underlined)

Philosophical underpinnings of psychological theories of meaning

It should come as no surprise that underneath any psychological theory of meaning you find a commitment to one or other philosophical school or theory of meaning. The philosophical enterprise itself is critically concerned with the analysis and investigation of what things mean in the world, and so in every culture you will find competing accounts, or philosophies, of how to make sense of things. Again at the risk of oversimplification, within philosophy it has been argued that there are two general orientations to the question of meaning: the direct and the indirect views. The direct view is often traced back to the Greek philosopher Plato and his theory of knowledge. Plato was concerned to show that knowledge of the world was knowledge of those things in the world that don't change. However, the meanings of such objects are treated as abstractions, they are ideal forms. The universe is to be understood as divided between appearance and reality. Although we can have views or opinions about the world of appearance, Plato believed only our souls can have true knowledge about the world. Thus our information about the universe is divided between opinion and knowledge. True knowledge about the world is knowledge about the world of Platonic ideas. The direct view asserts that meanings are abstract objects that exist independently of the minds that perceive them, and, furthermore, actual forms of language (in use) derive from a world of pure linguistic form. In a contemporary version of this approach, Katz (1981) asserts:

> Meaning is a transparent relation between signifier and signified. The signifieds of language (entities, dynamic relations, names) are recoverable from the signifiers (nouns, verbs, sentences). (p. 17)

In contrast to the indirect approach to meaning, adherents of the direct approach owe their allegiance to Aristotle. Convinced that Plato was mistaken, Aristotle argued that the everyday world we encounter can be accounted for without having to appeal to the notion of an abstract world of Ideal Forms. Historically, this view is expressed in a number of guises and is seen in contemporary psycholinguistics in the work of Lakoff (1987). Furthermore, we need to distinguish two general orientations within the indirect view of meaning: the individualistic and the societal. The individualistic would assert:

> Meaning in the natural world is an information structure that is mentally encoded by human beings.

whereas, the societal orientation supports the view that:

> Meaning is the relation between words and their referents and is conventional . . . social rules determine how meanings are paired with overt forms.

Frawley (1992) contrasts these different orientations as two instances of the 'semiotic triangle' (see Figure 3.3). In both instances the problem is posed as to what exactly is the relationship between a symbol and the thing (object, entity, relation) which it represents or stands for. The individualistic approach argues that it is the mental apparatus of the individual psyche which encodes or computes the meaning imputed in the relation between symbol and referent. The role of what Sinha (1988) calls the 'epistemic' subject becomes paramount in this case (i.e. some kind of 'logocentric' subject must exist in our minds, a subjective structure which does the processing). In contrast, the societal orientation asserts that the relationship between symbol and referent is a matter of social convention. So, in this second view the relationship is always arbitrary, i.e. interdependent with the way language is used in a particular social–cultural context. One implication of this for a distinctly psychological theory of meaning is that, in a curious sense, the thoughts in our heads are not our own. The language we use existed before we did, and while we may put words together in ways which are uniquely our own, the words, sentences and discourses are provided by the culture we live in. We are both limited

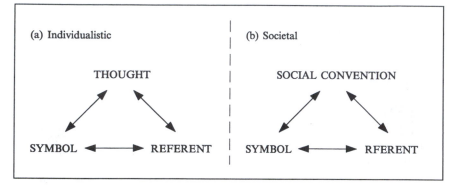

Figure 3.3   *The semiotic triangle*

and enlivened by our language. This view is echoed in literary criticism, where Selden (1985) argues that we cannot step outside, as if onto some neutral ground, the limits of our language in order to objectively analyse the nature of linguistic meaning. In the different approaches to indirect meaning outlined below, we will see that there are more adherents to the individualistic than to the societal orientation.

Five approaches to indirect meaning

Bearing in mind that we are concentrating on approaches to meaning which focus on the manner in which meaning (semantics) and form (actual syntax) must be linked in the act of speaking or understanding, the five approaches summarised by Frawley (1992) provide us with a useful overview. These are:

1   Meaning as reference.
2   Meaning as logical form.
3   Meaning as context and use.
4   Meaning as conceptual structure.
5   Meaning as culture.

Meaning as reference

The word 'reference' or the expression 'to refer to' is used by linguists in a number of ways, sometimes ways that are rather confusing. The logician Frege (1952) uses the term 'reference' with regard to any sentence's truth value (he distinguished between a sentence's 'sense' and its 'reference' – the former being what it means, the second what it refers to). Stevenson (1993) prefers to concentrate on the more everyday sense of reference, i.e. with regard to the specific situation that a sentence is said to 'refer to'. The important point for our purposes is to remember that this theory of meaning as reference is a theory of meaning as mental projection. 'The

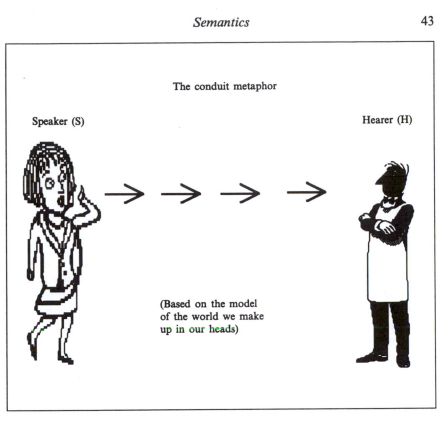

Figure 3.4 *Meaning as reference and the conduit metaphor*

contents of semantic representations (i.e. what we mean) is found in the components of the mentally projected world of reference' (Frawley, 1992, p. 25). So, the idea is that the meanings we have are tied up with our understanding of the constructions we 'impose' on the world through our everyday use of language. Consider a deep-rooted metaphor we often hold to in our discussions on communication, the 'conduit metaphor' (Figure 3.4). The general idea is that if I want to communicate something to somebody else, then I 'package up' my meaning in language and (through talk or text) communicate it to this person, who in turn unravels the 'package' (through listening or reading) and thus 'gets' the message. The language used to do the packaging only makes sense because it refers to things, objects, entities, and so on, in the world. My meanings (semantic representations) are made up of all such projects which link words with 'things in the world'.

Meaning as logical form

A second approach to indirect meaning stems from logic. Semantics here is defined as the study of the meaning of natural language expressions (and pragmatics the study of how such expressions are used). Zeevat and

Table 3.1 *Encoding events grammatically*

to run	versus	to slap	Question: Can we say this?
(non-punctual verb)		(punctual verb)	
(a) Alice ran on Tuesday		(a) Jenny slapped Fred on Tuesday	Yes
(b) Alice ran for an hour		(b) Jenny slapped Fred for an hour	Unlikely
(c) Alice ran in an hour		(c) Jenny slapped Fred in an hour	No
key: Semantic property absent		Semantic property present	

Scah (1992) comment, 'The meaning of a natural language expression is normally analysed as the *truth-conditions* of the (natural language) expression in so far as these can be analysed independently of its context of utterance' (pp. 18–19). And as logic is concerned with the conditions under which statements can be *truly inferred* from other statements, then given two sentences such as (a) and (b)

(a) Jenny bumped into Alice.
(b) Jenny made contact with Alice.

if sentence (a) is true, sentence (b) must also be true. On the other hand, if (b) is true, then it does not necessarily follow that sentence (a) is true. So, formal semantics is meaning as logical truth.

Frawley (1992) draws our attention to some interesting aspects of this approach to meaning. For example, he emphasises that meaning is 'grammaticalised', i.e. essential components of understanding what an utterance or sentence means are encapsulated in the grammar (rules of syntax) of any sentence. Consider the role of punctual verbs, and what is known as the implicit encoding of meaning. What is important to recognise is that the particular combination of words that make up the sentence is constrained by the presence or absence of a 'semantic property' that is not given explicit form. In Table 3.1, 'slapped' is the past tense of the verb 'to slap', known as a punctual verb. This verb encodes a momentary event. In other words it does not unfold over time or occupy an extended space. And arguably, only in the first instance (a) is the semantic content of the prepositional phrase (on) compatible with that of the verb. There exist implicit encodings of meanings in our everyday use of such expressions.

Investigations into the role that formal semantics plays for our everyday understanding of language have had a significant impact in the study of artificial intelligence (AI). AI was traditionally conceived as a branch of computing engineering concerned with robotics. However, as computing developed to the point where (a) sophisticated machines were being placed in the hands of the non-technical expert and (b) the 'computational metaphor' (human and machine as symbol-manipulating information processing entities) came to dominate psychology, AI has become a central part of what is known as cognitive science. Various semantically based models of language understanding can be found within AI. Schank and his co-workers (Schank, 1977; Schank & Abelson, 1977) made a significant impact on the development of this field. The central idea behind two of their more well-known models (one called MARGIE – Memory Analysis Response Generation and Inference on English; the other SAM, i.e. Script Applier Mechanism) was that of conceptual dependency. Conceptual dependencies are sets of representations which are said to arise from the semantic analysis we carry out when trying to comprehend any sentence. This is not meant to be a conscious process of any kind, rather the aim is to specify in a formal way semantic (meaning) processes and, at the very least, be in a better position to establish whether a particular semantic theory has any internal validity.

The study of meaning as logical form (i.e. where the emphasis rests primarily on the specification of truth-conditional semantics) is now being extended to, and incorporated with, areas of pragmatics (i.e. language use). Such efforts have been considerably facilitated by developments within logic which allow for the formal specification of 'non-probabilistic' logic (Ortony, Slack & Stock, 1992). Certainly, the boundaries between the strictly formal conceptions of meaning as logical form and other areas of pragmatics are becoming less rigid.

Meaning as context and use

A third approach to the study of indirect meaning concentrates on the function or use of language. Meaning as context and use was emphasised by Wittgenstein (1953) in his metaphor of language games. Language use can only be understood when it is integrated within patterns of everyday actions. 'Meaning is located in the function that words have as "signals" passed back and forth between people in the course of purposeful and shared activity. . . . Only in the stream of thought and life do words have meaning' (Wittgenstein, 1953, p. 180). Bloor (1983) points out that Wittgenstein was careful to emphasise that the term 'language game' was meant to bring into prominence the fact that the speaking of language is part of an activity or a 'form of life'. So, context and use determine meaning, and the meaning of an expression is a function of its use in particular context.

A useful way to think about this approach to indirect meaning is to consider the relationship between semantics, the study of the meaning of words and sentences, and pragmatics, the study of language use,[2] on a dimension from the 'language as formal object' through to 'language as practical activity' (see Figure 3.5). Underlying this semantics–pragmatics dimension, presupposition points towards our understanding of the relationship between language use and practical actions, certainly those actions and activities which, in any given culture, we assume other speakers

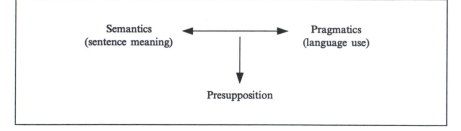

Figure 3.5   *Presupposition and pragmatics*

and hearers know and understand. Levinson (1983) notes that there is often some confusion over what is meant by the term 'presupposition', as the linguistic technical meaning often becomes mixed up with our everyday sense of the term. Consider how we might understand a sentence such as:

(A)   I'm sorry I'm late, I'm afraid my car broke down.

spoken by a student who enters a seminar some time after it has started (and maybe a little out of breath). This statement, at the very least, presupposes that the speaker actually has a car, even though this is not actually stated. However, if the same person has rushed into the seminar late and said:

(B)   I'm sorry I'm late, I'm afraid my fire engine broke down.

this statement presupposes that the speaker owns a fire engine or works on one part-time, probably a very unlikely scenario. In the latter case, at best we might view this statement as an attempt to make a joke, at worst as slightly insulting (i.e. a display of the disdain she holds for the seminar leader). The point here is that the meaning of this utterance is critically related to its context and use, and the mutual knowledge which is held between any speaker and hearer (writer and reader).

As an example of the importance and permeating nature of such presuppositions, Reason (1984) cites Sacks's (1980) noteworthy example:

(C)   The baby cried. The mummy picked it up.

where although we are told nothing about whether the baby and the mother were related, whether it actually stopped crying, whether it was lying in a cot, and so on, all such 'material presuppositions' come into play and provide for an understanding of the sentence (even in such a simple example). In other words, whenever we understand a sentence, it is a little like the sentence is the tip of an iceberg, where the hidden ice is a long history of use, action, comprehension, change, cultural convention, practice, and so on, i.e. all those activities which we simply accept as 'taken-for-granted' cultural practices, available and understood by each other when we communicate.

Language meaning and language use are irretrievably bound up together within this theory of indirect meaning. Underpinning the comprehension of any utterance (sentence) there are a host of presuppositions which come into play automatically the minute you understand any sentence. More often than not, they are not conscious inferences, rather the immediate bringing into play of our understanding of the mutual knowledge communicators possess about the social practices and activities associated with the particular words used. Mutual knowledge between speaker and hearer is critical here, and this knowledge is intimately bound up with the social practices and 'forms of life' shared by the users of the language concerned.

Meaning as conceptual structure

In this theory of meaning the orientation moves from use to conceptual structure. Starting from the position that all human minds are the same (or, at least, the structure and function of the neuronal substrate of mind, the brain, is shared by all), then the semantic properties of sentences, which underlie their meaning, are conceptual. As Jackendoff (1987) puts it, 'semantic information is conceptual information'. A good example of this notion of meaning underscores the research on metaphor by Lakoff and Johnson (1980). Their analysis of how people understand metaphorical expressions such as:

It was clear she was letting off steam when she jumped down his throat.

rests upon the fact that we possess core conceptual constructs for understanding metaphor. In this case the core constructs are ANGER IS HEAT IN A PRESSURISED CONTAINER (first part) and ANGER IS ANIMAL-LIKE BEHAVIOUR (second part). The conceptualist position is defined by Frawley (1992), where he notes:

> Linguistic meaning *precedes* and *enters into* a context of use because speakers bring this meaning with them, in their heads, into the context of communication. Context and use are relevant to meaning only because speakers have a prior conceptual structure. (p. 54)

The existence of propositional attitudes, conceptual categories and structures which can be utilised by speakers and hearers is supported by the work of cognitive psychologists such as Rosch and Mervis (1975) and Hampton (1988). Certainly, for this particular view of meaning the reliance on cognitive psychology as the ultimate arbiter in theoretical disputes is recognised by Frawley (1992). We should also keep in mind the fact that this approach favours the proposal that culture itself is a 'mental projection'. Certainly there will be continuing theoretical debate over whether observed consistencies across languages (i.e. with regard to the way that meaning is grammaticalised) point to the existence of universal internal categorisation processes or to a renewed emphasis on investigating whether social practices engender the similarities observed (e.g. in the work of Brown & Levinson, 1978, on politeness phenomena).

Meaning as culture

The fifth main perspective on meaning is diametrically opposed to the
preceding view. In the 'meaning as culture' approach, linguistic meaning is
entirely determined by the cultural context in which the language occurs. It
is more than simply saying, if you want to learn all about my culture then
learn my language, rather, the acquisition of language is coterminous with
the acquisition of a set of cultural practices. You cannot separate one from
the other. As Wittgenstein famously put it, 'the limits of my world are the
limits of my language'. Even a weak version of this view would propose
that language provides both the foundation of a shared cultural identity
and the means for the reproduction of social differences. DeBernardi
(1994), for example, makes the point that the acquisition of a language is
not only the internalisation of a linguistic code, but also entails the learning
of status and role, appropriate social affect and the foundation framework
for a 'world view'.

Earlier proponents of this view of meaning as culture developed the idea
that the parameters of language were interdependent with culture practices.
What was known as the Sapir/Whorf hypothesis (Whorf, 1956) was the
assertion that language shaped world view, a form of linguistic relativism.
Frawley (1992) argues that this orientation led to the view that:

> Language, culture and thought are all mirrors of each other . . . so it is possible
> to read thought off language, and language off culture because linguistic
> distinctions reflect cultural distinctions, which in turn generate distinctions in
> thought. (p. 46)

Certainly the most often cited example of linguistic relativism is the observation that Greenland Eskimos have approximately fifty words for snow
(Fortesque, 1984), whereas people in Britain may only have five or six (e.g.
slush, snow, sleet, hailstones, snowdrift, and so on). Care must be taken,
however, in distinguishing between this weak form of the 'meaning as
culture' theory (linguistic relativism) from the much more radical formulations apparent in post-structural linguistics and critical theory (e.g.
Barthes, Lacan, Foucault). We will go on to see (in Chapter 10) that the
strong version calls into question all claims regarding conceptual/linguistic
constructions per se. Linguistic relativity does not assert that language
reflects all thought, rather that there is cultural determination of habitual
thought through language. The existential status of the epistemic subject
remains assured in such a view of language (as noted earlier in Chapter 2,
page 27).

Post-script to an overview of theories of indirect meaning

Notwithstanding the observation that some of the theories of meaning
outlined above overlap (e.g. reference with conceptual structure; context
and use with cultural meaning), each one contains a distinct idea or set of
constructs. When we look a little closer at each one, however, we can

identify a number of problems which remind us of the incomplete nature of theories of indirect meaning. An account of meaning which rests on a simplified notion of reference would be incomplete. Our everyday understanding and use of language does suggest that there is some value in the 'sense/reference' distinction outlined by Frege (1952),[3] or at least the notion of reference. If you ask somebody what the word 'chair' means, then often he/she will simply point to one and say something like '*it means that* [thing over there]', i.e. by referring to an example of whatever it is, in context. Interestingly this slippage (meaning of word relating directly to a real object) is often employed by psychologists interested in the development of children's thinking. Vygotsky (1981), a well-known Russian developmental psychologist, would often use examples of the ways children confuse, or fail to recognise, the difference between a sign for something and the real thing itself. He describes a typical interchange between an adult and an eight-year-old child asked:

Why is a cow a word?

to which the child answers:

Because it has got horns.

Although this response is a clear indication of the child's understanding of those attributes which help define the category 'cow', strictly speaking she is incorrect. Of course, whether an adult could really provide a 'correct answer' to such a question (e.g. because of the spelling; because of the existence of a sign-system; because of use of the letters c-o-w in this combination) is another issue altogether. The reason why the notion of reference is itself problematic becomes apparent where we try to apply the 'sense–reference' distinction to understanding the meaning of words such as 'perhaps' or 'otherwise'. As a thing in the world a 'perhaps' is considerably more amorphous and ambiguous, obviously not a physical entity that somebody can point towards as an example. Whatever else meaning is, it cannot simply be explained by a theory of reference.

Truth-conditional semantics (meaning as logical form) creates problems of a different nature. It is difficult to establish the extent to which meaning itself can be reduced to a formally rigorous analysis of elements and rules which act upon those elements. Further, there is certainly little evidence that people actually utilise rigorous logical operations during ordinary comprehension, again reminding us of the limitations of an approach which considers language as a formal object, rather than as an everyday social activity.

Meaning as context and use brings with it a different problem, primarily the role of presupposition. It is not clear how presupposition relates to notions of mutual knowledge or common ground found in cognitive psychology. Clark and Carlson's (1981) proposals on the nature of mutual knowledge rest on unexamined assumptions about what we take to be 'mutually understood' as members of a culture. Although we have many ways of establishing criteria which lead to our feeling justified in making inferences about what somebody says or does, it is too easy to forget that it is impossible to access the 'intentionality' of another person. Levinson (1983) notes that although the logician Frege identified the problematic nature of presupposition nearly ninety years ago, it remains only partially understood, despite it being an important area for understanding how semantics and pragmatics interact.

Finally we noted that the 'conceptualist' and 'culturalist' theories of meaning appear directly opposed to each other. They again serve as expressions of the cognition-dominant versus language-dominant perspectives identified in Chapter 2. The conceptualist orientation will ultimately have to address the problems associated with uncritically accepting the existence of propositional attitudes, mental states, theories of mind, and so on. The culturalist tradition will have to find ways to address the problems raised by those who ask how is it possible to know anything outside of culturally delimited information, or why is it that I feel that I do indeed possess a rich cognitive life? Whatever else, the problems identifiable in the above theories serve as a useful framework for considering the extent to which any rationalist account of meaning (semantics) can avoid issues equally germane to pragmatics. Before concluding, one topic theorists of meaning continue to debate over is intentionality. Given that the meaning of an utterance (sentence) has to be bound up with the intention to communicate, the question we can pose is how are we to establish precisely what anybody means by saying (or writing) anything?

Implicature and the co-operative principle

A helpful way to begin to understand what linguists and psychologists mean by intentionality (and implicature) is to consider what exactly is involved in a very minimal interaction which might take place between two people waiting at a bus terminal. Let us imagine that the two people are strangers to each other, and one of them (person A) wished to find out if the other (person B) knows when the next bus is likely to come. What exactly is involved in finding out this information? Consider carefully what has to happen. First, person A has to turn towards person B, and look at him or her. Person B has to respond by looking in turn at person A, and indicating that he/she recognises A's intention to communicate. Person B has to display some sign that A's intention to communicate has been recognised as such, and has been accepted. This is quite difficult to think about, but it is certainly the minimal conditions that must be attained before any kind of communication can take place. Person B's display of his/her recognition that A has made an accountable attempt at communicating is a *cultural display*, difficult as this is to imagine. In other words, as a member of your culture, you have to learn how to indicate that you have recognised another's intention to communicate before actually starting the communication proper.

Once person A has received a recognitory display from B (a clear indication that A's attempt at beginning to communicate has been recognised, and accepted), then A can proceed by saying something appropriate like *'Excuse me, do you happen to know when the next bus is due?'* And then, of course, B can respond in an appropriate fashion. We might also note that the conventions surrounding displays of recognising intention are particularly powerful interactional mechanisms. That is, powerful in a normative sense of having to engage in interaction once these 'implicatures', as they are called, come into play. We are all quite conscious of how difficult it is in the 'standing at a bus stop' situation if we want to avoid at all costs the overtures being directed at us from another person (e.g. late at night in an unknown part of a city).

Conversational implicature at a general level can be defined as the force associated with the recognition (by the listener) of the intention (the speaker's) to communicate (see Levinson, 1983).[4] Grice argues that interactional purposes are fulfilled through an orientation participants have to fundamental conversational principles, outlined along such maxims as:

> make your conversational contribution such as is required, at the stage at which it occurs, by the accepted purpose or direction of the talk exchange in which you are engaged. (Grice, 1975, p. 45)

The Gricean account can be seen as a principled defence of the 'rationalist' position regarding social behaviour, the argument that conversation and related interactional rules are not merely derivable from accounts of social convention but are based on *a priori* rational principles.[5] The co-operative principle outlined by Grice (1975) states:

> Speakers try to be informative, truthful, relevant, and clear, and listeners interpret what they say on the assumption that they are trying to live up to these ideals . . . speakers and listeners adhere to the co-operative principle. (p. 89)

An important point to grasp here is that this is not really some kind of conscious process, much more of a general orientation that we all, as speakers and hearers, abide by without really thinking about it. Rather, precisely because we orient towards the co-operative principle (and associated maxims), we seek rational explanations when the maxims are flouted. Consider, for example, the four maxims outlined by Grice:

1 Maxim of quantity: make your contribution as informative as is required, but not more informative than is required.
2 Maxim of quality: try to make your contribution one that is true. That is, do not say anything you believe to be false or lack adequate evidence for.
3 Maxim of relevance: make your contribution relevant to the aims of the ongoing conversation.
4 Maxim of manner: try to avoid obscurity, ambiguity, wordiness and disorderliness in your use of language.

Imagine you overhear a conversation between two women, where one asks the other:

(A) Have you seen Rebecca?

and the other replies:

(B) There's a pink mustang at the back of Paul's flat.

How are we meant to understand this interchange? It would appear that speaker B is flouting the co-operative principle (e.g. the maxims of quantity, relevance and possibly manner) by answering in a fashion that is apparently unco-operative. It might even be seen as an attempt by B to ignore the topic of conversation altogether. However, as Levinson (1983) notes, despite the apparent failure of co-operation, we still tend to interpret B's response as co-operative somehow. So, as long as we can assume this is a normal conversation, we would continue to assume that the interchange is co-operative and ask what connection there might be between the statement that there is a car outside a flat owned by somebody called Paul, and then probably conclude that Rebecca is visiting this person. Levinson (1983) clarifies this point:

> In cases of this sort, inferences arise to preserve the assumption of co-operation; it is only by making the assumption contrary to superficial indications that the inferences arise in the first place. It is this kind of inference that Grice has dubbed an *implicature*, or more properly a *conversational implicature*. So Grice's point is not that we always adhere to these maxims on a superficial level but rather that, wherever possible, people will interpret what we say as conforming to the maxims on at least some level. (pp. 102–103)

Implicatures, then, are not to be confused with notions of logical consequence or entailment (within semantics). They are inferences which derive both from what has been said and from the existence of these underlying co-operative principles. This certainly locates the concern with meaning firmly with issues of function: what are people actually trying to do with language when they communicate? Functionalism in linguistic theory is concerned with looking beyond the purely linguistic system of signs for external pragmatic factors which relate linguistic structure to the way that communication is organised. We can see this at work in the theories of Austin (1961) and Searle (1969) and their concern with speech acts.

Speech act theory

During the late 1950s and early 1960s there was considerable research effort concentrated upon the development of a theory of language emphasising truth-conditional semantics. Within the philosophy of language Austin (1962) was sceptical about such a development and instead argued that, more than anything else, to *say something* is to *do something*. In his influential book *How to Do Things with Words* he outlined a theory which

Table 3.2 *Felicity conditions and speech acts*

	Directive (request) *Can you tell Jane I'm not* *going to the party?*	Commissive (promise) *I'll make sure that you receive* *the money tomorrow*
Preparatory condition	H is able to perform A	S is able to perform A H wants S to perform A
Sincerity condition	S wants H to do A	S intends to do A
Propositional content condition	S predicates a future act A of H	S predicates a future act A of S
Essential condition	Counts as an attempt by S to get H to do A	Counts as the undertaking by S of an obligation to do A

S = Speaker, H = Hearer, A = Act

focused on the motivation or force associated with making any utterance. This he termed 'illocutionary force', and as Levinson (1983) describes, he isolated three basic senses in which when you say something you simultaneously perform distinct acts. Illocutionary force is made up of three components:

(a) a locutionary act, which simply describes the fact that the speaking of a sentence involves the creation of a specific sense and reference;
(b) an illocutionary act, which, because of the force associated with performing an utterance, you make a statement, a promise, a request, or whatever;
(c) a perlocutionary act, which means that by uttering a sentence you are bringing about an effect on the audience, specific to the circumstances that they happen to be in.

The way illocutionary force is linked to the specific performatives was developed systematically by Searle (1969) through what became known as 'felicity conditions'. The four conditions were sincerity, preparatoriness, propositional content and an 'essential' condition. A useful way to understand how they help distinguish the relative illocutionary forces across different utterances (a request such as *'Can you tell Jane I'm not going to the party'* and a promise such as *'I'll make sure that you receive the money tomorrow'*) is provided by Searle (1975) (see Table 3.2).

In addition to this formulation of the underlying illocutionary force associated with any utterance, Searle (1976) argued that all utterances could be categorised into five basic speech acts, thus speech act theory. His interest was in finding a scheme reflecting the conditions influencing the effectiveness of illocutionary force. The five essential kinds of actions were as listed in Table 3.3. This framework was seen by Searle as the basic scheme within which all utterances could be categorised. It was not the word, or the sign, that was the basic unit of communication, rather it was the 'production of the token (word, symbol) in the performance of the speech acts' (p. 254).

Given the emphasis on action and speaking, psychologists, sociologists

Table 3.3   *Searle's (1969) five speech acts*

1	Representatives	. . . which commit the speaker to truth of the utterance (e.g. concluding, asserting, defining, and so on)
2	Directives	. . . which are basically attempts by the speaker to get the person addressed to do something (questioning or requesting)
3	Commissives	. . . which commit the speaker to a course of action in the future (e.g. promising, threatening, warning, offering)
4	Expressives	. . . which are said to express a psychological state or condition (e.g. thanking, welcoming, congratulating)
5	Declarations	. . . which in fact produce immediate changes in the institutional state of affair (e.g. declaring war, pronouncing marriage vows, conferring a degree, and so on). This last category of speech act depends on fairly complex extra-linguistic social institutions.

and linguists have utilised this framework in a variety of contexts. In child language, for example, it has been used extensively in studies which have concentrated more on what is being accomplished by the child than on their syntactic development (e.g. Bruner, 1975; Ervin-Tripp & Mitchell-Kernan, 1977; Forrester, 1989). Sociolinguists have found speech act formulations useful in cross-cultural studies (Richards & Schmidt, 1983) and education (Holmes, 1983). Within linguistics itself speech act theory has been applied to a number of areas, including syntax, second language learning and semantics. As Levinson (1983) argues, although there are key problems with the theory (see below), it remains one of the central phenomena that a general pragmatic theory must account for. An overview of what constitutes pragmatics will help locate speech act theory, and its relevance to psychology more generally.

Pragmatics

Pragmatics is both a field of research (largely found in linguistics departments in universities) and an approach to the problem of meaning. One of the most comprehensive books on the subject spends the first fifty or so pages trying to establish precisely what the term means. One common definition would say that pragmatics is meaning minus semantics, another that it is the study of the grammatical relations between language structure and context. The heart of the problem regarding definition is located by Levinson (1983):

> the term pragmatics covers both context-dependent aspects of language structure and principles of language usage and understanding that have nothing or little to do with linguistic structure. (p. 9)

Viewing pragmatics as a general framework within the study of language, we can identify some of the major topics as in Figure 3.6. Notwithstanding the proviso that other disciplines have more than a passing interest in this research domain (e.g. speech engineers, computer scientists), we can

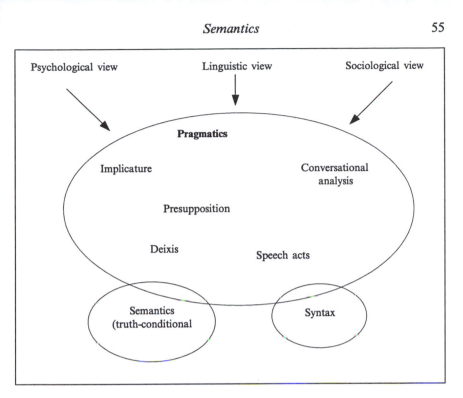

Figure 3.6 *The domain of pragmatics*

consider briefly how the psychologist, linguist and sociologist would address different topics. Linguistics, as the scientific study of language, has the greatest interest in the field, and a cursory consideration of topics found in contemporary linguistics journals would lend support to the argument that pragmatics is properly part of linguistics. We might note that there remain distinct divisions between areas which have clearly benefited from the adoption of a formally rigorous approach to the study of language (e.g. syntax and truth-conditional semantics) and the fundamentally functionalist concerns of topics which fall within pragmatics (thus the slight overlap in the circles in Figure 3.6).

In contrast, sociolinguists and sociologists interested in the social context of language use have contributed significantly to topics such as conversational analysis. Examining the ways in which participants in talk manage the ongoing interaction, and how they might overcome particular problems, rests upon methods of data collection and analyses derived from that branch of sociology/social anthropology known as ethnomethodolgy. This topic we will consider in more depth in Chapters 5 and 6.

A psychological view or interest in topics within pragmatics can be found in the developmental research on deictic terms (Tanz, 1980), the social psychological work on discourse analysis (Potter & Weatherell, 1987) and cognitive psychology in topics such as mutual belief (Clark & Marshall, 1981). Throughout, the psychologist's interest is generally focused upon understanding how language acts as a medium between the individual and other people, particularly how the relations between people become 'encoded' in language use during interaction. Again, these topics will be covered in what is to follow. For the present, it will be helpful to remember the distinction between pragmatics as a domain of inquiry, including at least those topics outlined in Figure 3.6, and as a technical description of a functional approach to language. Brown and Levinson (1978) argue that this more specific definition of pragmatics involves

> the search for a source outside the purely linguistic system that might motivate the bulk of grammatical constraints. ... Normally 'internal' cognitive explanations are favoured, but there are 'external' pragmatic theories that seek to link linguistic structures to the organisation of communication. (pp. 260–261)

and a strict definition of pragmatics which follows from this, would be

> the description of our ability to make *inferences* about the nature of the *assumptions* that participants are making, and the *purposes* for which utterances are used. (p. 286; emphasis added for key words)

Summary comments on the nature of meaning

There has always been a close, and occasionally complementary, relationship between psychology and philosophy. This is particularly the case within psychology of language when the question of meaning arises. It is simply impossible to discuss language as such without addressing the nature of meaning. Without some grasp of what is at issue when people use the word 'meaning', it is difficult to consider key topics within language, such as communication, language comprehension, language acquisition, and so on. In a well-known book on the development of language, Halliday (1975) conceived of the child's task as 'learning how to mean', which should help articulate the significance of meaning in our culture. Until we learn to speak in an appropriate way, our utterances cannot really be taken as 'meaningful' in an everyday sense. Using a word or phrase in an appropriate fashion makes us immediately accountable for what we say: in other words we assume that people 'mean' what they say – intend that others will understand the acceptable 'meaning' of the utterance and act accordingly. Language without meaning is not language at all (in the everyday sense of the term of course).

In this overview of the study of meaning (semantics) it should be clear that although there are particular gains in adopting formal approaches where appropriate (e.g. the particular engineering goals of artificial intelligence), any consideration of what language users 'mean' when they make an utterance in context forces us to go beyond truth-conditional semantics. The contemporary study of semantics (meaning) cannot be undertaken without due consideration of the function of language. This in turn implicates the importance of communication and social interaction. In one sense trying to understand meaning as if abstracted from the significance of the communicative context might strike us as rather curious, and this approach can be traced to the significance that has been placed on the study of the sentence (note the sentence as 'text' and not the 'utterance'). The study of meaning also raises questions about the value of presupposing the existence of cognitive states, propositional attitudes, mental models, or whatever. Leaving aside the temptation to phrase this problem by asking which comes first, thought or language, any consideration of meaning demands an investigation of communication and language function, forcing, if you like, the domain of inquiry away from 'in the head' concerns and onto issue of interaction and participation with others. We move from the individual to the social, from thinking to talking, and in closing the first theme of the book we anticipate the second.

Notes

1. It is helpful to distinguish the theoretical sense of Meaning (with a capital M), from particular instances where any specific sign has meaning in context (small m).

2. See p. 54 for more details on the domain of pragmatics.

3. The distinction between sense and reference is best thought of as one between our understanding of the ways in which sentences 'work' together (the words, phrases and rules which apply to language), all of this amounting to 'sense'; and the relationship between language itself and external things in the world, or 'reference'.

4. Whatever else communication might be, its purpose is achieved in part through being recognised as such (as an attempt to communicate) and the very recognition of intention is a central part of any theory of speaker meaning. From this view it is clear that we need to be aware of a particular distinction between speaking and communication, in that although speaking (and being exposed to speech) can be conceived of as a process whereby opportunities for 'conversation' are made available (to both speakers and listeners), communication (at least verbal) must combine speech with clear indications of intention (i.e. the display of intentional signals).

5. However, it is often forgotten by those who favour Gricean rationalist accounts of communication and co-operation that Grice himself stressed that, ultimately, emergent forms of categorisation (e.g. illocutionary force) rest upon evaluative criteria, i.e. are open to non-rationalist conventions (moral or otherwise). Also, his outline of implicature (Grice, 1957, 1982) invites an ironic reading: in part, as a parody of recursivity favoured Chomskian structuralism.

4

Deixis: The Interface between Language and Social Interaction

Clarifying what might be called 'in the head' approaches to the psychology of language can serve as a useful introduction to the study of deictic terms – particular forms of language which, in a sense, bridge the gap between language concerns focused on thinking and those converging on talk. We have been concerned so far with topics close to the interests of cognitive psychologists and experimental psycholinguists. Compositional theories of language comprehension such as Chomsky's (1957) transformational grammar rest on explanatory accounts of mind and thinking which predicate the significance of the 'logocentric' subject. Similarly, theories of semantics (meaning) are in the main concerned with the nature of abstract entities such as propositions and take the sentence as the basic unit for analysis. It has been suggested that semantics is not really interested directly in natural language, but rather is concerned with the way in which sentences operate within contexts so as to pick out propositional content (that essential meaning element said to underpin the particular sentence used). Certainly, whatever else, contemporary psycholinguistics attempts to address the problematic relationship between thinking (cognitive activity going on inside an individual) and language. The prevailing metaphors (information processing, neural networks, mental models, and so on) are firmly rooted in the cognition-dominant view of language. In many instances the aim is to uncover how language 'hooks on to', underpins or influences mental states, propositional attitudes, states of mind, or whatever.

However, within the recent history of linguistics there has been increasing interest in a functionalist account of language: what language means in context. The emphasis changes from concerns with individual thinking and its relations to language, to considerations of why we might use any particular utterance in context. We noted earlier that as soon as you ask this question then you move the spotlight away from certain forms of formal analysis (e.g. truth-conditional logic) onto topics such as communication, intentionality, interaction and principles of co-operation. If our aim is to understand the function of language in context, then one of the most promising routes for doing so is through the study of deictic terms.

Deixis

Deixis, derived from the Greek word for pointing or indicating, is a grammatical term for a group of words and phrases which anchor an utterance to the context of its occurrence. Deictic terms can only be understood with reference to the situation in which they are used. Levinson (1983) provides an interesting example where he asks us to imagine finding a bottle at the seaside, and in it there is a note which reads:

(1)   Meet me here in a week with a stick about this big.

How are we to understand what the writer meant when he/she penned this note? Who is the 'me'? Where is the 'here'? When was this note written (which week)? Relative to what is 'this' stick big? Although we might be able to infer certain things about such a note, it is simply impossible to fully comprehend the communicative intention of the person who wrote the letter. Likewise, consider the occasional confusion we feel when somebody asks us to move something from over 'here' to over 'there. As long as we are correctly distanced from each other (as speaker and hearer) in an appropriate way, and in proximity of the objects in question, then there is usually no problem. However, if it is not clear whether the speaker's *here* is close by or distant from your *there*, then clarification is sought (i.e. 'Do you mean over by your elbow or under the chair' etc.). Expressions such as 'here' and 'there' are deictic terms of place. Again, we are all familiar with the potential confusion where somebody says to us 'I'll see you next Wednesday, OK?' If we hear this expression on a Thursday, Friday or Saturday, then we will assume that they mean Wednesday of the following week. But if we hear the expression on a Sunday, Monday or Tuesday, then, more often than not, we will reply 'Oh, do you mean *this* Wednesday coming or *next* Wednesday?' This is an example of time deixis: the use of the word *next* has to be understood relative to the immediate moment when the utterance is being made.

Deixis concerns the encoding of many different aspects of the circumstances surrounding any utterance with the actual utterance itself. It is in this way that many natural language utterances are 'anchored' directly to aspects of the 'real' context. There are many examples in English (as in all other languages).

> Deictic expressions serve to direct the hearer's attention to spatial or temporal aspects of the situation of an utterance which are often critical for its interpretation. They serve as a meeting point for syntactic, semantic and pragmatic aspects of language. (Lyons, 1977, p. 637)

Words and phrases such as 'I/you'; 'this/that'; 'here/there'; 'in front of/ behind'; 'yesterday/next week'; ' come/go'; 'under/between', and so on, are all deictic expresssions. There are also forms of deixis knows as social honorifics which encode aspects of the status or rank of the person being addressed (e.g. the way in which you are meant to address someone of considerably higher social rank – the Queen of England would be addressed as 'Ma'am', the chief executive of the American government, Mr President). The study of deictic terms has become a key topic within pragmatics because it brings together aspects of syntax, semantics and pragmatics, all three domains influencing comprehension and use. Levinson (1983) suggests that pragmatics is really all about understanding the way in which a given context determines how a sentence spoken in that context specifies what propositions are being expressed on the occasion of its utterance. Needless to say, this helps explain why deixis is an area of language which is conceptually complex and has evaded concise analysis by philosophers of language and psychologists.

Over and above the observation that the study of deictic terms serves as a fruitful way of bridging the gap between the first two themes of this book (thinking and talk), there a number of other reasons why deixis is important to a psychology of language. First, it lies at the interface between language comprehension and social interaction. It is impossible to understand these expressions without also understanding the roles, rules and circumstances surrounding their expression in context. Second, developmental psycholinguists are particularly interested in the acquisition of deictic terms as they offer an avenue for studying how children learn to understand that other people have a different perspective than their own. Pre-school-aged children have particular difficulty with using expressions such as 'here/there' and 'this/that' (Tanz, 1980), and many argue that this is because they have not reached the appropriate level of cognitive development.

A third reason for the interest in deictic terms arises from the controversy over whether people possess a 'universal grammar'. In the previous chapter we noted that Chomsky's theory rested on the assumption that the mind is a computational entity. Chomsky also argued that the only way you could explain how a young child could learn language (in the time it appears to take) was by proposing that he/she is genetically predisposed to acquire it. This innatist view of language acquisition can be found in the contemporary work of Pinker (1984) and Karmiloff-Smith (1983). In contrast, linguists who favour a functionalist account of language understanding argue that a structural analysis of the similarities of deictic expressions across the world's languages holds out the promise of a 'universal grammar' of language use. Brown and Levinson (1978), for example, argue that the way social honorifics (another form of deixis) operates can be explained as a politeness phenomenon related to 'saving face'. Their cross-linguistic analysis highlights how a 'social-discursive' universal grammar might be formulated.

Many forms of deixis also allow us to examine how social rules and relations are encoded in language. Johnson (1994), for example, notes that the way in which people giving important public speeches will utilise the pronominal deictic term 'we' so as to index social relationships. He points out that rhetorical goals are often achieved by a careful manipulation of the shifting meanings of deictic terms in discourse. The analysis of kin terms (expressions we use to refer to our relatives) is another form of social deixis which provides a useful avenue to study social relations. In addition, examining how children acquire social deixis has been studied in a number of languages (Carter, 1984, in India; Hollos, 1977, in Hungary; Tanz, 1980, in England).

A fifth reason why deixis is important to the psychology of language derives from the relationship between deixis and reference. Levinson (1983) notes that contemporary philosophy has a renewed interest in this issue, arising in part from the recognition that if a word can be said to have 'sense' and 'reference', then how did it become associated with the particular object referred to in the first place? For example, when children are learning their first words they invariably accompany the sound they make with a pointing gesture (a deictic act if you like). Golinkoff's (1983) detailed analysis of how children acquire some of their earliest words shows how, first, the child makes a gesture, then a gesture accompanied by the sound for the word, and then finally the sound replacing the gesture completely. Sign language research also has an interest in the deixis/ reference issue, given that the study of sign language provides a context for investigating the relationship between language and gesture (e.g. Haukiouja, 1993; McNeill, 1985). Studying communicative development where the grammar is so clearly 'external' provides a unique opportunity for those debating issues in language acquisition research.

A final reason why we might be interested in deixis is that deictic terms are of course used in writing as well as in speech. What is often called discourse deixis considers how deictic and anaphoric terms help create cohesion in text. Anaphora describes any situation in which a word is used as a substitute for a preceding word or group of words. So, if somebody was telling a story and began by saying 'Once upon a time there was a princess called Snow White . . .', then more often than not in one of the following sentences you would find the deictic pronoun 'she' employed anaphorically, as in 'One day **she** went for a walk in the woods . . .' (she referring to Snow White). The study of anaphoric relations is a key part of experimental psycholinguistics, particularly in studies of sentence and extended text comprehension (Garrod, Freudenthal & Boyle, 1994; Williams, 1993). We will go on to look a little closer at the role of dis- course deixis particularly as it helps clarify important distinctions between talk and text.

Deictic comprehension and conceptualising the deictic centre

Keeping in mind the idea that deixis serves as a good topic for examining the relationship between 'thinking' and 'talk', we can consider the relation- ship between the event of making an utterance (saying something) and the speaker who actually makes the sound. A useful way to conceive of what is involved is by thinking of what is known as the deictic centre:

- The central position is the speaker.
- The central time is the moment when the speaker makes the utterance.
- The central place is the speaker's location at the time of the utterance.
- The discourse centre is the point which the speaker is currently at (or has reached) at the moment of the production of his/her utterance.
- The social centre is the speaker's social status or rank, to which the status or rank of the addressee is relative.

Outlined in this way, the complexity of deictic comprehension seems to defy description, which is curious given that most of us appear to use deictic terms unproblematically when we communicate. However, this should remind us that we have all spent a very long time acquiring language, and Karmiloff-Smith (1983) notes that even at age seven or eight years, children still have difficulty with deictic expressions. Levinson (1983) highlights the complexity of deictic comprehension by asking us to imagine some sort of four-dimensional space:

> [It may help] readers to visualise this unmarked deictic centre if they can imagine a four-dimensional space, composed of the three dimensions of space plus that of time, in which a speaker stands at the centre. Radiating out from the speaker are a number of concentric circles distinguishing different zones of spatial proximity; through the speaker passes a 'time line', on which events prior to his present utterance, and events prior to those, can be linearly arranged, and similarly events at points and spans in the future; while the discourse to which the speaker contributes unfolds along this same time line.
>
> To capture the social aspects of deixis, we would need to add at least one further dimension, say of relative rank, in which the speaker is socially higher, lower or equal to the addressee and other persons that [sic] might be referred to. Now when the speaker and addressee switch participant roles, the co-ordinates of this entire world switch to the space–time–social centre of the erstwhile addressee, now speaker. Such a picture makes the acquisition of deictic terms seem a miracle. (p. 64)

The remainder of this chapter will describe in more detail the main types of deixis, consider in brief how children appear to acquire appropriate use of these terms, and conclude by examining how deictic terms are employed in conversation. One issue which underpins how the topics below are outlined is the relationship between **thinking** and **talk**, as domains of inquiry for the psychology of language. Deictic comprehension and production certainly seem to rest upon our ability to make inferences, take another's perspective, understand how things would look from another location, and so on. At the same time, the dynamics of talk itself appears to defy prolonged cognitive considerations (talk is dynamic, immediate or 'on-line'), and for the most part we utilise deictic terms without effort. In fact, some languages encode the semantics of space and interaction simul-taneously, calling into question assumptions about cognition–language separation in the first place (e.g. for Mopan Maya spoken in Yucatan, space and place are not objectively 'out there' but much more fluid and dynamically related to the ongoing interaction). However, this pre-empts our outline description of the main types of deixis.

Person deixis

When we are interacting with one another, the deictic centre changes quickly from person to person. And obviously my use of the word 'I' is interchangeable with your use of the word 'you'. This pronominal shifting is best understood within a pragmatic framework of participant roles as Levinson (1983) argues. The basic grammatical distinctions which encode participant roles are the first, second and the third person. So, normally when in the role of speaker we use the first person, as addressee second person, and when neither speaker or addressee, the third person. However, interaction contexts can have speakers, addressees, spokesperson who is distinct from utterance source (e.g. newsreader), recipients distinct from addressee or target, and overhearers (see Goffman, 1976, for clarification of participant roles). Although many languages have a basic first, second and third person category scheme, this is not always the case. Japanese, for example, uses pronouns which distinguish sex of speaker, degree of intimacy with person addressed, social stutus of speaker, and so on,[1] and Brown and Levinson (1978) note that Tamil has six singular second person pronouns which indicate relative rank between speaker and addressee. The use of the deictic pronoun 'we' can also be an important marker of social identity and group membership (Johnson, 1994).

How you learn to use personal pronouns highlights the significance of interaction and the participant role you happen to be in. Arguably, it is very difficult to see how you could learn the 'pronominal shifting' (I'm 'I' and you are 'you' during my turn, and then 'you are 'I' and I'm 'you' when it's your turn) if you don't have many opportunities for watching other people do this first (and your earliest examples are heard where somebody picks you up and says to you, 'Who's a pretty girl, then Jenny? Aren't you?' – i.e. who's the girl, who's Jenny, never mind 'you'?). The role of overhearing and the acquisition of first and second person pronoun forms was investigated by Oshima-Takane (1988). By comparing children who had exposure to other people using personal pronoun forms with children with very minimal experience, she established that acquisition is facilitated by overhearing and observing talk. In other words it is much more difficult to learn pronominal shifting through face-to-face interaction. Although the data are somewhat difficult to interpret, there is little doubt that over-hearing and observing others plays a part in the acquisition of deictic terms. This is further supported by Fox (1980), who has highlighted the problems hearing-impaired children have with certain deictic terms, particularly where they are constrained by face-to-face interaction dynamics.

Likewise, we can ask how you acquire an appropriate understanding of the deictic term 'we', say during your earliest experiences of being a group member (e.g. in pre-school). Exposure to group-addressing speech can be seen as a unique situation where participation can be optional, i.e. either as a possible 'next speaker' participating listener or as a more passive 'overhearing listener'. As a member of the group a young child has to simultaneously comprehend that as part of that group, she can fulfil the role of participating listener, as in the two-party encounter (and in her response talk 'for' the group), while at the same time perceiving her potential role as only one of many 'overhearing' listeners. In effect there is the possibility (unlike two-person encounters) of being freed from certain participation requirements. Somebody else in the group can make the necessary reply, not her. In fact one skill to be acquired is how to recognise situations where it would be wiser to 'stay mum'. Another is to know that as a group member you are a member of a participation context which has quite distinct social participation rules (to those previously encountered). In a study of group-addressing speech in the pre-school by an adult to children aged between two and five years, I came across many interesting (and potentially confusing) examples of 'we' (see Forrester, 1989):

(2) Right, boys and girls, we are going to tidy up now.
(3) We'll just have Ian in the middle.
(4) I think we'll have this story . . . there are too many people sitting chattering.
(5) Well some of you have got your fingers on your lips anyway.
(6) We won't get any sweets if we carry on like this, will we Brenda?

Certainly, we should not be suprised that learning the subtle distinctions implicit in the use of specific deictic terms in context takes a considerable length of time. When we also recognise that in many instances deictic terms for person are used alongside deictic terms for space, time and status, then we might begin to wonder how we ever learned to use them appropriately at all.

Place, space deixis

There are a whole range of words in the English language which are generally only understood if we know the position of the speaker making the utterance. Spatial locations relative to principal speakers and hearers would include *here* and *there*, *this* and *that*, *in front of* and *behind*, *below* and *above*, *inside* and *outside*, and so on. Lyons (1977) suggests that there are two ways in which we refer to objects in the world – either by describing and naming them (the red box), or by locating them (it's over there). As we noted earlier in discussing the relationship between deixis and reference, obtaining a sufficiently rich theoretical understanding of space and location is not without its problems. It has been argued, for example, that there are at least two ways to understand how anybody manages to locate an object in space (see Verjat, 1994). One idea, described as the 'spatially pure' approach, suggests that the frame of reference can either be egocentric (focused on the subject) or allocentric (focused on the outside). The metaphor of spatial purity is employed so as to emphasise the fact that this approach is independent of language. An

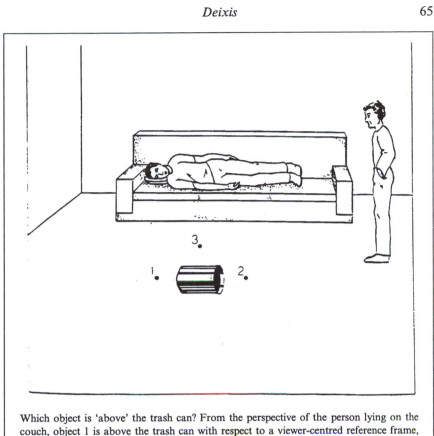

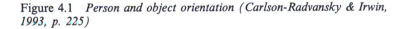

Which object is 'above' the trash can? From the perspective of the person lying on the couch, object 1 is above the trash can with respect to a viewer-centred reference frame, object 2 is above with respect to an object-centred reference frame, and object 3 is above with respect to an environment-centred reference frame.

Figure 4.1 *Person and object orientation (Carlson-Radvansky & Irwin, 1993, p. 225)*

alternative idea is that of the 'spatio-linguistic' approach which describes the frames of reference as being either deictic (focused on the subject) or non-deictic (focused on the object).

Consider how this is taken up in a study by Carlson-Radvansky and Irwin (1993), who asked people to locate an object above another object (see Figure 4.1). In a series of experiments designed to test whether comprehension of *above* was dependent on either a deictic or an object-centred frame of reference, the results indicated that what really mattered was a spatial assignment procedure. In other words, people first had to establish their own paramaters for spatial location in context, and then comprehend expressions such as *above* and *below* relative to this assignment. Certainly this accords with our everyday experience of the potential confusion when somebody asks us to give him/her an object equidistant from both of you, while saying something like

(7)   Oh, can you put *this* over *there*?

Our understanding of *this* and *there* is, in the above example, dependent on our comprehension of the speaker's perspective and mutual knowledge of shared conventions for proximity (when something is reasonably far away from somebody to be 'there' and not 'here'). People also have considerable difficulty with deictic expressions for place such as *in front of* and *behind* (Abkarian, 1982), primarily because of the independent nature of our knowledge of WHAT something is, compared to WHERE it is. However, Brown (1994) points out that in the Mayan language Tzeltel, object configurations and locations are encoded in verb roots, and the language has three distinct systems for specifying geographical anchorage, deictic viewer-centred perspective and object-centred orientations, reminding us that deictic comprehension may not be dependent on underlying spatial abilities but interdependent with lexical distinctions encoded in whichever language is being used.

Alternative conceptions to the English demonstrative and deictic terms for space can also be found in American Indian languages. In Haida, for example, there are at least thirteen directional suffixes which encapsulate relations between space, person and spirits. Enrico (1985) analyses the suffix distinctions between *gat*, which means 'towards the edge of a clear space', and *sa*, which means 'towards the centre of a clear space'. The first would help describe the boundary of the clear space intrinsic to the four walls of a room; the second the clear unbounded space of the sea. In Haida, the significance of fire (normally at the centre of a square room with a roof opening for smoke) was that it was the medium of transfer and communication between the everyday and the spirit world. The encoding of suffix terms which fulfilled a deictic function is reflected in myths which describe how hunters could escape into the spirit world by entering the fire:

> This conception of the fire as continuing beyond the focal point of the house interior into another world brings into approximation the two chief members of the set of clear spaces, the house interior and the sea, the bounded with the unbounded. (Enrico, 1985, p. 402)

Suffice it to say, that such radically different ways of carving up our experience of space, place and location in the world should caution us against assuming that the 'account' encoded in our own deictic schema somehow reflects a real objective world of objects.

Time deixis

For many English-speaking people, one fairly obvious way in which our understanding of deictic terms is linked to how utterances are 'anchored' in context is with the many words which encode time (just now; then; last night; tomorrow morning; next month, and so on). Many languages have particular ways for encoding our natural experience of time (day/night; lunar cycles, etc.) relative to when an utterance is made. The most common distinction, as Levinson (1983) notes, is between measures which focus on time relative to a fixed point of interest such as the speaker ('I'm going to go the cinema in half-an-hour'), and calendrical time, which encapsulates time measures relative to some absolute origin (such as the birth of Christ). Consider how the significance, or otherwise, of the immediate present (now) is encoded in the following sentences:

(8) I'll cook dinner now.   [possibly uttered just before you start]
(9) I'm cooking dinner now.   [uttered when you're cooking]
(10) I can't go down to the shop. I'm cooking dinner now.
(11) I was going to cook dinner now.
(12) I've cooked dinner now.
(13) I cooked the dinner. Now I'm going to eat it.
                        Now I am eating it.

                                             (Wright, 1987)

Or, as we noted above (p. 59), notice how when we are arranging a forthcoming meeting with somebody we might find ourselved asking for clarification if we are told:

(14) I'll see you next Thursday, OK?

In other words, if we are addressed in this way on a Thursday, Friday or Saturday, then we are much likely to answer 'Oh, do you mean this Thursday or next Thursday?' – a very common request for clarification if we are spoken to on Sunday, Monday, Tuesday or Wednesday. A related participant role distinction that Levinson (1983) draws our attention to is the difference between when an utterance is actually spoken (coding time) and when we actually receive the utterance (receiving time). Notices on shop-doors which read 'Back in 20 minutes' alert us to this, and only if we wait for the period indicated could we be assured that the writer's 'coding time' corresponds in some way to our receiving time.

Part of the problem with time deixis is that present time is something that we experience as continuous and ongoing, and yet we can talk of time as if bounced around relative to points in the past and the future. Wright (1987) looks carefully at the way we use the deictic term 'now', and considers how it demarcates the moment of an utterance, relative to an emphasis that the speaker intends:

(15) She's been seeing this psychiatrist now for three months.
(16) She's been seeing this psychiatrist for three months now.

MOMENT OF UTTERANCE

And note how this demarcation can be modified with reference to the time before the current utterance:

(17) I finished cooking the dinner, vs
(18) I finished cooking the dinner just now.

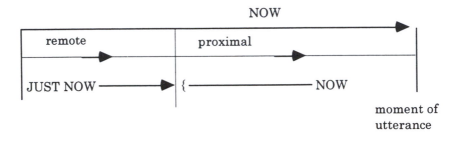

Wright (1987) comments that South African English has a unique segmentation phrase (now now) signifying a maximally proximal temporal point, 'thereby setting up a three point scale of futurity . . . demarcating and separating immediate from remote proximal future points' (pp. 173–174):

(20) I'll finish washing the car just now.
(21) I'll finish washing the car now now.

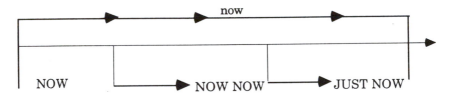

The study of time deixis highlights the difficulty of attempting to articulate a general linguistic theory to explain language understanding, as Levinson (1983) notes. Deictic words as linguistic entities interact with any given culture's conception of time and the specific usage of these terms cannot be easily explained along universal formalisms.

Discourse deixis

Whenever you are talking (or writing) there are many occasions where you refer back to some topic or item of discussion which has already taken place. Your discourse unfolds over time, and forms of discourse deixis indicate or point to a particular aspect of the preceding discourse. So, you might use the phrase:

(21) Well, that's the silliest joke I've ever heard [after somebody has told you a joke]

where *that's* is a discourse deictic expression pointing back to the previous chunk of talk. Such terms are always anchored to the discourse location of the current utterance. Many are found in 'utterance initial position' such as *but, anyway, therefore, look, after all, however*, and they fulfil a number of functions such as indicating how the present utterance might relate topically to what has come before. We have to be very careful not to confuse discourse deixis with anaphora, which is a linguistic term describing circumstances where a word is used to refer back to (or is a substitute for) a preceding word or group of words. This is not easy, again as Levinson (1983) notes, where he gives the example:

(22)   I was born in London and have lived there ever since

where **there** simultaneously refers anaphorically to the word 'London' (note the speaker could have said *in London* again instead of there), and deictically contrasts with **here** to indicate that the place 'London' is not where the current utterance is taking place. Words such as *then* and *that* are particularly open to simultaneous anaphoric/deictic use (see Reichmanandar, 1984, and Schiffrin, 1992), and anaphoric relations in text have become a major focus for experimental psychologists interested in how people comprehend extended written text (Williams, 1993).

An additional way in which aspects of discourse deixis have a close affinity with space or place deixis can be seen within the context of story-telling. In a series of studies looking at how people narrate everyday events and stories, McNeill (1985) and his colleagues (McNeill, Cassell & Levy, 1993) have shown that there is a very close relationship between deictic gestures and the introduction of characters in a story, plot development and important 'meta-narrative' events. For example, when a story-teller wishes to make an interpretative comment on some aspect of the story she is herself narrating, then she will often do so accompanied by pointing in the direction of the person listening to her. In contrast, when describing the context which surrounds where the story took place, she might point at the empty space between herself and the listener. Similarly, in everyday conversations when a new topic is being introduced this is often accompanied by deictic gestures, which then disappear or are replaced by other more metaphoric gestures (such as a shrug of the shoulders) when the shared topic is being oriented to by those concerned. McNeill et al. (1993) comment:

> The reason people seem to point at an empty space [during story-telling] is that, thanks to the creative work of gesture, the space is not in fact empty! (p. 17)

We can also note that discourse and time deixis are interrelated in the act of story-telling given that the narrator creates a 'time line' where the non-verbal pointing gestures accompanying the story frame the discourse deixis as the story unfolds. Such actions can be likened to the 'discourse scaffolding the speaker must be constructing to support and clarify the core story' (McNeill et al., 1993, p. 18).

Social honorifics

A fifth key area of deixis is what has been called social deixis or social honorifics. Levinson (1983) restricts the definition of social deixis to 'those aspects of language structure that encode the social identities of participants or the social relationships between them' (p. 89). Fillmore (1975) defines social deixis as 'that aspect of sentences which reflect or establish or are determined by certain realities of the social situation in which the speech act occurs' (p. 76). Certainly in recent decades there has been an increasing interest in studying the role of linguistic categories in establishing and maintaining social relationships (see Agha, 1994, for a useful review of 'honorification'). Social constructionist and discourse analysts often argue that there are many situations where we only have to start talking and immediately what we say, and how we say it, reflects (and reproduces) the social relationships we hold with one another.

We need to be careful here to distinguish between social deixis (specific deictic terms which 'grammaticalise' social relations between people) and honorification language processes more generally, which would include register shifts (e.g. changes in the way you might say something depending on who you are talking to), bi-lingual code switching and politeness phenomena. With regard to social deixis, Levinson (1983) distinguishes between relational (or participant role) honorifics and absolute honorifics. The former, for example, can be differentiated between:

(a) referent honorifics: which involves the speaker referent (who is actually speaking – e.g. the *tu/vous* distinction in French); and
(b) addressee honorifics: which involves both speaker and addressee relations.

Levinson (1983) notes that in languages such as Korean and Japanese it is possible to use an expression such as 'The soup is hot' and encode respect to the addressee without actually referring to him or her: 'in general, in such languages it is almost impossible to say anything at all which is not sociolinguistically marked as appropriate for certain kinds of addressees only' (p. 90).

Absolute honorifics, on the other hand, are expressions which are reserved for authorised speakers. Fillmore (1971), for example, notes that there are very specific particle forms (first person pronouns) confined for use by the Emperor of Japan. Likewise authorised recipient honorofics are familiar to anyone in England who is going to meet the Queen in person. He/she would be taught beforehand not just what to do on meeting the Queen (e.g. bowing or curtseying), but also how to speak, and to take care to use the social honorific 'Ma'am'. It would simply not be permissible to say 'Hi, there. How's things with you then?'

Studying such words grammatically and considering how they are used in practice can often be a little confusing. Levinson (1983) notes that we should be careful to differentiate between how social honorofics are employed in service of a specific social function and how they are encoded in the structure of whatever language is being used. Sociolinguists are primarily concerned with how honorofics and other related politiness phenomenon reflect social relations between people. Linguists are less concerned with functional rules, and more with how it has come about that language structure encodes social information in the first place.

Honorofic process more generally extends the boundaries of social deixis (or social honorofics). Honorification includes pronoun and address forms, politeness phenomena, honorofic register, social indexicality and code-switching. Agha (1994), for example, defines honorification as any linguistic means whereby social relations can become marked – linguistic encoding which marks relationships involving social status, respect or deference between communicative interactants. In order to obtain a better under-standing of honorofic language processes, we can consider two of these in brief: politeness phenomena and code-switching.

Many languages use very specific forms of address and reference in order to encode politeness. For example, in many instances politeness is related to power, influence and deference: and you might be much more polite to somebody who has some power over you, particularly where you want to obtain something from that person. Likewise, you are much more likely to respond positively to somebody who has asked you politely, 'Excuse me, could you spare me 10p for a cup of tea', compared to receiving a demand such as 'Give me some money, I'm hungry'. Brown and Levinson (1978) have developed a model of politeness phenomena which they say can explain many of the consistent patterns of politeness observed across cultures.

Resting on the Gricean ideas of co-operation and implicature which we summarised in Chapter 3, Brown and Levinson (1978) argue that forms of politeness (and the likelihood of their occurring) rest upon certain rationalist rules of conversation that people hold. Underpinning many of our social conventions is the notion of 'face', and politeness phenomena exist as a protective mechanism against threats to one's 'face'. Their interactional pessimist orientation is implicit in their suggestion that:

> Normally everyone's 'face' depends on everyone else's being maintained . . . and since people can be expected to defend their 'faces' if threatened and in defending their own to threaten others 'faces', it is in everyone's best interest to maintain each other's faces . . . that is, to act in ways that assure the other participants that the agent is heedful of the assumptions concerning face governing conversation. (p. 59)

This notion of face is universal and is further sub-divided into negative (the desire to be unimpeded by others) and positive (the need to have one's wants desired by others) face. For example, using familiar forms of the second person pronoun (the *tu/vous* distinction in French) indicates an assumption of positive politiness, while, in contrast, reciprocal use of the formal pronoun emphasises the social distance of 'negative politeness'. So, the general idea is that everybody has certain wants and desires, and the only way of maintaining or achieving these needs is to be sensitive to whether other people's actions serve to threaten our interests, or, in turn, whether our desires are seen as potentially threatening by others. We don't just rush up and demand something from somebody; rather we recognise that we will increase the chances of obtaining what we want by using language in a 'face-saving' way (e.g. 'Excuse me, I know it is a lot to ask, but I was wondering if you could possibly lend me some money').

Brown and Levinson (1978) argue that for any given face-threatening act (FTA) any speaker can work out the potential risk of face-loss in terms of three variables: social distance, relative power and the significance of the particular imposition in that specific culture. Their paper provides many examples of how their formula works in practice across different cultures (in different languages). Certainly in terms of other theorists of politeness phenomena, Brown and Levinson include a wide range of utterance types (including many examples of the social honorifics referred to above) in their analysis. And underpinning their social calculus formulation of 'frozen conversational implicature' (p. 23) is their dissatisfaction with theories of grammar which overemphasise cognitive rather than social factors. Their concern is with

> the search for a source outside the purely linguistic system that might motivate the bulk of grammatical constraints. . . . Normally 'internal' cognitive explanations are favoured, but there are 'external' pragmatic theories that seek to link linguistic structures to the organization of communication. (p. 82)

Code-switching is another interesting example of honorification language processes, although in this instance it amounts to a much broader meta-pragmatic phenomenon (i.e. a language process which people themselves monitor and employ in deliberate ways so as to accomplish a particular goal). Commentators argue that bi-lingual code-switching reflects the close relationship between language use and politics (e.g. DeBernardi, 1994). In other words, ways of speaking often mark out personal and social identities such that language realises and reproduces the power structure of a given society (Halliday, 1978), and in many multi-lingual societies the use, or not, of the 'standardised' or 'officially ratified' language can indicate a great deal about the social identity of the speaker. Emphasising the social function of code-switching Romaine (1989) notes that in Norway a switch from the local dialect to 'official' Norwegian (e.g. in the post office) serves to indicate to the person addressed that the topic has now moved from simple everyday talk between equals to the formal relation of customer and shopkeeper engaged in a business transaction.

Defining code-switching formally as 'the use of two or more linguistic varieties in the same conversation or interaction', Scotton and Ury (1977, p. 5) consider the general hypothesis that code-switching occurs because at least one speaker wishes to redefine the interaction by moving the topic they are discussing into a different arena or discourse. Examining the relationship between linguistic code and the social meaning of the conversation,

Scotton and Ury investigated naturally occurring conversations among the Luyia of Western Kenya where at least three languages are spoken: Swahili, the national language and also the language of business and commerce; English, considered as the language of power and officialdom; and a Luyia dialect, i.e. the language used by people simply chatting to each other. They report many interesting instances where the switching from one language to another serves quite specific functions, and the people taking part in the study showed strong agreement over such functions. For example, a bus-driver and a passenger are chatting in a friendly way in Luyia (the local dialect) as they drive along, occasionally changing into Swahili when negotiating the price of the fare. When the passenger is nearing his stop, and has yet to be given his change, there is an additional switch from Swahili ('I want my change') to English ('I'm nearing my destination') so as to emphasise the role of power, i.e. the passenger has a right to his change before he has to get off the bus.

Redefining the ongoing social interaction is one of the most important functions of bi-lingual code-switching, although recent commentators have raised questions over whether code-switching is really a form of register variation. Register is a technical term in linguistics which refers to a dialect associated with a particular social function. So, we all have a range of different registers to cope with the wide variety of social roles we find ourselves in. Geerhardt (1995) has noted the particular register shifts that young mono-lingual children employ when moving from pretend play to negotiating with each other. Halmari and Smith (1994) studied in detail code-switching and register shift in bi-lingual Finnish–English children. They found that for serious negotiation ('What shall we play now?') they would code-switch from their second into their first language. When in character mode (during play) they would use their second language. Furthermore, while code-switching was most often associated with shifting from one conversational task to another, it was also marked prosodically (changes in intonation, pitch and stress) and grammatically through the use of particular deictic terms, shifts in tense, and so on. All of this, Halmari and Smith suggest, is evidence that code-switching may be conceived as a marker of register change, relevant to the study of all populations (not just bi-lingual cultures). However, this suggestion may be somewhat overstated given the grammatical distinctions involved with bi-lingual code-switching. Mid-sentence bi-lingual code-switching does not occur, yet register shifts are quite possible during a single utterance.

Social honorifics or social deixis is a term covering many aspects of language use. It encodes social identities and interaction relations on occasion through the grammaticalisation of deictic terms (e.g. pronouns), at other times through more general meta-pragmatic factors such as politeness phenomena. Social deixis also bears upon other social functions of language such as register shift and code-switching, topics which predicate the significance of language use in context. Furthermore, honorification processes themselves not only help maintain social relations between people, but also serve as one site for challenging such relations, as the historical analysis of the development of the pronominal contrast (*tu/vous*) in Europe has shown (Brown & Gillman, 1960). Finally, exposure to social honorofics provides an ideal context for inculcation into the conventions, rules and relations of any given culture. Hollos's (1977) study of pronoun use with Hungarian children brought up either in the town or the country-side emphasises the interdependent nature of language acquisition, social-cognitive development, and the social context. The complexities of such deictic categorisation schemes have led commentators to ask how children manage to understand and use deictic terms in the first place, which brings us to our next topic.

The acquisition of deictic terms

Investigating how children manage to acquire deictic terms is of interest to psycholinguists and developmental psychologists because it provides a 'way-in' to examine the relationship between language acquisition and cognitive development. Developmental psychology throughout the 1970s and 1980s was critically concerned with the extent to which children under the age of seven years were intrinsically egocentric in the way Piaget (1932) originally described (i.e. conceived of the world from their own point of view, with considerable difficulty in understanding somebody else's per-spective). Donaldson (1978) and others called into question the experi-mental rigour of Piaget's studies and the ensuing debate focused on what children at various stages of development could accomplish. The study of deictic terms offers a unique method of teasing out the relative importance of perspective-taking abilities and language understanding given that adequate comprehension depends on the child recognising the anchorage point of the speaker (and corresponding shifts to the listener as turn-taking proceeds).

Psycholinguists investigating child language have a particular interest in the acquisition of deictic terms because they offer a way to examine the extent to which language learning is dependent upon innate or environ-mental factors. The structure of deictic systems can indeed be considerably complex (pronominal, locative, and so on) and appropriate use would imply possessing fairly sophisticated cognitive abilities. On the other hand, comprehending and using deictic terms is interdependent with the social interaction context, as we noted earlier: it is simply not possible to under-stand and use such terms except with regard to participant role during the ongoing interaction. Learning a language goes hand in hand with learning all about social rules, conventions and interaction practices.

Research work on the acquisition of deictic terms can be divided into three different themes: acquisition studies, perspective-taking investigations and participant role research. Acquisition studies concentrate on precisely when children begin to understand and use various different deictic terms (e.g. Chiat, 1981, and Tanz, 1980, on pronouns; Collis, 1991, and Charney, 1979, on locatives). Considerable attention has been paid to the strategies children use in order to learn the contrastive aspects of locatives (*here* and *there*), and demonstratives (*this* and *that*). Starting from the notion that the most critical issue for the child is cognising specific location with respect to the 'anchorage point' of the speaker's utterance, various studies have attempted to map out what is involved (Clark & Sengul, 1978; de Villiers & de Villiers, 1979) and outline the stages the child moves through. Wales (1983), for example, suggests that the child moves from an early 'functional' recognition stage, through a spatial/locative/person contrastive stage, and from there on to 'typical' adult forms. More recently, Choi and Bowerman (1991) found very different patterns of acquisition across English and Korean for deictic words of motion (*come/go*), which they say reflected the different lexical distinctions in the two languages. This, they say, challenges the common assumption in the research that children map spatial words onto underlying non-linguistic concepts. Rather, children are influenced by the semantic organisation of their language right from the beginning.

Perspective-taking and proximity studies focus instead on the questions of the child's egocentricity. Karmiloff-Smith (1983), for example, notes that children do not acquire full adult use of many deictic terms until aged eight or nine years (which would correspond to Piaget's concrete operational stage formulation). Proximity is emphasised in studies examining the contrastive spatial function, i.e. where *here* is taken to be the space near a speaker and *there* defined as locations distant from the speaker (Clark & Sengul, 1978). A common finding is for the young pre-school child to adopt a 'position strategy' (i.e. whenever in doubt choose a location near the speaker), and Charney (1979) argues that the comprehension of *here* and *there* involves the child recognising that *there* most often describes somewhere away from self and other (speakers), whereas *here* is sometimes near self and sometimes near other people. It remains an unresolved question whether proximity interacts with perspective-taking in line with the notion of egocentrism (Tanz, 1980).

Participant role studies of the development of deictic comprehension focus primarily on the discourse context. Oshima-Takane (1987) and Forrester (1988) have drawn attention to the facilitative nature of the overhearing/observing context for the young child's acquisition of pronouns. The idea that I/you shifts (pronoun reversals) are easier to learn if the child can first watch others using these terms in ongoing dialogue is supported by Pine's (1995) study of first- and second-born children. He found that a significantly greater number of deictic personal pronouns in the first 100 words of second- compared to first-born children. They benefited by being exposed to an increased number of instances of overhearing and observing pronoun reversals. Correct use of the third person pronoun also requires a fairly sophisticated understanding of the relationship between speaker, addressee and the third person. Brener (1987) and Tanz (1980) both report the particular difficulties children up to aged six have with this personal pronoun form, although Forrester (1992) reports on the skills pre-school children have in utilising opportunities for interruption after hearing others use their own name in the third person.

It is also noteworthy that there are deictic contrast problems related to the complexities of participant role and turn-taking in conversation. On the one hand there are issues which highlight the relationship between the discourse context and a given deictic expression in a (usually) single sentence utterance. At the same time there are factors surrounding conversational coherence and changing speaker–listener roles. Goodell and Sachs (1992) note the particular problems young children have with deictic shifting in their story-telling (i.e. changing from direct speech – the original speech of a character – to indirect speech – their current reporting). Complete mastery of such an ability extends over many years.

Many issues are thrown up by the study of the acquisition of deictic terms. Some work seeks to solve questions over whether children map particular expressions onto underlying non-linguistic concepts; other research focuses on whether children learning language really are as egocentric as has been suggested; and yet other work attempts to consider the role of participation. Certainly when we remind ourselves of the complexities of the 'deictic centre', never mind the myriad deictic forms the child will acquire by the time he/she is nine or ten years old, we can concur with Levinson's (1983) assertion that sometimes it seems a miracle they manage to acquire correct use at all.

Deixis and the conversational context

Fully understanding the relationship between comprehending and using deictic expressions remains a challenge for psycholinguistics. A cross-linguistic analysis of many deictic forms would highlight the fact that different cultures encode category distinctions in quite distinct ways (personal pronouns, time deixis, social honorifics, and so on). Moreover, investigating such forms would reveal the ways in which these distinctions are systematically encoded grammatically. At the same time understanding the meaning of such expressions demands that we know something of the roles of the speaker, addressee and anybody else involved in the interactions. But it is not only syntax and semantics which come together in the study of such expressions: we also need to know something of the principles of communicative organisation and the social rules and conventions of the given culture, i.e. additional pragmatic and meta-pragmatic factors which contribute to how the terms are used.

It is for this reason that deixis serves as an important example of the interface between language understanding and social interaction. Certainly it is reasonable to argue that any given individual would have to possess fairly sophisticated cognitive abilities to understand the distinctions encoded by deictic expressions. At the same time the dynamics of the ongoing interaction are critical for both understanding and employing such forms. We have noted how communicative principles bear upon social deixis, how time and discourse deixis interact during the telling of a story, the significance of recognising the 'anchorage' point of the current speaker and numerous other instances predicating the importance of the conversational context. It is simply not possible to use deictic expressions in an appropriate way without an understanding of the dynamics of the ongoing interaction. During conversation, participation is constantly shifting and changing, and deictic comprehension often requires an immediate cognisance of who said what, where, when and in what way, never mind the status of the person talking and the background institutional framework against which the interaction is taking place. We open the door on the second theme of the book – the study of talk.

Notes

1. Levinson's (1983) excellent chapter on deixis provides many details of the deictic terms described here.

5

Conversational Analysis and Accountability in Everyday Talk

It is clear that many linguistic expressions cannot be adequately understood except with reference to the context in which they are used, i.e. people using language to communicate with each other. The second theme of this book is critically concerned with talk, probably the most frequent activity we all participate in every day. The study of talk or conversation is approached in a number of different ways by disciplines within the cognitive and social sciences. Researchers in artificial intelligence, for example, will seek to encapsulate formal aspects of intentional communication to aid their understanding of how artificial systems might 'talk' to each other. Social psychologists and discourse analysts often look very carefully at the content of talk, in order to examine the ways in which people's concerns are linked to ideological constructs within society. Linguists might be more concerned with the fine-grained analysis of prosody (pitch or loudness) and how this is used by conversationalists so as to add emphasis to something being said. And developmental psychologists often look for evidence of how children acquire social and cognitive skills by considering how they manage to enter into (and subsequently direct) conversations with peers and parents.

Arguably, however, the contemporary study of conversation is dominated by the work of conversational analysts, a group which encompasses sociologists, psychologists, scholars from humanities and, increasingly, researchers in human–computer interaction and other applied areas of the social sciences. In this and the following chapter we will be looking in some depth at the work which has emerged from conversational analysis, as well as critically considering the contribution this approach has made to the psychology of language. First, however, our understanding of the theories and methods of conversational analysis would be incomplete if we overlooked the tradition they emerged from: a branch of sociology which encompassed ethnomethodology and ethnography.

Ethnomethodology can be traced to a group of dissatisfied sociologists who, during the 1960s, began to call into question the way quantitative sociology imposed arbitrary categories in their classification of sociological phenomena. Building in part on the work of social anthropology and ethnography, ethnomethodologists insisted on placing centre-stage participants' own formulations of their everyday interactions. In other words, the object of sociological inquiry should be 'the set of techniques that the members of a society themselves utilise to interpret and act within their own social world' (Levinson, 1983, p. 295). Ethnomethodology can be defined as the study of 'ethnic' (the participants' own) methods of production and interpretation of social interaction.

In order to understand why this approach is considered uniquely qualitative and 'inductive', consider first how a quantitative social scientist might study conversation. An experimental social psychologist with a particular hypothesis in mind would seek first to record a representative sample of conversation between people, transcribe the words spoken into lines of analysable text, and then categorise the utterances according to some *pre-determined* classification system. The frequency of this or that category would then be amenable to statistical analysis and interpretations made regarding whether there was a significantly greater amount of category x in one context compared to another, ultimately lending support to the original hypothesis or not.

In contrast, an ethnomethodological approach to the study of conversation would insist that unless the participants themselves display an orientation to some category, model or rationale underpinning the activity of their ongoing talk, then no 'outside' analyst is in any position to emphasise one classification system over any another. Ethnomethodology is always centrally concerned with the rational analysis of the structures, procedures and strategies that participants themselves employ so as to make sense out of their everyday world. Beattie (1983) notes that for ethnomethodologists conversation is simply there, not to be approached with pre-conceived constructs, and Levinson (1983) succinctly summarises this outlook where he notes:

> Out of [ethnomethodology] comes a healthy suspicion of premature theorising and ad hoc analytical categories: as far as possible the categories of analysis should be those that participants themselves utilise in making sense of interaction; unmotivated theoretical constructs and unsubstantiated intuitions are all to be avoided. (p. 295)

Related to this emphasis upon the rational analysis of participants' own constructivist processes, two other issues for the study of conversation derive from ethnomethodology: *the architecture of intersubjectivity* and *accountability*. The significance of the 'architecture of intersubjectivity' is apparent where we recognise the impossibility of obtaining access to (truly knowing) anybody else's intentions, thoughts or feelings. However, although we cannot access another person's private thoughts and experience, nevertheless we can obtain an 'intersubjective' shared world as an ordinary practical accomplishment. During everyday communication we operate under the common assumption that there are no interactionally relevant differences between our experiences, i.e. for all intents and purposes we more or less believe that we all have similar experiences of the real world. And if we have any interactionally relevant differences between our experiences, then these differences will be made public through our own behaviour and its normative *accountability*. We adjust our understandings and bring them to a 'common ground' that is 'identical for all practical purposes'.

Accountability is the other important notion. Here it is important to recognise that people design their behaviour with an awareness of its 'accountability'. In other words they orient to whatever rule is relevant to the situation they find themselves in, and they choose to follow (or not to follow) the rule in the light of what they expect the interactional consequences of that choice to be. Taylor and Cameron (1987) clarify the importance of this where they note:

> [Participants] assume that their co-interactants also know the rule and will be judging their behaviour accountable for its conformity or non-conformity to the relevant rule. Ordinarily, the relevant rules will be followed; but when they are not followed, the co-interactions can be expected to look for the reasons why (is the actor? angry? sloppy? inattentive? rude? and so on). (p. 134)

So all behaviour which is concerned with communication will be accountable and will follow appropriate conventions for display, signalling, and so on. Goffman (1976) has considered in detail the nature of accountable displays in his analysis of those odd moments where we find ourselves slightly 'out of control' (e.g. accidentally stumbling when walking along the street). Goffman stressed the 'immediacy' and confrontational character of conversational contexts with his suggestion that individuals are compelled to 'chronically display' agency to one another, in other words no matter how small or insignificant a behaviour might be, in each other's company we are always accountable for it. Giddens (1988) argues this point on the strength of what happens in situations where an individual experiences a lapse of control and the concomitant display of 'response cries'. So, for example, if you are chatting with somebody and accidentally drop some papers you are holding, you are very likely to make some kind of minimal response such as 'oops, sorry; hold on a minute; silly me' as an explanation for this unintentional act. Many of us know how odd it feels where we accidentally bump into a lamppost or letter-box and, before we realise it, find ourselves apologising or something similar. We have just made an 'accountable' display for an object, and of course we are struck by the incongruity of our response. Such minimal comments (sometimes simply a sound will do) have 'the consequence of demonstrating to others awareness of the lapse, and that it is only a lapse, not a sign of generalised incompetence of bodily management' (Goffman, 1981, pp. 101–103).

The twin pillars of 'accountability' and the 'architecture of intersubjectivity' underpin and inform the ethnomethodological approach to conversational analysis. In the next chapter we will consider instances of everyday talk where this becomes apparent. Before doing so, however, conversational analysis is now being used as a methodological tool in many applied areas of social psychological research which traditionally have emphasised the importance of non-verbal behaviour (e.g. Argyle, 1975;

Rutter, 1987). In order to better understand the relationship between conversational analysis and the psychology of language more generally, we need to consider in a little more detail what constitutes non-verbal behaviour. It is interesting to note that although many people have considered non-verbal behaviour as somehow communicative, its study has remained within social psychology, largely ignored by mainstream psycholinguistics.

Prospects for the study of non-verbal behaviour

For many, non-verbal behaviour brings to mind such phrases as 'body language' or 'body signalling', and there is certainly a common-sense view that we communicate to each other (at least in part) by what we do with our bodies. Certainly in social psychology there has been a tradition which asserts that the non-verbal channel serves particular functions, and this has often been taken to mean *distinctly different* communicative functions compared to verbal behaviour or speech. Applied researchers (e.g. in forensic psychology and marketing) continue to emphasise the significance of our body displays to each other, whether conscious or unconscious. Argyle (1975) suggests that there are four specific functions carried out by non-verbal behaviour: elaborating verbal utterances; showing attentiveness; self-presentation; and to help synchronise our speech with our bodily movements. We can consider each of these functions in turn:

Completing and elaborating on verbal utterances: Although there might be something in this (and note on occasion we often try to embellish our talk on the telephone with gestures and physical emphasis), by definition a separate communicative function cannot be at issue here. If non-verbal behaviour was in any sense an essential function, then communicating on the telephone wouldn't be possible at all. It remains uncertain how significant it is to be able to embellish and elaborate our talk with non-verbal gestures and the extent to which this is a culturally determined phenomenon.

Evidence of attentiveness on the part of the listener: Again this looks interesting, particularly in that we know that we are compelled to at least look up and gaze at the speaker when listening to somebody. However, as we will go on to consider, care must be taken to distinguish between non-verbal behaviour and non-verbal communication. It is much more likely that this function is part of the latter.

Self-presentation: The way we walk, sit down and generally give off a sense of 'presence' has been a topic of considerable interest to social psychologists and psychotherapists. As yet there are few studies which have considered whether the 'presentation of self' in everyday life is irretrievably bound up with what somebody communicates. And it is not very clear what it is we are orienting to, for example, in contexts where we know somebody only through his/her voice or words (telephone or electronic mail). Do we build up a picture of some kind of generalised 'other' through his/her speech style, and is this part of the reason we are often surprised when we eventually meet him/her? One of the few studies of 'style' displayed through non-verbal behaviour seems to indicate that there are four dimensions we are sensitive to: expressiveness, animation, expansiveness and co-ordination (Gallaher, 1992), although such constructs are very likely to be culture-specific.

Managing synchrony of utterances: This fourth function is concerned with the orientation of physical gesture, movement and, most of all, the timing of engaging in everyday talk. Interesting here is to consider the criteria we seem to employ where we meet somebody and later on think there was something rather curious about the way he/she interacted with us. Research in conversational analysis indicates that we are very sensitive to 'exceptions to the norm' when interacting with others (e.g. if somebody seems to interrupt at all the wrong points, or seems to look away at those moments where we expect to be gazed at). It is also noteworthy that many adults and children with learning disabilities are often assessed on criteria which emphasise the significance of synchronic interaction (Wing, 1988).

This brief examination of Argyle's (1975) key functions of non-verbal behaviour raises the question whether any of them are unique to non-verbal communication. Beattie (1983) is somewhat critical of what has emerged from this research, noting that no adequate attempt to connect the descriptions of non-verbal behaviours to any detailed analysis of the linguistic aspects of the interaction has ever been undertaken. Before summarising why there are some key differences between non-verbal behaviour and non-verbal communication, it might help if we consider at least six distinct activities which are visible during talk: gesture; proxemics; gaze; touch and body contact; posture or body orientation; and facial expression.

Visible activity in talk: the significance of non-verbal behaviour in communication

Visible activity in talk: gesture

The first thing to recognise with gesture is that principally we are concerned with hand and arm gesture, although we might note that body orientation might be conceived as a form of 'whole-body' gesture. There are certainly a number of quite diverse approaches to the study of gesture, given that it touches on questions of the evolution of language, whether gesture is 'natural' or learned, whether it could be an independent language, and so on. The first point to note is that it is principally about speakers, i.e. the gestures people make when directing their talk at somebody else. As Schegloff (1984) points out, it would be particularly curious when we are speaking to be distracted by the actions of a very 'gestural' listener. There are considerably fewer conventionalised gestures for the listener to display attentiveness (e.g. head nod), and there has been considerable interest in the relationship between gesture and speech. Gesture which accompanies speech might be seen as the part of the physical syntax of talk, and the suggestion is often made that gesture and speech share many underlying qualities. Studies of everyday conversation, particularly where people are telling each other stories, indicate that when people are introducing a new topic into a conversation they have a tendency to gesture more than usual. It seems that executing gestures helps indicate the shared background information the participants assume (Levy & McNeill, 1992; McNeill & Levy, 1993).

Gestures can easily be differentiated into those hand and arm movements which occur alongside speech, and other very ritualised gestures (many people can think of a number of rude or contemptuous gestures quite easily). As signs and signals, certain gestures have the status of public ritualised acts – saluting, waving, two-fingered hand gestures, and so on – and in some cultures gesture use is very prominent and has a particularly marked role in indicating not only the type of communication but also its content. Kendon (1995), for example, describes in detail the gestures used in Southern Italy, noting how particular gestures will signify the intent behind the actual utterance spoken (such as a 'praying hands' gesture), while others mark out the focal point of a topic being discussed (the index finger to thumb 'ring' gesture). Research of this nature has led some commentators to argue that the manual gesture was the evolutionary precursor of proper syntax. In other words the essential sentential structure of agent–verb–object has evolved from manual gesturing where 'a hand (as agent) moves (what verbs imply) and may act on another part of the body (as patient) . . . entailing a preadaptive elementary syntax' (Armstrong, Stokoe & Wilcox, 1994, p. 349).

One last point to note about gesture is that it appears to play an important role in how children actually acquire the meaning of a word. Golinkoff (1983) has described how the way children learn to use their first words is closely linked to their abilities in transforming gestures (e.g. pointing) into sound (give me some object). The relationship of gesticulation to speech remains an important part of language acquisition research, particularly where such studies inform our understanding of sign-language acquisition by hearing-impaired children (Marschark, 1994).

Visible activity in talk: proxemics

Proxemics is the study or description of the ways in which people employ and interpret physical and spatial distance as part of their ongoing interactions. It is probably useful to think of proxemics along at least two dimensions (and there are probably more) (see Figure 5.1). On one axis you have physical space – clearly there are demarcations between being too

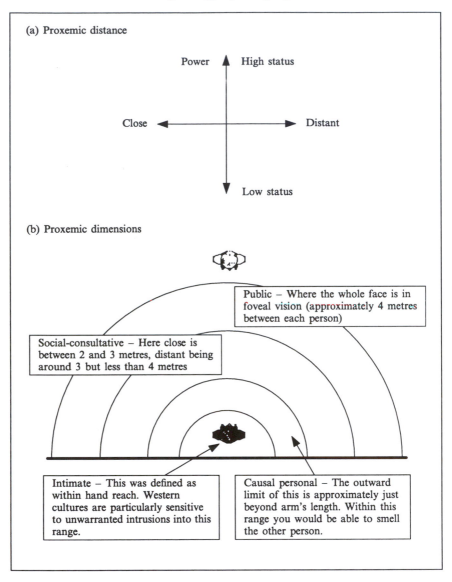

Figure 5.1 *Hall's (1963) analysis of proxemics*

close and too far away during this or that interaction. On another axis there is what might be termed social distance or power relations and here we are concerned with status or social hierarchies (see Hall, 1963). Beattie (1983) makes the point that although proxemics appears to be an elemental dimension and concerned with what appears 'natural', it turns out to be surprisingly complex, ambiguous and open to a variety of other causal factors (such as the size of the room you happen to be in or the sex of the person you are talking to). Furthermore, gender seems to be a major factor in determining whether you will sit next to the driver when riding in a taxi (Kenner & Katsimaglis, 1993). We might note finally that proxemics also has its psychological correlate in figurative language. We often use the terms *close*, *distant*, *above* and *below* in describing certain aspects of our relationships, where closeness can be understood both as loving and comforting but also as threatening and overbearing.

Visible activity in talk: gaze

One of the most researched areas of activity in non-verbal communication (in conversation) has been eye-gaze. Typically many elaborate experiments will involve having people interact in various ways in specially constructed observational rooms so that they can be observed through a one-way mirror and the patterns of eye-gaze recorded. There is no other aspect of non-verbal behaviour (except maybe touch) capable of arousing quite the same intensity and subtlety of reaction for participants. It really does matter if you stare at somebody too long, or make pointed efforts not to look at them. Possibly one way to think of the significance of gaze is to imagine the minimal conditions which might apply where you are in a situation on your own, and then another person comes into the room you happen to be in (e.g. you are sitting alone in a railway station waiting-room and somebody else enters to await his/her train). At the very least, even if you wish to avoid actually having to speak to the person, you would feel compelled to look up or over at the person and then maybe look away. This would be the least you could do simply to be polite, and Goffman (1979) emphasises that we are compelled to both monitor each other in this way, and act in such a way that others can monitor us. If we were to deliberately not look up (and were not obviously involved in doing something else), then this might itself be taken as a display as far as the person entering the room is concerned (rudeness, oddness or whatever).

During talk there are at least three important ways to think of gaze: where the speaker looks at a listener; where the listener looks at the speaker; and mutual gaze. When listening you tend to look much more compared to when you are speaking (Kendon, 1967) and speakers will often alter their talk if they do not experience mutual gaze with the listener. Moreover, where you are talking and interacting in a dyad (only two people), or in a triad, or in groups of more than three, clearly a number of different factors are involved. Studies have shown that leaders in group discussions tend to exhibit prolonged gazes during their turn-taking behaviour, and Kalma (1992) reports that in free-ranging discussions (where nobody is taking the active role as leader) the prolonged gaze acts as a powerful turn-signal when a speaker wishes to end his/her turn at talk and hand over to somebody else. The timing of the gaze or look is also very critical in situations where you wish to interrupt somebody else or prevent another from interrupting you. In an earlier study of pre-school children's turn-taking behaviour I found that children as young as three years of age were sensitive to the appropriate synchrony of eye-gaze (turning and looking) as well as being able to time their interruptions appropriately where somebody was talking about them (Forrester, 1988). Furthermore, throughout literature writers and poets have highlighted the significance of mutual gaze where attraction and sexuality are concerned. There is no other non-verbal behaviour which is capable of arousing the same intensity and subtlety of reaction.

Visible activity in talk: touch and body contact

Body contact (sometimes referred to as haptics) includes both intentional and unintentional touching of various kinds. Graddol, Cheshire and Swann (1987) remind us that body contact is related to proximity, in the sense that you can only touch if you are near enough to another person, and they suggest that the significance of certain proximities may derive from the potential for body contact. Fisher, Rytinne and Hesling (1976) have found that you do not even have to notice you have been touched to be affected by it. They found that women responded more warmly and positively to a library assistant who made contact when returning a library card even if they reported being unaware that any touching had occurred. Many forms of touch are viewed as having such 'consensually recognised' meanings. Burgoon (1991) has studied the relationship between touch, posture and proxemics, noting that although in most instances all three factors affect our 'haptic' perception, it was the form of a touch that was most important. Not unexpectedly for the American group studied, hand holding and face touching expressed great intimacy, whereas handshaking indicated receptivity and trust (and a slight degree of formality).

A good deal of research has found that touching is related to status and power, where those with higher power and status appear to have touching 'privileges' over those of lower status. More recently, and in the light of equal opportunities, there has been much discussion over the nature of unsolicited touching and contact. Nguyen, Helsin and Nguyen (1975) argue that men are, on the whole, rather more attuned to the kind of touch involved (when they noticed it), whereas women are slightly more concerned with where the touch occurred. This is borne out by studies reporting a greater proportion of women (compared to men) perceiving touching by strangers as a violation (Tang, Critelli & Porter, 1995) and different gender perceptions of the significance of being touched (Crawford, 1994). Women have been reported to be more positive about same-gender touch, although cross-cultural studies suggest that this is not a universal phenomenon (e.g. see Willis & Rawdon, 1994). Whatever else, positive perception of touching has been linked with notions of intimacy, curiously a topic rarely addressed in studies of non-verbal behaviour.

Touching and intimacy   Psychoanalysts have long discussed the importance of touch and body contact during early development. Clearly the first more important form of contact between mother and child is touch (e.g. note how common the practice has become of immediately placing a new-born on the mother's stomach after birth). Before we can really see and hear, our skin receives information about texture, pressure, and so on. Contrasting claims have been made about the special status of this touching bond between mother and child, not least in work which seeks to link later pathology with earlier touch deprivation (Gupta & Schork, 1995; Polan & Ward, 1994).

Touch has also a very ambiguous quality in adult love, affection and sexual attraction. Note Roland Barthes's (1990) comments on the nature of body contact:

> Accidentally, Werther's finger touches Charlotte's, their feet, under the table, happen to brush against each other. Werther might be engrossed by the meaning of these accidents; he might concentrate physically on these slight zones of contact and delight in the fragment of inert finger or foot, fetishistically, without concern for the response. But in fact Werther is not perverse, he is in love: he creates meaning, always and everywhere, out of nothing, and it is meaning which thrills him: he is in the crucible of meaning. Every contact, for the lover, raises the question of an answer: the skin is asked to reply. (p. 67)

Visible activity in talk: posture and body orientation

How people sit, stand and generally hold themselves has often been seen as an indication of their innermost feelings and the state of their relationship with others. Graddol et al. (1987) suggest that we should be cautious when interpreting posture and body orientation, noting that what seems import-ant is whether the person is displaying general features of tension or relaxation. There has been some attempt to isolate particular aspects of body orientation, for example Scheflen (1964) notes (with reference to the direction of leaning when sitting in a chair): 'such postural behaviours occur in characteristic, standard configurations, whose common recogni-sability is the basis of their value in communication'. Such postures are, he claims, governed by rules which determine where and when they can occur: 'a posture such as sitting back in a chair rarely occurs in subordinate males who are engaged in selling an idea to a male of higher status' (p. 241).

Whether this is always the case is clearly open to debate; however, it remains an interesting question whether such postures reflect a person's level of anxiety, or whether they form part of conventional ways of signalling attention or status. The term 'postural congruence' was coined by Scheflen (1964) to describe the observation that many people seem to shift posture in a kind of synchrony, i.e. if your friend leans forward slightly, then you will imperceptibly (and unconsciously) shift your posture in the corresponding way.[1] It would also seem that if you are a waiter and wished to increase the chances of getting a large tip, then at least in certain Midwestern American cities you would be better squatting down near your customer's table rather than standing slightly away from it (Lynn & Mynier, 1993).

Visible activity in talk: facial expression

Facial expression has been of interest to scientists and academics for well over a hundred years. We are all so familiar with what it is to 'pull a face' or display one particular facial expression while feeling something else that it is hard to imagine how one could ever have learned how to deceive or pretend without developing a sophisticated repertoire of face-pulling skills. In the study of facial expression as a non-verbal behaviour two issues stand out:

(a) the extent to which our facial responses to emotional stimuli are innate and at least build upon (in an evolutionary sense) similar responses observed in animal behaviour (most of all primates); and
(b) the question of how facial expressions convey meaning to people.

The research work can be divided into two camps, the biological and cultural views:

The biological view: Darwin (1872) was one of the first to scientifically study facial expression. His main argument was that emotional displays by animals served a variety of functions which aided species survival. It seemed possible that certain displays were biologically programmed and subject to processes of natural selection in the same way as other behavioural dispositions which had survival value. Graddol et al. (1987) make the point that some research would lend support to the claims Darwin was making.

> Ekman, Sorenson and Friesen (1969) sifted through over 3000 photographs to obtain *'those which showed only the pure display of a single affect' and presented these to people in many cultures, literate and pre-literate, around the world.* Each person was asked to categorise the emotion as one of six (happy, fear, disgust–contempt, anger, surprise, sadness), and the results were very similar across the cultures. They say, 'our findings support Darwin's suggestions that facial expression of emotion are similar among humans, regardless of culture, because of their evolutionary origin'. (p. 144)

More recently Matsumoto (1992) has looked carefully at the material used in Ekman's early studies, replicated the work in four non-American cultures and suggested that the data provide strong support for there being a universal facial expression for disgust–contempt. Ekman (1992) recognises the considerable debate his work had engendered and advocates a somewhat less extreme innatist view than originally formulated.

The cultural view: Other researches dispute the suggestion that facial expression is biologically based. Birdwhistell (1970) reviewed a large body of the then available research and suggested: 'Although we have been searching for 15 years, we have found no gesture or body motion which has the same social meaning in all societies . . . that is, we have been unable to discover any single facial expression which conveys an identical meaning in all societies' (p. 134).

Certainly a socially motivated account of facial expression would emphasise the observation that many people, when they have extended relationships with each other, often begin to make very similar kinds of facial expressions, and Ekman (1973) argues that both culture and biology are important in that although displays of emotion have an innate basis, this is filtered by cultural learning (the context within which you grow up). Graddol et al. (1987) summarise their review of these ideas by noting

> one reason why the 'meaning' of a particular facial expression may vary across cultures is that in each culture the social contexts in which such an expression could be freely and appropriately displayed will be very different. The primary affect and facial expression of a bereaved person may be, in principle, similar around the world but some cultures may construe death as an occasion for celebration not distress, or may require the bereaved person to censor or exaggerate their display of emotion. (p. 146)

Other commentators are more critical of facial expression research. Reviewing the wide range of methods, procedures and facial expressions employed in the most often cited studies, Russell (1994) comments that while facial expression and emotion may be linked in some way, the association varies with culture and the results are consistent with biological, cultural and one or two other accounts which fall in-between. Motley (1993) is more concerned that the kind of material employed in facial expression research has little bearing on how facial expressions are interpreted in actual conversations. In other words the photographs and pictures used as the testing material in facial expression studies are static and germane to the recognition of material in textual domains (such as 'mug-shot' research in journalism – see Lain & Harwood, 1992). In contrast, in conversations facial expressions are not used as display signals of emotional states, but as a particular non-verbal type of interjection (similar to saying 'Gosh' or 'Really' as a turn-taking 'filler' in a conversation).

This brings us to the question of why there is a problematic relationship between definitions of non-verbal behaviour and non-verbal communication. One reason for this is that we do not pay enough attention to an important distinction between the two phenomena. Implicit in the word 'communication' is the notion of intention. When we communicate we intend that somebody else understands what we wish to inform them about, and whatever form of 'language' we employ (actual speech or 'body language') what really matters is whether one person (the speaker) has carried out a clearly identifiable intentional act of communication.

What is also critical to the interaction is whether the listener or person for whom the message is intended recognises the intention of the speaker to engage in communication. And in turn, the listener is required to display the appropriate recognition of that (the speaker's original) intentional display. Finally, the speaker must then recognise his/her (the listener's) display of that recognition of intention (whew!!). Part and parcel of any communicative act is the presence of reciprocal acts of recognition display behaviours. Linguists use the term 'implicature' to describe this phenomenon, and in Chapter 3 we emphasised why implicature is an important idea for understanding the co-operative principle. Again here, it helps us recognise why *communicative behaviour* and simple *behaviour* are two quite distinct things. The United States Supreme Court has recognised the importance of making clear this distinction with regard to whether the Free Speech Clause applies to non-verbal communication. Tiersma (1993) notes that non-verbal conduct can only be described as communicative where the actor intends to communicate, quite distinct from contexts where observers feel justified in making inferences about somebody simply as a result of watching his/her behaviour: 'It is necessary to distinguish when people communicate by means of conduct from when people merely draw inferences from conduct' (p. 1525).

Summarising the distinctions between non-verbal behaviour and non-verbal communication

In this overview of visible activity in talk there are a number of instances where the object of the 'non-verbal' inquiry is clear. In the study of where people sit when riding in a taxi (proxemics), the investigators simply recorded the behaviour and then infer from the observed gender differences certain factors about sexual relations. Likewise, in the non-verbal analysis of 'style', people were asked only to categorise the observed behaviour on a number of indices, and from the resulting recorded ratings the investigators went on to identify certain key dimensions. In contrast, we noted in the study of facial expression in conversation that making faces had a quite distinct communicative function (similar to a reply) and was not simply any old behaviour. It was part of an ongoing dynamic communicative interchange and was employed intentionally by participants. The most important difference between non-verbal behaviour and non-verbal communication is the role of intentionality, which in part brings us back to where we started: the twin pillars of accountability and the architecture of intersubjectivity.

Without an ongoing orientation to the display of intentional signals and the recognition of such displays by participants it is very difficult to argue that communication has taken place at all. Many non-verbal signs and signals are intentional in this sense: the developed gestural system of Southern Italy; the timing of a look or a gaze at key points during a conversation; the use of gesture to emphasise topic or theme during story-telling. The recognition of all such behaviours depends on their being seen as accountable (explanations would have to be forthcoming if they occurred at the wrong time or in the wrong context), and on the background set of assumptions and presuppositions shared by members of any particular community. Remember, the architecture of intersubjectivity highlights the fact that for all intents and purposes people will act on the assumption that others share the same sort of background knowledge about their world and community. And if somebody acts in a way that is in discord with these shared assumptions, then (unless they are somehow indisposed) this act in a communicative context would itself be 'read' as meaningful in some way ('Why are they acting silly just now? Are they being ironic or sarcastic?', and so on).

We must be very careful, then, in using the expression 'body language' when referring to certain types of non-verbal behaviour. Without communicative intention a token in such a 'language' (e.g. stooping over slightly) does not warrant the status of a 'sign' or signifying act. It remains simply behaviour, and whether you wish to make inferences on generalisible patterns of such behaviours rests on a quite different set of criteria. Increasingly, many aspects of non-verbal communication (e.g. gestures) may be better understood within the framework of conversational analysis, rather than through principles which derive from applied behavioural analysis. Some of the confusion over what is properly non-verbal behaviour research and what is communication can be traced to a failure to recognise the quite distinct methodological traditions each area has emerged from (behaviourism and linguistics in turn). Throughout this and the previous chapters the research studies cited have often rested upon quite distinct methodologies and procedures. Given the nature of our inquiry into the study of language and the significant role methodology plays in psychological research, this issue needs to be addressed more directly, notwithstanding the fact that a full account of this topic is beyond the confines of this text and is covered in much greater detail by Neuman (1993).

Methodology in language research

One of the challenges for the student of language is to find a way of understanding the diverse range of methods and procedures employed in language research. On the one hand studies of word recognition will typically employ the fine-grained hypothetico-deductive methodology of cognitive psychology. Likewise, studies of reading which concentrate on patterns of eye-movements adopt a similar approach, and it is not uncommon to hear proponents defend theories on the grounds that such procedures facilitate the application of rigorous formal principles (e.g. Gough, 1972). In complete contrast, a conversational analyst will use inductive methods and on occasion insist that his/her data collection is atheoretical: he/she is simply identifying pre-existing patterns in the regularity of everyday talk. And again, a psycholinguist interested in certain aspects of formal semantics will conceive of his/her data as the already existing grammatical structures of a target language. Analysis of language structure might be the first point of departure. Child language researchers might use all of the above methods as well as additional ones borrowed from developmental psychology and ethology (e.g. a longitudinal study of language acquisition might typically be a single-subject case study and employ observational methods first developed by ethologists).

As a way of gaining an overall picture of the different approaches used in language research at least four principal outlooks or pre-theoretical frameworks can be identified:

1   The hypothetico-deductive methodology familiar to cognitive psychology and experimental psycholinguistics which focuses upon theory formulation hypothesis testing, refutation, replication and related statistical procedures. The search for evidence based on quantitative methods is viewed as the appropriate tool in such an outlook.

2   The inductive methodology typical of ethnography and conversational analysis, where, rather than approaching a topic with a specific hypothesis, substantive amounts of 'data' are collected and, by a process of analysis, regularities, rules and patterns are identified, analysed and described. Explanatory accounts of the data are then formulated and the generalisability of the data considered. Qualitative methods of this type can also lend themselves to statistical analysis (e.g. non-parametric methods).

3   The formal-analytical approach utilising methods and procedures from logic, linguistic analysis, mathematics and formal methods. Chomsky's formulation of transformational grammar is a good example of this linguistically based methodology. His original theory was a mathematical model of what would be required for any system which wished to display grammatical competence. Formal modelling is the principal focus here and a particular theory might be rigorously analysed to establish whether or not it exhibits internal validity. Many contemporary connectionist studies of language would fall into this category, as would certain topics within semantics.

4   Analysis of textual material through comparison, critique and argumentation. The study of language within the humanities would come into this category, including critical and literary theory, linguistic philosophy, semiotics and feminist criticism. Many of the most influential contributors to language research (e.g. Saussure, Wittgenstein, Derrida and Eco) are to be found within this tradition. A cursory examination of a topic such as reading would quickly demonstrate that contemporary literary criticism rests upon ideas some distance from those to be found in experimental psycholinguistics.

If we were to go through many of the topics in this book we would find that reading research falls largely into category (1), alongside experimental studies of sentence processing, deixis and writing. Conversational analysis, discourse analysis and many studies of how power relations are expressed in language employ the inductive methods of category (2). In contrast, formal analysis of recursion, syntax and semantics relies on the analytical approaches found in logic and linguistics, and maths. Certain areas of pragmatics would also fall into category (3), particularly as developed with artificial intelligence approaches to language. Finally, social semiotics, feminist criticism and critical approaches to writing and reading are firmly rooted in the 'textual comparison' tradition (4), i.e. critical inquiry through argumentation, debate and analysis of literary and related works.

Equally, however, there are many topics which utilise methods and procedures from two, and sometime three, of the categories above. The acquisition of deictic terms, for example, is just as likely to employ an experimental approach (e.g. Charney, 1979) as naturalistic and inductive methods (Oshima-Takane, 1988) or formal analysis (Jarvella & Klein, 1982). Furthermore, other areas, such as the discourse-analytic approach in social psychology, while borrowing from inductive methods, exhibit an orientation towards analysis through textual comparison. All of this should draw our attention to the importance of recognising the relationship between theory, method and data.

The connection between underlying philosophical position and instantiated theory helps determine the domain of any framework, and subsequent analysis in a way that we need to recognise. This is emphasised by Williams (1989), where he comments:

> The formation of a theory is a twofold process. The theory begins with some object of study, or unit of analysis: for example a reflex, an introspectible subjective state, a behaviour, a cognitive capacity. It then develops a general explanatory principle: for example, appeal to conditioning, introspection, flow chart model, and so defines itself from the perspective of the logic of this philosophical tradition. This view of the relation between psychological theories and philosophical perspective underscores the importance of developing a critical awareness of the presuppositions that support the content of a particular theory. (p. 111)

In the study of language the position taken is always defined with reference to the logic of a particular underlying 'philosophical' orientation (such as the four categories defined above). Students of language must be particularly careful when attempting to evaluate the status of a given theory, the research evidence it might rest on, or some other related criteria. Researchers in lexicalisation processes in neurolinguistics would find it particularly odd if they were being criticised for not using inductive methods in their data collection. And ethnomethodologists would find criticisms that they were not being 'scientific' enough simply irrelevant. Within disciplines, espousing the benefits of methods not conventionally used will often lead to controversy, as can be seen in contemporary debates in memory research (e.g. Edwards et al., 1992, and see Chapter 11). It is particularly important to be aware when investigating subjects that cut across boundaries and utilise different methodologies that one is not simply comparing like with like (even if they appear at first to be on the same topic).

Part of the answer to the problem of understanding multiple methods, theories and data collection procedures, is to develop a critical awareness of the presuppositions that support the content of a particular theory. Of course there are occasions where researchers will assert that they don't really have a theory, they are simply collecting data, observing behaviour, analysing events, or whatever. What this indicates is that they themselves may have lost sight of the underlying theoretical position they have assumed. To decide to investigate one phenomenon rather than another already signifies a theoretical orientation. And to record one set of 'data' and not some other will again be informed (implicitly or explicitly) by the supporting ideas which underpin any theoretical view. We will go on, in Chapter 11, to reconsider the significance of developing a critical awareness of the underlying ideas which inform theories. For now, we can conclude by noting that although examining the underlying presuppositions of a theory can be difficult, it will also lead to our being able to develop a critical awareness of the questions at issue. Students of language should always remember that it is never possible to 'step outside' language on to some neutral ground and then somehow investigate language processes.

Note

1. As Graddol et al. (1987) note, a phenomenon borne out by the extensive research carried out by Beattie and Beattie (1981) in a naturalistic setting.

6

Processes and Procedures in Conversational Interaction

The analysis of everyday conversation might strike many people as the study of the commonplace, the prosaic and the obvious. It is one of those phenomena whose structure and function you rarely notice until something starts to go wrong with it. One aim of this chapter is to show that the study of conversation is fascinating in itself, providing unique insights into how people manage their interactions, conceive of their roles and relations with each other, and maybe even contest and re-conceptualise their identities. Moreover, it will become clear that within the psychology of language the use of conversational analysis is having considerable influence on many applied problems, for example in health, developmental, clinical and forensic psychology. It is also beginning to have an influence on other more tangential areas such as human–computer interaction, psychotherapy and management science. Why should a specialist topic somewhere in-between sociology and linguistics begin to exert such a strong influence on psychology and related social sciences? In order to provide an answer to this question we need to begin with an outline of the conversational analysts' position and an overview of the basic phenomena they are concerned with.

As we noted earlier, conversational analysts trace their emergence to the ethnomethodologists, who found the quantitative leanings of sociology much too presumptive, i.e. their pre-theoretical identification of demographic and related socio-economic categories which determined the kinds of questions that a social scientist could ask – and answer. Remember, one of the principal theoretical constructs conversational analysis (CA from this point on) borrowed from ethnomethodology was the focus upon the participants' own model building, metaphor construction and rationalisations during their own ongoing interactions. In other words, where you are concerned with studying human behaviour, if the people themselves do not display an obvious orientation to the ideas and concepts that the analyst thinks might be important, then it is hardly a tenable position to insist that such constructs are critical or even important.

The first thing to note is that CA is concerned with how people manage to conduct their everyday interactions in an orderly way. Numerous interactions certainly exhibit a 'turn-taking' form: greeting ceremonies, boxing matches, playing a card game, interchanges at the market, and so on. One of the earliest questions Harvey Sacks[1] and his colleagues asked was how do participants manage the business of turn-taking in everyday talk, and, basing their analysis on a large collection of conversations recorded over a five-year period, Sacks, Schegloff and Jefferson (1974) developed a model of the organisation of turn-taking which emphasised its 'locally managed' nature. What they established was the fact that talk is a highly organised system of interaction that displays many structural properties which participants themselves are oriented towards and utilise in the 'doing' of a conversation. What they mean by the term 'local' is that the business of handling who has the current turn at talk, who might have the next turn, and so on, is conducted 'locally' on a 'turn-by-turn' basis in the immediate setting of the interaction.

The model of the local management system is itself based on two components, and a set of rules which operate on them. The two components are:

(a) a turn-constructional element, which can be a unit composed of a sentence, a word, a phrase or even a gesture or sound (such as 'ehm'); and

(b) a turn-allocation unit, itself composed of two sets of techniques:
   (i) those where a next turn is allocated by a current speakers choosing the next speaker and
   (ii) those where the next turn is allocated by a speaker self-selecting.

Keeping in mind Sacks et al.'s (1974) argument that participants are oriented towards a principle of economy and that participants will seek to maintain and share conversational resources, during conversation a speaker is assigned a 'turn-constructional' unit designating him/her as current speaker. At the end of such a unit (which can be a long sentence or simply one word) speakers may change, the change-over indicating or marking a transition-relevant place. It is important to recognise that the speaker is initially entitled to one such 'turn-constructional' unit, and the first possible completion of such a unit constitutes a transition-relevant place. Of course in many instances the current speaker keeps going, i.e. self-selects, but this self-selection is made clear even in the act of indicating potential speaker selection (as the transition-relevant places are being projected as the talk proceeds). All turn-taking transfer is co-ordinated around transition-relevant places, which are themselves determined by possible completion points for instances of the unit types (turn-constructional components).

What is critical, then, is that participants must be able to predict and project such transition-relevant places. Consider for a second what you do when you ask somebody a question. Towards the end of the question the pitch and stress of your voice will change (even before you actually get to the end), making it very clear that as the current speaker you are now going to hand over the floor to the next speaker. And as a listener, you know precisely when to 'come into' a conversation and 'self-select' yourself as next speaker (e.g. if somebody else has not handed the 'floor' over to you). Sacks et al. (1974), in identifying the turn-taking constructional and allocation units, specified a set of rules operating on them:

RULE 1: *This rule applies to the first transition-relevant place of any turn*

(a) If the current speaker selects the next speaker during the current turn, then the current speaker must stop speaking and the next speaker must speak next. And he/she must speak next at the first transition-relevant place after this 'next speaker' selection

(b) If the speaker does not select a next speaker during a current turn, then anybody else present (other parties) can self-select and the first person to do this will gain 'speaker rights' at the next turn.

(c) If the current speaker has not selected the next speaker and nobody else self-selects, then the speaker can continue (although this is not a requirement). In doing so he/she gains a right to have a further turn-constructional unit.

RULE 2: When rule 1(c) has been applied by the current speaker, then, at the next transition-relevant pause, rules 1(a) to 1(c) apply again, and keep reapplying until speaker change is accomplished.

It is important again to stress that the model is a description of key features of conversation such that the interaction can be conceived as 'locally managed'. The set of rules and components described above are all parts of this system – a system which is designed to solve the 'turn-taking' problem of interaction. The *problem* itself is composed of many obvious features of conversation which have to be explained (adapted from Sacks et al., 1974):

1 Speaker changes occur with relative ease.
2 Most of the time only one speaker has a turn at talk.
3 Transitions (from one turn to the next) are exceptionally sophisticated and very often occur with no gaps or overlaps.
4 Turn order and turn size are not fixed and the length of conversation is not specified in advance.
5 The distribution of turns is not specified in advance nor what people will say during a turn.
6 Repair mechanisms exist for dealing with turn-taking errors and violations (e.g. when two people inadvertently start talking at exactly the same time, then one of them will invariably stop and let the other person continue).

The local 'interactionally managed' system, then, is focused upon how turn-constructional units and turn-allocation techniques follow specific normative conventions and rules making possible the everyday flowing conversational interchanges we are all very familiar with. The system deals with single transitions, one at a time – and thus only with how the two turns which a single transition links together actually function. It is important to understand that this 'system' is not somehow abstract and something only suddenly discovered by conversational analysts. Rather conversational analysts have made a significant contribution to the study of talk by showing that it is participants themselves who are oriented towards locally

managed techniques and devices for the 'doing' of a conversation. Amongst
many other things, the model provided by Sacks et al. (1974) can account
for the remarkable sophistication in speaker transition and demonstrates
how participants themselves must be able to predict and project the
transition-relevant places which make turns at talk realisable at all.

There are two senses in which to think of the nature of conversation. One
is to consider it as a micro-sociological context where different factors (such
as the relative ages of participants or their status) will have a bearing upon
the interchanges. This is not to say that external variables determine the
nature of the interchange in any direct way, only that the interaction will
proceed with reference to those 'extra-linguistic' interactionally relevant
factors which influence both the content and, to some extent, the structure
of the talk. There is always a background context of institutionally relevant
phenomena which underpin and inform our everyday interactions. A second
element to conversation is what it means to participate 'within it'. In other
words we need to recognise that as participants ourselves in conversations
we orient to the structural aspects of conversation described in this chapter,
and we also contribute to making such structures available so that others
can recognise their relevance. What does this mean exactly? We need to
turn to some of the techniques employed in the turn-allocation component
of the local management system to get a flavour of how this works.

Mechanisms and procedures within conversation: adjacency pairs

It should come as no particular surprise to note there are many turn-
allocation phenomena which come in two parts, sequentially organised. A
question to somebody normally requires that the recipient provides
answers. And a greeting is likely to be followed by a greeting, a summons
by an answer, an end of a conversation with two-part farewells, an
invitation by an acceptance. Take, for example, a typical opening telephone
conversation between two friends, composed of many pairs of utterances
adjacent to each other (thus termed in CA as adjacency pairs):

(1)		Telephone rings	SUMMONS	1st PP*
(2)	(Dave picks it up in the conventional fashion) Dave:	Hello?	Answer to summons	2nd PP to (1)
(3)	Chris:	Hello, there:	Greeting	1st PP
(4)		is that Dave?	Question	1st PP
(5)	Dave:	Yea,	Answer	2nd PP to (4)
(6)		hi	Answer	2nd PP to (3)
(7)	Chris:	How are you?	Question	1st PP
(8)	Dave:	Not bad,	Answer	2nd PP to (7)
(9)		how's yourself?	Question	1st PP
(10)	Chris:	Good	Answer	2nd PP to (9)
(11)		Look, the reason I'm calling is		Topic initiation

*PP = pair part

The first thing to note is that the ring of the telephone acts as a kind of summons (the acoustic analogue of being nudged on the shoulder by someone to get their attention!), and Dave answers it (in the conventional fashion) with a greeting which acts as an answer. The two parts to this adjacency pair are complete and follow the conventional form. This is then followed by a greeting 'proper' from Chris and a question which also acts as a first pair part of an adjacency pair, embedded within the greeting–answer pair (note lines 3 to 6). A second and a third set of question–answer pairs then follow (lines 7 to 10) before Chris finally introduces the topic, the reason for the phone call, in the last line above. There are a number of key elements of adjacency pairs of this sort:

1   They must be adjacent.
2   They must be produced by different speakers (it might be viewed as very strange if you started answering your own questions while talking to somebody).
3   They are always ordered as first pair part/second pair part.
4   The two pairs are conditionally relevant in the sense that the first pair sets up what may occur as a second, and the second will depend on what has occurred as the first (as Pathas, 1995, notes).

Schegloff and Sacks (1973) argue that adjacency pairs follow a rule such that, having produced a first pair part of some pair, the current speaker must stop speaking and the next speaker must produce at that point in the interchange a second pair part to the same pair. It is the participants themselves who are very sensitive to the structural form of these inter-change formats. As Pathas (1995) puts it:

> If next speaker is not to produce the appropriate next [turn], they may have to show in some way why they have not done so, for example, a failure to under-stand, a nonhearing, a misunderstanding or a disagreement. Because the first pair part implicates what is appropriate for the next turn, what occurs in the next turn is closely monitored for its relation to the first part. Even slight pauses or hesitations can be indicative of some sort of interactional troubles. (p. 18)

This is seen in cases where a person's non-response is itself perceived as an accountable response:

(from Atkinson & Drew, 1979, p. 52)[2]
(1)   A: Is there something bothering you or not?
            (1.0)
(2)   A: Yes or no
            (1.5)
(3)   A: Eh?
(4)   B: No.

Here the speaker asks a question, does not receive a response in the time normally expected (one whole second elapses), such that the gap becomes an attributable silence followed by demand for a response, again followed by an even longer silence, finally culminating in the question/answer adjacency pair of lines 3 and 4. The role of 'silence' itself is an aspect of the ongoing conversation that participants orient to. Consider the following interchange between a doctor and a 71-year-old woman:

(from Coupland, Robinson & Coupland, 1994, p. 97)
(1)   Doctor: (brightly) hello Mrs Howard (.) nice to see you

                                                                   [   ]
(2)   Patient: hello
(3)   Doctor: you remember me of course?
(4)   Patient: yes I do (1.0)
(5)   Doctor: just two seconds (doctor reads notes) (45.0) right (.)
(6)   how have you been?

Here we can note the classic forms of adjacency pairing of the greeting exchange in lines 1 and 2, followed by a question–answer sequence (lines 3 and 4), and then a silence which is something that needs to be accounted for. The doctor orients to this attributable silence at the beginning of line 5, says something so as to pre-empt an additional task at hand (actually reading up on the patient's notes before proceeding further into the consultation). This takes approximately 45 seconds moving finally to the assertion 'right' and into the next question in line 6.

Adjacency pairings can also have four-part structures. Many invitations take a form similar to the following:

(from Pathas, 1995, p. 19)
(1)   A: Are you busy tonight?
(2)   B: No
(3)   A: Wanna go to a movie?
(4)   B: Sure

where although there are two distinct sets of question–answer pair parts, the whole scenario forms a four-part structure, consisting of a pre-sequence which is significant for what is too follow. Clearly if in line 2 B had answered with something like 'I'm off to the football tonight', then lines 3 and 4 would either not have occurred or have taken a very different form. This example also indicates what conversational analysts called preference organisation. Levinson (1983) notes that this has got nothing to do with the psychological sense of the speaker's desires, but describes a phenomenon where dispreferred 'second pair parts' exhibit many common features. Compare the following two examples:

(from Atkinson & Drew, 1979, p. 58)
example 1.
(1)   A: Why don't you come up and see me some time?

                                                    [   ]
(2)   B: I would like to

example 2.
(1)   A: Uh if you'd care to come over and visit a little while this morning
(2)   then I'll give you a cup of coffee
(3)   B: hehh. Well that's awfully sweet of you,
(4)   I don't think I can make it this morning
(5)   .hh huhm I'm running an ad in the paper and- and uh
(6)   I have to stay near the phone

The first example is 'preferred' in a structural sense. The invitation is followed by an acceptance (question–answer). It is noteworthy that this acceptance is not only quick but actually overlaps slightly with the first speaker. In contrast in the second example, the 'dispreferred' second pair part (to the invitation) contains first a delay ('hehh. Well') followed by an appreciative comment on the invitation, then in line 4 an actual refusal followed by an account of why B feels she has to decline. Levinson (1983) studies this and other examples in detail and emphasises that dispreferred second pair parts exhibit many of these features, i.e. delays and hedges; prefaces (such as 'Well'), accounts or reasons for the refusal, and the actual declination component itself. Preference has been described as a 'system that organises certain types of second actions in a way that gives a kind of priority to one particular choice from a set of alternatives and relegates other choices to being delayed, structurally complex and appearing "reluctant"' (Nofsinger, 1991, p. 75).

Closing sequences: how to end a conversation

Another very familiar form of adjacency pairing is found in closing sections of talk. The sequential order of turn-taking itself creates a problem for participants which becomes clear when we consider the nature of ending a conversation. The sequential nature of 'talk as action' means that one turn will always follow another (your turn, my turn, your turn, my turn and on . . . and on . . . and on), and, as participants, we have to create the possibility of stopping this potentially never-ending process in a realisable and accomplished way. Remember it is important to recognise that at all times conversationalists construct conversations dynamically and immediately, and they are always oriented to achieving the continued occurrence of the turn-taking machinery which makes conversation possible (adjacency pairs and so on). The problem of closing is summarised by Schegloff and Sacks (1973) as:

> How to organise the simultaneous arrival of the co-conversationalists at a point where one speaker's completion [of a turn-constructional unit] will not occasion another speaker's talk, and that will not be heard as some speaker's silence (i.e. as a turn-taking attributable silence). (p. 294)

There are many situations where we can recognise that the business of 'closing' a conversation is problematic. Many of us are familiar with going to a teacher or colleague and making some request (e.g. more time to complete some work and so on) and there comes a point in the conversation where you realise that the business at hand is finished, and it would be seen as rather unconventional to simply say 'Bye', turn and abruptly walk out of the door. You and the person you are talking to must somehow 'work' towards making the end of the conversation possible in an easy, smooth and acceptable way. So, whoever is first concerned with stopping the conversation must produce a 'first pair part' which has a certain kind of special status; a first pair part which, when uttered, indicates a desire to move towards finishing the conversation. But the sequential placing of that first pair part is critical as it is the orientation of the second pair part to the first which signifies whether the 'next speaker' to the current speaker has taken up the offer of a possible closing. Typically, a speaker (who wishes to move towards creating the possibility of a 'closing') will initiate a pre-closing sequence of the form 'Well' or 'Alright' accompanied by a downward intonation, for example:

(from Schegloff & Sacks, 1973, p. 307)
(1) Dorrinne: Uh, you know, its just like bringing the blood up.
(2) Theresa: Yeah, well, THINGS UH ALWAYS WORK OUT FOR THE (.) BEST (topic completion)
(3) Dorrinne: Oh certainly. Alright (.) Tess
(4) Theresa: Uh, huh,
(5) Theresa: Okay,
(6) Dorrinne: G'bye
(7) Theresa: Goodnight

Here in line (3) Dorrinne uses 'Alright' ending with a rising intonation followed by a pause then 'Tess', and Theresa takes up the 'offer' of the move towards a close, following which very typical forms of closing adjacency pairs complete the interchange. In line 6 the speaker initiates a final (terminal) first pair part following the pre-closing offering 'Okay' by Theresa in line 5. Of course, it may be that, following the production of a first pair part pre-closing turn, the person spoken to indicates in some way that he/she is not finished yet and doesn't wish to take up the offer:

(from Pathas, 1995, p. 20)
(1) Geri: Oka:y
(2) Shirley: Alright?
(3) Geri: Mm.h [m:?
(4) Shirley: [D'yih talk tih Dayna this week?
(5) Geri: hhh Yeh . . .

Here, although in line 2 the speaker provides a pre-closing first pair part unit, the offer is not taken up. Rather, in line 3 the response is a rising intonation question sound, and the response to this in turn introduces a new topic and the conversation continues. Participants' orientation to the formulation of this 'closing problem' is often marked, particularly in circumstances where there has been some degree of acceptance of a pre-closing first pair part offer. Take for example the next stretch of talk:

(adapted from Schegloff & Sacks, 1973, p. 321)
(1) A: You don'know w-huh what that would be, how much it costs.
(2) B: I would think probably, about twenty five dollars
(3) A: Oh boy hehh hhh!
(4) A: Okay, thank you.
(5) B: Okay, dear
(6) A: OH BY THE WAY. I'd just like tuh say thet uh, I DO like the new programming. I've been listening, it uh (.)
(7) B: Good girl!

(8) B: He listen, do me a favor wouldja write Mister Fairchild 'n tell im that,
         I think that'll s-shi-break up his whole day for im.
(9) A: ehh, heh heh, hhh!
(10) B: Okay, ?
(11) A: Okay.
(12) B: Thank you
(13) A: [[bye, bye
(14) B: Mm, buh(h) bye

Leaving aside the observation that the end of the conversation provides another nice example of how adjacency pairs work in talk, after turn 4, the next speaker offers a pre-closing sequence ('Okay, dear') which in this instance is not taken up. However, its very existence provides an opportunity for speaker A to introduce another topic before moving again to a pre-closing sequence. Thus the sequential placing of a first pair pre-closing part makes available a slot for previously unmentioned topics to be brought in (in turn 6). The very expectation that a pre-closing second pair part is being violated is oriented to by the person not taking up the offer. Schegloff and Sacks (1973) examined numerous conversational endings and noticed that this orientation to the 'problem of how to close' was itself a factor that participants marked. Having a pre-closing first pair part made a slot for 'previously unmentioned mentionables' possible. And very often it will be marked by such phrases as:

Oh, there was one more thing . . .
Ehmm, by the way, I just wanted to say . . .
I just wanted to mention one other thing . . .
By the way, I meant to say . . .

What is significant is that here we have an interactional system which is sensitive to the needs of the participants and where the sequential ordering of adjacency pairs is something that participants themselves orient to. As Pathas (1995) notes, the study of such phenomena as greetings, questions–answers and closings achieved considerable significance in the study of talk because these represented the first discoveries of orderly interactional phenomena whose methodical procedures, rules or sequential structures could be analysed and formalised.

Turn-taking and interruption

Another instance of the importance of the sequential nature of turn-taking is observed in interruption. It is important to distinguish between an overlap and an interruption. Although speaker changes are accomplished in a very smooth fashion by participants in talk, there are many instances of minor overlaps. Keeping in mind the one-speaker-at-at-time and other associated speaker assignment rules specified above, what is often significant in the next-speaker selection process a current speaker displays is the forward projection of the transition-relevant place. Typically the current speaker will change the intonation of his/her voice in a particular way (upwards or downwards), might put stress on a specific word, and so on. For example:

>   (from Sacks et al., 1974, p. 17)
>   (1) Uh you have been down here before (.) havenche . . .
>   [   ]
>   (2)   Yeah

The rules outlined above (p. 97) lead to certain predictions regarding the nature of interruption. For example, inadvertent interruptions will tend to occur as competing first starts (two people beginning at the same time). In nearly all such cases one person will drop out. Jefferson and Schegloff (1975) called this the 'initial drop point', suggesting that it is better to consider such instances as false starts. Only if there is a continuation beyond this drop-off point could such an overlap be considered a true interruption. The turn-taking rules also make it possible to discriminate between an inadvertent or neutral interruption and a violation interruption. A typical example of the first would be as follows:

>   (from Goldberg, 1990, p. 888)
>   (1) P: Okay, the doctor wz uh, doctor Eddington
>   (2)   He's the first one that told-
>   [   ]
>   (3) D: Ehrinton?
>   (4) P: Eddington. He works out've . . .

where speaker D interrupts simply for clarification about the person P is talking about. A violation interruption will often be marked in quite a different way, for example:

>   (from Goldberg, 1990, p. 897)
>   (1) M: As a matter of fact, I'm going to switch my optician not because of
>   (2)   that. I'm switchin for another reason.
>   (3) S: Why?
>   (4) M: Well, first of all, he's very sarcastic and-
>   (5) S: =Oh, well, if they've gottn- made
>   (6)   so much money maybe we can find
>   [   ]
>   (7) M: Well, wait a minute
>   (8) S: =somebody that uh so that, support
>   [ ]
>   (9) M: No
>   (10) M: =Wait. Wait a minute. Wait. There's another guy in town and he's
>   (11)   got cancer

In this context speaker M violates the speaker-centred rule in line 7 (the speaker rights of the person holding the floor), and even though speaker S responds by continuing very quickly after the next transition-relevant place, M again interrupts in line 9, finally succeeding in taking over speaker rights in lines 10 and 11. In such instances it is very common to find assertive expressions such as 'wait a minute' and 'hold on'. Distinguishing between

various types of interruption is important because the participants themselves will make normative decisions on the basis of how the interruption
occurs and what can be inferred from it, as Nofsinger (1991) notes:

> Overlap can be a tactic for dominating a conversation, but it can just as well be a
> tactic for showing vigorous support of a speaker. Participants with different
> conversational styles may have trouble co-ordinating their turn taking and may
> attribute sinister motives to each other when overlap occurs . . . the turn system
> in conversation is a normative system in the sense that participants orient to its
> rules – by designing their behaviour so that it conforms, by sanctioning or
> demanding an account of behaviour that seems not to conform, or by providing
> accounts for, or initiating repairs of, such behaviour. (p. 104)

A number of studies have considered the nature of interruptions and
hypothesised that it is the power relations between participants that help
determine the distribution of interruptions in conversation. Keeping in
mind Sacks et al.'s (1974) original formulation that participants are
oriented to sharing the resources of the 'floor' (turns at talk will in general
be equally distributed between participants), investigations of everyday talk
have looked at whether variables such as gender, status, age and socio-
economic class are reflected in the frequency and form of interruption.
Early studies have indicated that men interrupt women, adults interrupt
children, doctors interrupt patients and more powerful spouses tend to
interrupt the less powerful partner. Zimmerman and West (1975), for
example, studied conversations between men and women and reported that
men talk more, often assume a leadership style, and are more likely to
interrupt women than other men. Smith-Lovin and Brody (1989) argue that
men discriminate by sex in their interruption attempts (much less likely to
interrupt another male than a female), whereas women interrupt and yield
the floor in a way that does not discriminate between males and females.
And doctors have been shown to dominate their patients through assuming
and asserting rights over the management of turns at talk (Drew &
Heritage, 1992), although there are at least some patients who are well
disposed to their doctor behaving in this way, as it can provide a sense of
authoritative security (West & Frankel, 1991). We will go on to consider
these studies in greater detail in the following chapter and reconsider the
relationship between interruption and the 'speaker-centred' nature of the
CA position.

Topic selection, narrative and topic change in conversation

Early research on conversation simply assumed that talk was always about
'something' and every conversation was always focused on one topic
or another. Maynard (1980) notes that this explains why many of the earlier
studies of talk consisted of content analysis (e.g. Watson & Potter, 1962),
methods where conversations were simply coded for the principal themes
identified in the utterances. Sacks et al. (1974) and other conversational

analysts, however, began to show that topics were entities that conversationalists had to work at. We only have to think of many of our own telephone conversations to notice that after preliminary 'greeting' adjacency pairs, if we are the caller we have to establish very quickly what it is we are phoning about (p. 98 above). However, topic is not simply a matter of content, but is also constituted by the procedures and structures provided and produced by the participants. On the one hand, a speaker is very likely to partially fit what is currently being said with what has just gone before, while, on the other hand, there are ways in which completely new topics can be brought in: 'Oh, by the way, I was wondering if . . .'. And again, structural entities such as silences can indicate that a topic is finished with, as in the following:

> (from Maynard, 1980, p. 279)
> (1) Tom: Yeah I'm a bio sy major I kinda wanta get inta some research
>   work so=
> (3) Bill: =Yeah=
> (4) Tom: =At's why I'm kinda here
> (5) Bill: = See I sorta want to get OUtta research work=
> (6) Tom: =Outta-outtah research huh
> (7)   (1.2)
> (8) Tom: hmm::
> (9)   (2.4)
> (10) Tom: Hh psho:oo
> (11) Bill: Do you live on campus?

In this example two students meeting on campus first introduce the topic of research work, with Tom talking about how he wants to get into it, and then it transpires that Bill actually wants to get out of doing research work. This is then followed by a silence and a long outbreath by Tom, indicating that the topic is something neither of them wishes to pursue further. Maynard suggests that not only does the silence indicate neither person has elected to talk, but that such non-election is a way of avoiding the consequences of the participants' divergent views on the topic. Topic change (in line 11) is a means whereby conversationalists can re-engage formal turn-by-turn talk when disagreement results in a failure at speaker transition (lines 6 to 10).

The sequential nature of turn-taking itself helps determine the form in which topics will be formulated, introduced, ratified or ignored. However, a large number of interruptions do not appear to be specifically precipitated by what has gone before. There is a certain paradox here in that the structural elements of conversation both provide the mechanisms which make topic formulation and change possible at all, but at the same time should not be seen as determining the flow from topic to topic. For example, an interrupting speaker can say something brought to mind by the whole nature of the conversation, an instance where he/she might be ignoring the specifics of what has just gone before, but nevertheless orienting towards the general nature of the topic. Of course, instances where somebody interrupts and introduces a very divergent topic (completely removed from either the general thrust of the talk or the specific prior turn) would be marked for its very oddness. At the same time, as participants we are often in contexts where we have no idea (specifically) regarding what the next 'topic' is going to be about. This potentiating and facilitative nature of the conversational context is another important interactional aspect of talk, particularly in educational and learning environments.

Arguably, conversational learning contexts indicate and specify a range of possible developments which are permissible and 'likely' to take place. Consider, for example, a typical dialogue which might take place between a teacher and a student engaged in discussion around a somewhat obscure topic. Putting ourselves in the role of teacher, we can imagine being sensitive to the direction in which the pupil's understanding or thinking is going, and through the dialogue one would attempt to hint, invoke, suggest and attempt to get the pupil to see things in a different light. It is precisely in the response (i.e. the teacher's response) to the fact that 'I'm not getting through here', or 'He/she is really not getting the drift', that *teacher learning* can and does take place.

In other words, by having to construct novel forms of conversational structure (to overcome the pupil's response along the lines of 'No, I don't quite see that' or whatever), new possibilities or ways of seeing the problem are made available to the teacher (i.e. not necessarily to the pupil). Whatever else is going on in conversational teaching, one is attempting to set up those aspects of the conversation which have to be noticed. However, it is in the very process of their not being taken up, combined with the interest expressed via your participant's dialogue, that you, as teacher/learner, recognise the necessity to restructure whatever conversational topics are at issue.

There may also be an important relationship here between restructuring and narrativity or narrativisation (structuring the point to be conveyed around a story). It may very well be the case that a good teacher is one who can engage in the 'narrativisation' of ongoing discourse such that he/she adequately predicts the way a listener/learner will view his/her (the teacher's) developing topic – through the conversation – knowing that when the appropriate 'punchline' or point of the story is delivered this will result in the learner 'seeing' the connection to previously (for the listener) unconnected topics in a newly structured or newly conceived way (e.g. resulting in 'Oh, I see! **That's** very interesting, I'd never thought of **it** like **that** before').

This raises a final aspect regarding topic in conversation: the relation between topic formulation and story-telling or narrativisation. During a conversation the occurrence of any given utterance is always accountable, which gives rise to the observation, as Jefferson (1975) has noted, that the local occasioning of a story is often triggered in the course of the turn-by-turn talk and is methodically introduced into the talk. Consider, for example, the following:

(from Jefferson, 1975, p. 220)

(1)   Roger: The cops don't do dat, don't gimme that shit I live in the
(2)   Valley
(3)   (0.5)
(4)   Ken: The cops, over the hill. There's a place up in Mulholland where
(5)   they've - where they're building those housing projects?
(6)   [
(7)   Roger: *Oh*, have you ever taken them Mulhallan' time trial? 'hh You
(8)   go up there wid a girl. An bucha guys'r up there an [. . .]

Studies of the placing of stories in ongoing talk demonstrate that the occasioning of the story is exhibited by elements such as the 'Oh' in line 7, accompanied very often with an 'embedded repetition' (in this case Mulhallan) which locates but does not explicitly cite the element of the prior talk which 'triggered' the story (in this case for Roger in line 7). Furthermore, the way people return to the normal sequential turn-taking after an extended section of story-telling has also been shown to be methodical and 'worked at' by those involved (Jefferson, 1975).

The role of the hearer in conversation

The study of conversation has been criticised by some as being over-concerned with the role of the speaker (e.g. Goldberg, 1990). When we are interacting with others we alternate the roles of speaker and hearer/listener, yet it can be argued that one fundamental assumption of the CA position is the 'centrality and sanctity of the singular speakership code' (Goldberg, 1990, p. 884). When we consider what is involved in the role of the hearer the first thing to note is the difference between participants and bystanders, a distinction that warrants closer attention. Goffman (1976) asks us to pay more attention to the specific role of speaker/listener and participant where he distinguishes different listener roles:

> those who *over*hear whether or not their unratified participation is inadvertent and whether or not it has been encouraged; those who are ratified participants but (in the case of more than two-person talk) are not specifically addressed by the speaker; and those ratified participants who *are* addressed, that is, oriented to by the speaker in a manner to suggest that his words are particularly for them, and that some answer is therefore anticipated from them, more so than for other ratified participants. (p. 260)

Developing Goffman's (1976) distinction between non-ratified and ratified overhearing bystanders, McGregor (1983) suggests that 'eavesdroppers' comprehend their own roles as listeners depending on whether they know neither, one or more than one of the participants in exchanges they over-hear. The skills of the hearer, McGregor (1983) argues is 'fundamental to our understanding of conversational activity' (p. 302) and only recently has this become a major concern in linguistics and CA (e.g. Humphrey-Jones, 1986). Others have pointed out that as analysts we are overconcerned with the speaker utterance to a degree which mitigates against our under-standing communication:

Ours is a speakers' civilization and our linguistics has accordingly concerned itself almost solely with the speaker's problems. This accounts for the rise of generative grammar and the prestige attached to this particular facet of the speech process. The skilful speaker wins praise; the skilful listener despite the mystery of this achievement is ignored. (Parker-Rhodes, 1978, p. xiii)

There are a few studies within cognitive and developmental psychology which address issues surrounding overhearing. Schober and Clark (1989) and Clark and Schaefer (1987) discuss the role of meaning and discourse, with reference to the roles of overhearer or addressee, suggesting that the process of understanding is dependent upon participant roles in such contexts. Speaking is not conversation, and recognising the communicative opportunities inherent in talk may be linked to a distinction between hearing the sounds of speech and listening to talk. Talk provides opportunities for conversation, and successful participation implies a social-cognitive skill which may be better explained, or at least investigated, from principles of detection and recognition rather than construction. The mechanisms described within CA (such as gaining the floor or conceiving talk as turn-constructional units) help to highlight its dynamic project-ability. In other words participants are particularly adept at knowing when turns at talk change, or when a topic is foregrounded or presupposed, how to maintain topical coherence (and recognise when coherence is not being maintained), and so on, all to a degree which defies explanations based on information processing models found in the psychology of language.

For example, according to Clark and Carlson (1981), in order to establish 'common ground', hearers must be able to listen, decode and interpret communication attempts against a cognitive model. However, this cannot accommodate findings which document the sophisticated nature of children's communicative skills at an early age (e.g. Craig & Washington, 1986; Dunn & Shatz, 1989). In order to better understand what it is to be 'inside' a conversational context the last section of this chapter considers a model of conversational participation which bring together certain ideas from perceptual psychology and CA (see also Forrester, 1992).

The predictability and projectibility of talk: affordances in conversation

Talk is always dynamic in the sense that as participants we are engaged in an ongoing immediate interaction which, as we have seen, has its own rules, procedures and mechanisms, yet nevertheless provides for serendipity and the unexpected. How we act and what we say are immediately accountable in the sense of both the content of our discourse and the way in which we conduct it (Goffman, 1976). As participants we are exceptionally good at predicting the end of somebody else's turn at talk, a skill we seem to acquire in the first two or three years of our life. At the same time we are very skilled at projecting the end of a 'turn-constructional unit', making it clear to those around us that the 'floor' is again potentially available. One way of understanding the significance of our engaging in procedures which exhibit a high degree of structural complexity is by considering an 'internal' model of conversational participation. To understand this we need first to consider one or two ideas from perceptual psychology, particularly what has become known as the ecological approach to visual perception.

In contrast to the information processing 'constructivist' account of visual perception, Gibson (1966, 1979) argued for an ecological perspective which emphasised the 'coupling' of organism and environment. The emphasis is on the symbiotic relationship between animal and environment, and to consider one without regard to the other is both misguided and ecologically invalid. In this view, one does not have to construct a picture of the world based on the impoverished perceptual information (as the constructivist position would argue): rather, the visual system (and Gibson's original argument is with respect to perception) and the structured information available in the visual field available to an orienting person specify the perceptual world in a much more direct fashion. The environment, perception of it and action within it are all directly tied up with an organism. One resonates with the environment and the environment 'affords' sets of actions and events. Learning, then, involves detecting the 'invariant' and 'transformational' aspects of events (i.e. the things and events that always stay the same and those that often change).

One important aspect of this perspective is the relationship between the perception of objects, events, and so on, and what such objects 'afford' in terms of activities. Aspects of situations, events or objects permit or sustain certain forms of activity for the perceiving organism. So, a square solid object of sufficient strength and durability will afford sitting on, trees afford climbing, and so on. However, square solid objects will only afford sitting on for an adult if they happen to be about knee high, otherwise (if smaller) they might afford being stood on, used as a ladder, or whatever. The point here is that 'affordances' offer, or have the potential for, sets of actions: they don't cause or require them. Thus this model is not a stimulus–response kind of approach, cloaked in the language of the 'ecological niche' and animal–environment synchrony. Rather it is a framework which allows for, and more importantly emphasises, the dynamic potential of social interaction.

Following from this, the suggestion is that the predominant orientation of our sensory–cognitive processes (i.e. arising from, but not exclusively, visual perception) leads to our engaging in constructivist conversational practices which build upon our skills, or predispositions, to detect and extract affordances. In conversations, and in the construction of them, we make available and use patterns and structures (of talk/language) so as to signal and identify those aspects of the ongoing talk which have to be picked up, ignored, made recognisable, or whatever. In other words, many of the structural patterns identified by conversational analysts could be considered from an ecological viewpoint, i.e. as affordances and affordance structures. Furthermore, participants themselves utilise the affordance structures in talk such that they both recognise their occurrence, produce them and employ an orientation to their occurrence and ongoing development during participation in conversation.

Consider again the structures identifiable in talk. Schegloff and Sacks (1973), in their analysis of the closing of a conversation, demonstrated that it is the presupposed nature of the very recognisability of the adjacency pair sequence which had a direct bearing on the evolving pattern and coherence of talk. What is interesting from the point of view of 'affordance structures' in conversations is that the participants oriented the production of their discourse to their ongoing perceptions of the talk not only as the 'unit of reference', but also as the act to be accomplished.

So, adjacency pairs, transition-relevant places, summons–answer sequences, opening and closing sections of talk, and so on, are all recognisable structural patterns of talk, realisable as conversational affordances. Sacks et al. (1974) argue that such patterns are manipulated, used and produced by participants as part of a local management system, and there are a number of studies testifying to the split-second timing and 'on-line' perceptual abilities of participants orienting themselves to such mechanisms (Goodwin, 1981; Rutter, 1987). The studies of conversation described above make it clear that the overall coherence and manageability of talk (as an accomplishment between participants) is a highly conventionalised and socially instituted form of interaction. In addition the synchronistic interaction abilities of young infants in pre-linguistic proto-conversations (Stern, 1974; Trevarthen & Hubley, 1978) and the sophistication of young children's timing in their early conversations (Garvey & Berninger, 1981) lend support to the 'directly' perceptible affordance nature of conversational contexts. More recently Wootton (in press) demonstrates that the pre-school child's early attempts at projecting structural aspects of conversations can often lead to misunderstandings by their caregivers – and result in the often reported 'tantrums' displayed by two- to three-year-old children. Arguably, the invariant and transformational elements of such phenomena could be considered as affordances, particularly where this would help to highlight the sense of potential, and the immediacy, of conversations.

Here, the idea of participant 'structuration' serves as a good metaphor, i.e. the production of affordance-like conversational structures by participants for co-participants. We noted that the study of closing sections in talk serves as a useful example where the problem was posed as to how it is that two people manage to succeed at closing a conversation, given the observation that the continuation of speaking turns could go on indefinitely (without a precise mechanism for solving the closing problem). As Schegloff and Sacks (1973) put it:

> Our analysis has sought to explicate the ways in which the materials (units and exchanges) are produced by members in orderly ways that exhibit their orderliness, have their orderliness appreciated and used, and have that

appreciation displayed and treated as the basis for subsequent action . . . simply it is the closing as the problem for the participants which is our interest. (p. 290)

Given that it is the production of recognisable 'affordance structures' in conversations which is of interest here, the participants must somehow organise their co-convergence at a point in the conversation where one speaker's turn completion will not occasion another speaker's talk, and will at the same time not be heard as the other's silence. As we noted, what is needed are techniques or methods for providing ways to introduce previously unmentioned mentionables (such as 'Oh, by the way, one of the reasons why I came by to see you to-day was . . .') which makes recognisable the structural properties of a closing section, itself then permitting appropriate 'terminal exchange' adjacency pair inclusion. The importance of the adjacency pair format as a technique derives from the fact that it provides

a deterministic 'when' for it [the closing section] to happen (i.e. 'next') . . . a means for handling the close order problem, where that problem has its import through its control of the assurance that some relevant event will be made to occur. (Schegloff & Sacks, 1973, p. 297)

The specific way in which adjacency pair sequences are used as a technique by participants as 'affordances' requires that the first utterance of such a pair is recognised as having a particular 'first pair part' status. It is in this sense that we can consider the relationship between the recognition of 'structural affordances' in talk and procedures and processes produced by participants in order that they can accomplish necessary moves in conversation. The term 'structuration' is employed so as to help articulate how this operates, and highlight the fact that the participants are oriented towards the accomplishment of talk and themselves provide and produce 'structuration' strategies. Recognition and display of conversational patterns can be considered not only for their 'structural regularities' but also as dynamic potentiating 'on-line' affordances oriented to by participants.

Concluding comments

One aim in outlining examples of the processes and procedures identifiable in talk has been to make clear that the most significant contribution that conversational analysts have made to the psychology of language has been to uncover the nature of the 'local management' system itself. Demonstrating that talk is an accomplished activity produced by participants who exhibit a sophisticated orientation to the processes and mechanisms involved has opened up opportunities for many researchers within the social sciences. As a micro-sociological context, the study of conversation has increasingly been adopted as a key method for understanding the relationship between the individual and the social. Moreover, the methodology itself is conceived as being somehow uncontaminated and atheoretical, or at least less influenced by the analyst's pre-theoretical assumptions. In other words the significance of applying ethnomethodo-logical principles to the study of talk helps redress the balance of the cognitivist leanings of psycholinguistics. Remember, the underlying position of CA is that if the people whose talk is being studied do not themselves display an accountable orientation to any given phenomenon (model, construct, metaphor), then, as analysts, we must be very cautious with our interpretations of their interactions.

In this chapter we have covered the basic formulations of the CA position. The elements identified by Sacks et al. (1974) serve as the building blocks for many different structural components which can be found in conversation. Turn-taking itself and the significance of interruption rely on certain key aspects of the local management system, as do adjacency pair sequences, topic selection and change, closing scenarios, greetings and other related phenomena. Increasingly, many disciplines adjacent to psychology and sociology are recognising the methodological potential of CA, particu-larly as the *conversation* can serve as the 'site' for uncovering the rela-tionship between sociological, ideological and psychological entities.

The affordance model of conversation outlined above provides one way to bridge the gap between the micro-sociological and the psychological in the study of talk. On the one hand the study of talk makes clear that social relations between people are paramount: the implicit rules and conventions participants orient to; the on-line criteria of accountability; and the underlying assumptions regarding intersubjectivity. On the other hand, as individuals we all have a good (if intuitive) understanding of what it is to be 'in' a conversation. Unfortunately, contemporary psychological models of communication (Rafaeli, 1988) continue to treat the study of talk as if it was something to be viewed through a passing window (i.e. as if from outside). The significance of bringing together the notion of the affordance with the analysis of conversational structure is that it provides a way to accommodate the dynamic nature of our own conversational experience. As conversationalists we both recognise, produce and contribute towards the ongoing creation of structural entities (e.g. adjacency pairs, side-sequences, and so on) such that conversations as social activities can be realised at all. We can predict the end of a turn-at talk with considerable ease and project the endings of turn-constructional units without ever giving them a thought.

Structuration was described as the production of affordance-like conver-sational structures by participants for co-participants, the making available of structural patterns of talk which allow our predisposed 'perceptually biased' cognitions to take expression and function. An adequate concep-tualisation of what is involved in identifying the affordances of talk may require an 'internal' account of conversational participation, somewhat at odds with the methodological tradition of psycholinguistics. The question why we might require an 'internal' account derives first from the recog-nition that it is questionable whether one can establish what anyone knows 'extra-discursively'. Furthermore, ascertaining whether somebody knows something can only be established with reference to our own participation in that particular social-discursive context, a point reiterated in the following two chapters.

Appendix

Code	*Transcription conventions employed:*
CAPITALS, *italics* or <u>underlining</u>	Used for emphasis (parts of the utterance that are stressed)
::	Sounds that are stretched or drawn out
([ ])	Overlaps, cases of simultaneous speech or interruptions
(.)	Small pauses
(1.4)	Silences with the time given in secs
=	Where there is nearly no gap at all between one sentence and another

Notes

1. The principal researchers involved in establishing CA as a research methodology were Sacks, Schegloff and Jefferson (1974). See also Schegloff and Sacks (1973) and Sacks (1972).

2. In the Appendix at the end of this chapter there is a summary of the transcription conventions employed with the examples of conversation.

7

Power Relations in Language

Power in conversational contexts

The small group of sociologists who helped shape the emergence of CA were dissatisfied with their contemporaries during the late 1960s and early 1970s. They were unhappy with the heavily laden assumptions of quantitative methodology and the excessive formalism they found in linguistics and psycholinguistics. Ethnomethodology offered an alternative to the positivist leanings of language research, particularly through the adoption of principles of accountability and intersubjectivity. Conversation could simply be studied for 'what it is' and approached in an apparently atheoretical fashion. The people involved in the study of talk (the subjects) would themselves validate the data underpinning any analysis of models, processes or procedures said to be in play. However, as we noted earlier, it is simply not possible to investigate any phenomenon without some theoretical assumptions coming into place (even if only implicitly). A significant extension of the CA perspective is now emerging within sociolinguistics and feminist social psychology which, although applauding the efforts and contributions made by conversation analysts, criticises some of the underlying assumptions. The aim is to incorporate within the approach a greater understanding of the role of ideology and power.

This brings us on to a consideration of some of the more problematic assumptions underlying CA. While emphasising that there are many advantages in adopting the approach, Cameron (1989) and Taylor and Cameron (1987) point out that the explanatory accounts are in danger of simply being circular. There is a naïve appeal to examples of the phenomena as explanations for their expression, and analysts uncritically emphasise principles of negotiation and agreement. Sacks et al.'s (1974) proposal that turn-taking rules in conversation are based upon principles of 'economy' and sharing 'the floor' is questionable given that often participants are not oriented towards equality and a fair distribution of resources (Zimmerman & West, 1975).

We can note that the way in which turn-taking resources are provided is likely to be critical for defining power relations in the ongoing conversations. For example, invitations to contribute might be offered by speakers in a very offhand way, indicating a certain attitude or display of power towards other participants. Fisher (1976) describes how power relations are expressed through a very sophisticated form of conversational insults by

Barbadian speakers. In Barbadian a popular way to insult a person is to speak with somebody else (while clearly in earshot of your intended target) in a very ironic and sarcastic way about that person. Again, and with reference to the use of the first pair part as a pre-closing initiation attempt by a first speaker, a second speaker might assert or indicate power by displaying her failure to understand (before we can go on to the closing section, please be much more specific about *x*), or simply pretend she misunderstood so as to carry on the conversation (this being somewhat more insidious of course). Further, the 'pretence' can be either displayed (so as to exert power over the first) or disguised (simply to exert power but not to let the first speaker know that this power is being employed). Such considerations support Cameron's (1989) call for an analysis of the institutional nature of talk:

> Conversational rules are postulated on the basis that orderliness can only proceed from our sharing the same view of what is going on [the architecture of intersubjectivity]; without some means of bringing about this shared understanding, communication will break down. But the literature on unequal encounters suggest that this is not necessarily the case. Communication does not depend on perfect mutual understanding and awareness. We must ask new questions about the nature of intersubjectivity: we must construct new accounts which do not leave out or render inexplicable the discursive operation of authority or power. (p. 7)

Certainly we need to investigate the presuppositional basis of conversational procedures, i.e. the social–cultural practices which provide and establish the parameters of our communications. We must not lose sight of the fact that talk itself is a social practice, and rather than just saying that our behaviour is always accountable the central notion of accountability should be politicised, as Cameron (1989) suggests. The argument that powerful speakers are able to impose their version of reality and marginalise alternative accounts has a particular appeal as it is something many of us have experienced (in one context or another). People in positions of power have the authority to call others to task and hold them accountable for their behaviour. Feminist critics remind us that reality is as often 'contested' as it is shared, and the reason why most of the time it appears consensual is precisely because a certain version of reality is 'extruded' as the talk proceeds. We are all familiar with the experience of being in a conversation where although we find the 'version of the world' being discussed somehow at variance with our own, the nature of the encounter somehow forces us to go along with it. The conversation seems to make demands of its own.

One social scientist who helps us understand the relationship between the conversational context and background institutional factors (e.g. power relations, gender, class, and so on) is Goffman. Goffman's work has a curiously marginalised status across the disciplines of psychology and sociology, possibly because psychologists consider his writings to be too sociological (rarely amenable to quantitative analysis), while sociologists view his approach as over-individualistic. Schegloff (1988) points out that Goffman's psychology was one of the relations between an individual and 'ritual' interaction, and one element of Goffman's work which warrants our attention is his concern with the 'display' of behaviour and what he called the doctrine of natural expression. In outlining this idea he noted:

> we assume that among humans a very wide range of attributes are expressible: intent, feeling, relationship, information state, health, social class and so on. Lore and advice concerning these signs, including how to fake them and how to see behind fakeries, constitute a kind of folk science. (p. 7)

Goffman (1979) proposes that we routinely seek information about properties of objects that are enduring and in some way read as naturally basic, some information about the characteristic or 'essential nature' of people and objects. The fact that such information as 'signs' both exists and is displayed is a central tenet of his perspective. In an essay on the recognition and display of that essential characteristic 'gender', Goffman (1979) points out that although this most cherished distinction is taken as the prototype of expression, 'something that can be conveyed fleetingly in any social situation and yet something that strikes at the most basic characterization of the individual', it is nevertheless complicated:

> The human objects themselves employ the term 'expression,' and conduct themselves to fit their own conceptions of expressivity; iconicity especially abounds, doing so because it has been made to. Instead of our merely obtaining expressions of the object, the object obligingly gives them to us, conveying them through ritualizations and communicating them through symbols. (p. 7)

What is important here is that these configurations of what we take to be natural expression are not simply elements passively processed in an everyday fashion, but are an integral part of what we produce or what can be generated in social situations. The parallels between this line of argument and the notion of affordance discussed in the previous chapter should be emphasised, i.e. affordances as those participatory and conversational display structures produced by participants in particular social–cultural settings. While they are available as directly cognisable phenomena, they are not necessarily 'simplistic' or obvious, and we employ them so as to exert power and influence over others.

What is also interesting about Goffman's work is the utilisation of a 'dramaturgical' metaphor within an evolutionary framework. Collins (1988) asserts that Goffman did not support any simplistic 'processualism' or reality constructionism, arguing that his contribution was the application of a kind of social determinism constrained by the structural realities operating at the micro-behavioural level. Again we can consider his notion of 'frames' and framing and power relations in language. Working on three levels (the physical, social-ecological and institutional), frames are not cognitive objects or mental rules but rather behavioural scenarios tied to the dynamics of unfolding conversational contexts. They are alignments to situations such that there is a compulsion to behave in some, and not other, specific ways, and where the constraints at one level of a 'frame' are breached or extended there remain in place other boundaries which allow for change only in predictable and recognisable ways. Goffman (1979) defended the 'realist' view that the physical world exists and has a primary reality, 'situations . . . are something that participants arrive at, rather than merely construct' (p. 50). The mental realm, he points out, is not free-floating but derived, and it is out of the basic physical frame that the mental emerges, always anchored to it. The second, social-ecological frame emphasises Goffman's evolutionary position, where the importance of 'display' is paramount, and so:

> When nothing eventful is occurring persons in one another's presence are still nonetheless tracking one another and acting so as to make themselves trackable. (Goffman, 1979, p. 103)

The third, institutional frame exemplifies the 'institutional' nature of talk, in a way, however, which again does not imply a causal dependency. Collins (1988) once more:

> The rituals of social life should not be regarded as an 'expression' of the properties of institutions; it is a form of activity established 'in regard' of those institutions. There is only a loose coupling to the qualities of the institutions themselves. (p. 53)

This leads to the argument that each participant can orient towards several different 'role-definitions' during any interchange. The observation that these social roles or identities have a structure in relation to one another suggests that they are not simply created by the observer. Moreover, the relationship between the performance of this or that role highlights the importance of power relations, particularly with one of our most enduring of social roles, gender. The significance of Goffman's analysis of gender role was his insistence that such expression is not instinctive (i.e. biological sex) but socially learned and socially patterned. Gender is a socially defined category which employs a particular expression, and a socially established schedule which determines when these expressions will occur:

> insofar as natural expressions of gender are – in the sense here employed – natural and expressive, what they naturally express is the capacity and inclination of individuals to portray a version of themselves and their relationships at strategic moments – a working agreement to present each other with, and facilitate the other's presentation of, gestural pictures of the claimed reality of their relationship and the claimed character of their human nature. (Goffman, 1979, p. 7)

Against this 'three-frame' analysis provided by Goffman, we can consider how the idea of role relations and power has been studied in the social psychology of language and linguistics, beginning first with gender relations and then looking briefly at parent–child talk and doctor–patient encounters. In all contexts we can find good examples of the relationship between power and language use.

Power and role relations in language

Ever since the pioneering work of Zimmerman and West (1975), many studies have reported the asymmetrical relationship between the language of men and women (and here we are principally concerned with their everyday conversations with one another). In some instances men are said to interrupt women more than would be expected (e.g. West & Zimmerman, 1985); in other studies the opposite has been found (Murray & Covelli, 1988). It has been claimed that because of their disadvantaged position women's voices become louder and more dominant sounding when talking with unfamiliar men (e.g. Hall & Brainwald, 1981) and women with more feminine voices are perceived as weaker and warmer than their male peers (Montepare & Vega, 1988). One problem with many of these studies is how conversational competence is defined in the first place (e.g. Smith-Lovin & Brody, 1989). In a summary of the major findings in this area, West (1995) points out that the whole notion of 'competence' is derived from what men say and do, i.e. there is an assumed superiority of men as speakers. She argues that a careful examination of the demands made on participants in conversation

> demonstrates women's abilities to guide and organize the flow of messages between speakers, to achieve smooth transitions between conversational topics, to maintain a polite accord in conversation, and to elicit compliance with their directives . . . a very competent force indeed. (p. 124)

Another problem with definitions of interruption (e.g. Smith-Lovin & Brody, 1989) is where it is employed as an index of power. One central tenet of the Sacks et al. (1974) model was that participants were oriented towards principles of economy and 'sharing the floor', i.e. the major resource available in any interchange. Holding the floor for more than one's fair share has thus been viewed as an expression of power, reflecting the wider social and institutional frames at play. Typically, interruption as a measure of power has been derived from studies where the frequency of interruption is simply recorded (i.e. context and content-free analysis where an interruption is defined as the distance from a transition-relevant place) and the distributions between participants compared. However, in a recent study of interruption which combined a CA approach with the idea of 'face' outlined in Chapter 5 (Brown & Levinson, 1978), it was found that women primarily employ interruption as a means of support and ratification (affiliative), while men use interruption both to agree and to disagree (disaffiliative) with anybody who happens to be speaking (Makritsilipakou, 1994). An affiliative interruption is one which displays 'positive politeness' and agreement, while a disaffiliative would exhibit 'face-threatening' qualities.

Other researchers have also become aware that interruptions need not be synonymous with power. Employing a cross-cultural comparison of everyday conversation, Murata (1994) notes that there has been an over-concentration on English. English ways of speaking (American and North European) exhibit a pattern of interruption which indicates conversational participation and listenership, simultaneous speech showing interest and involvement with each other. In contrast, an examination of Japanese conversational style shows that interruption is very rare, in this case indicative of a high regard for co-operation in turn allocations. Such findings accord with our own experience of contexts where, although somebody may be interrupting a great deal and otherwise 'violating' turn-taking procedures, it does not necessarily mean they are more powerful or dominant. As Goldberg (1990) argues, interruptions arise from a multitude of personal, relational and conversational sources, and what we need to do is distinguish between interruptions which seem linked to the ongoing 'moment-to-moment' interactional rights of participants, and other forms which may arise from individuals' desires or demands.

In questioning the 'centrality and sanctity of the speakership code' – unimpeded single speakership – found in CA, Goldberg (1990) outlines criteria for distinguishing different types of interruption on a power/non-power axis. A neutral interruption is one where there is no intention to wrest control of the talk from the speaker, nor any indication of a threat to the speaker's 'face'. In contrast, non-neutral interruptions can be designed either to wrest control of the floor (power-oriented) or as acts of support or collaboration (rapport-oriented interruptions). Instances of the former will be marked by other participants' orientation to them as rude, impolite, intrusive and often as competitive. The latter will generally be viewed as acts of collaboration, mutual orientation, and may, for example, elaborate on the prior speaker's topic. In providing examples of each, and formulating criteria for such a classification, Goldberg (1990) succeeds in showing that while interruptions can indeed be used to display power, they can also indicate other role relations relevant to the ongoing conversation.

Another context where power relations are very clearly expressed in language is that between parents and children (particularly where children are learning language). Since the early work of Snow and Ferguson (1977) on 'motherese' or 'baby-talk', developmental psycholinguists have noted that when children are exposed to speech (either directed at them or overheard) they are not just learning language, they are also being given lessons in social relations, roles and culture. In many cultures, the child's acquisition of language is interdependent with learning codes and conventions for interrupting, taking turns, introducing topics, and so on (Ervin-Tripp & Mitchell-Kernan, 1977). Exposure to, and participation in, talk provides the young child with lessons not only in how conversations are structured, but also in the rights and responsibilities regarding turns at talk. In the cross-cultural literature on language socialisation, parents from Polynesia to the United States have been shown to provide explicit instructions in what to say and how to speak in a range of activities and events (Lutz, 1983; Scheifflein & Ochs, 1981).

We should not be surprised by the asymmetrical relationship of adult–child talk. The speech modifications of adults to young children are in some sense directed at socialising the child into cultural meaning systems and social roles. This 'language of socialisation' has been described by Farris (1992) as the voice of authority – the speech of caregivers to children which has the intention to direct and control the child's behaviour and socialise him/her into specific cultural meanings (see also Slomkowski & Dunn, 1992). Whether the asymmetrical language relationship between adult and child ends in childhood is itself open to question. A recent study of how young adults speak to their grandparents highlighted asymmetrical power relations (e.g. manipulating their talk for specific ends, rather than engaging with them as they would their own parents – Montepare, Steinberg & Rosenberg, 1992). There is also a large body of work in family systems theory pointing to the significance of power relations in family conversations (Fitzpatrick & Ritchie, 1994; Haremustin, 1994).

Another context in which we can study the relationship between power and language is the doctor–patient interview. Studies have reported on doctors' overbearing questioning style, their tendency to interrupt and otherwise control the ongoing interaction (Mishler, 1984; Todd, 1984). Other work has indicated that doctors can have a tendency to slip into a certain form of medical discourse (often using highly technical terms) which, although conveying a sense of authority, can simply result in patients feeling they are being treated as medical 'objects' (Fisher & Todd, 1983). Undoubtedly there is a certain ambivalence between the aims of both parties in the interaction. From the doctor's point of view he/she must obtain as much information as possible in often a limited amount of time. At the same time in many instances, the actual conversation (or at least that part which requires a diagnostic/interrogative style) may not proceed until after the actual physical examination has taken place, and may be supplementary to the doctor's interpretation of the signs and symptoms already observed. In contrast the patient is in the position of wanting a cure or at least a solution to the problem that has brought him/her to the interview/examination. In many instances the patient seeks medical help only after his/her own solutions (however minimal) to the problem have failed. While in one sense the doctor has authority and power (i.e. possesses the knowledge/solution the patient needs), the doctor can find him/herself constrained by the difficulties inherent in encouraging the patient to provide information. This is particularly the case in situations where the problem is not physical. Part of the asymmetry, then, is due to the nature of the topic (i.e. the patient's health, not the doctor's), and part to the circumstances of the tasks at hand (making a diagnosis, providing information, and so on). Viewed in this way, ten Have (1991) argues that much of the asymmetry derives from expectations both parties bring to the encounter, which sometimes allow consultations to be almost conversation-like, at other times more akin to interrogations. Consider the following examples:

(from West, 1990, p. 91)
example 1.
(1) Patient: So, if I fe- ee:l this coming on, an' I'm sidding up in a pla:ne, 'r
             I'm out
(2) somewhere in a car., .h'n I can't lie dow-
             [
(3) Doctor: LIE DOW:N

(from West, 1990, p. 91)
example 2.
(1) Patient: I'm trying' tuh (.2) sid o::n this tailbone duh tyr and get it bedder
(2)   an' eviry chance I could I try duh
                                       [
(3) Doctor: oh:: don' even try . . . if it hurts when yuh
                                       sid on it, stay
(4)   off of it

where the doctor in example 1 commands the patient to change his or her
posture, or in the second example, where again he (and West argues that it
is significant that it is a male doctor) simply tells the patient that if something is hurting him or her, then stop doing it. Patients have no choice but
to do what they are told. Interestingly in West's (1990) analysis of the
difference between male and female doctors, it is the latter who can
encourage a more symmetrical and equally participative encounter, as in
the following:

(1) (from West, 1990, p. 91)
(1) Doctor: .h Let's talk about cher press:ure for a minnut 'r two
                                       [
(2) Patient: '.h .h . . . chhhew Okay ((sound-
                                       ing congested))
(3) Doctor: Oka:y! Wull let's make that our pla:n
(4)   .h Let's get a fa:sting sugar nex'time too: (2.) Okay?

Here, not only does the doctor use phrases such as 'let's' to facilitate a
compliant response from the patient, but she also engages in the conversation as if the task is a joint venture. In this case the women doctors were
much more likely to produce polite rather than impolite directive forms.
    It can be argued, then, that whenever we engage in conversation with
others we bring to the context certain assumptions, presuppositions and
other background 'framing' influences which find expression in both the
content and form of the talk (i.e. what we actually say and how we say it).
Note that this is not to argue that 'extra-conversational' institutional
factors force or determine us to interact in a particular way, only that we
engage in the constructive production of talk with reference to outside
background frames. Not only are many of the power relations which hold
between people brought into play during conversation, but the conversational site itself serves as the context for such relations to be established
and (re)produced. Goffman's (1979) analysis of our 'role-performance' in
the act of speaking emphasised distinct frames of influence (the physical,
the social-ecological and the institutional) which can help differentiate

important elements of the interchange, e.g. the way two people of different rank might work towards closing a conversation.

Certainly the physical 'frame' might be paramount in instances such as the doctor's interaction referred to above (asking somebody to move) or how Barbadians use the overhearing context; the 'social-ecological' frame is more prominent where participants are monitoring the significance of the types of interruption uncovered by Goldberg (1990); and the 'institutional' frame can be utilised successfully by participants in medical encounters. The work of West (1990) above reminds us that Goffman suggested that we can move in and out of different frames, or occupy more than one, during any single interchange. However, Goffman (1979) was careful to highlight the dynamic and unpredictable nature of the conversational context. It is not too difficult to imagine a situation in which somebody may appear to have control of the floor during a conversation (e.g. a double-glazing salesman at your door), yet ultimately not be able to exert a great deal of power over the other person. And likewise, there are many situations where power can be expressed as much by what is not being said rather than the other way around (e.g. a suspect's refusal to incriminate him/herself during an interrogation through remaining silent).

Talk and text: expressing power in different discursive domains

When considering the association between power relations and language we need to be careful to distinguish between language as 'talk' (conversation and the parallel performance of role relations) and language as 'text' (including written texts, visual images and text produced in non-interactive contexts, e.g. radio or television). Although both talk and text are forms of communication concerned with discourse, all too often students (and researchers) combine both together as *language* and then proceed to exhibit confusion over phenomena they are dealing with (e.g. calling non-verbal behaviour 'language' as if it was composed of grammatical elements). In the remainder of this chapter we will consider how some of the power relations identified above find complementary expression in text. The study of text is the third major theme of this book, and just as deixis served as a topic to bridge the gap between thinking and talk, so power relations in discourse serve as a way to articulate continuities and discontinuities across talk and text.

In order to emphasise the significance of the distinctions between talk and text, we can summarise a number of distinctions made by Ricoeur (1970), a philosopher of language concerned with this issue (see Table 7.1). First, talk is dynamic in the sense that as participants we are engaged in an ongoing immediate interaction which has its own rules, yet provides for serendipity and the unexpected (Sacks et al., 1974). Second, as we noted, how we act and what we say are immediately accountable in the sense of both the content of our discourse and the way in which we conduct it.

Table 7.1   *Distinguishing characteristics of talk and text*

Talk	Text
(1) Dynamic	(1) Free of presence and also free of authority
(2) Accountable	(2) Formal – how does the text function?
(3) Intersubjective	(3) Historical – what does the text speak about?
(4) Interdependence of explanation and understanding	(4) Reading experience – text–reader strategies: what does this text say to me that is common to the reading experience of other readers?
	(5) Interpretation level – dialogic engagement with the text is crucial; how has my world changed because of the reading of the text?

Source: Adapted from Ricoeur, 1970

Third, conversational analysts informed by the ethnomethodological tradition remind us of the intersubjective nature of talk. The fourth distinct characteristic of talk is the interdependent nature of explanation and understanding. During talk as activity, if we do not understand something a speaker says, we can demand clarification and a more detailed explanation. Finally, the criteria for what counts as an 'adequate' explanation will rest upon the shared reference of the immediate situation (the surrounding physical and the unfolding discursive context). The world of text clearly does not possess such a characteristic.

Moving to the right-hand side of Table 7.1, texts are, of course, free of presence (i.e. the speaker) and free of his/her authority as the originator of the discourse. Clearly the actual author is not present and there can always be a question mark over whether the author is the originator of the text. A second characteristic of text is its formal nature, which asks the question 'how does the text function?' The rules of operation, the linguistic interrelationships and related structural features all provide a formal dimension for the text, with syntactic, semantic and text-world levels of analysis providing the bread and butter of linguistic analysis. It is worth noting that although talk does possess a rule-governed and formalisable dimension (Schegloff & Sacks, 1973), this does not lend itself to those logico-mathematical procedures used so successfully within structural linguistics (Allwood, Andersson & Dahl, 1977).

Texts also always have a significant historical dimension (point 3 in Table 7.1) which derives from the fact that all readers and texts will have a history. Readers adopt a mode of semantic inquiry which 'seeks to bring the dialectic of past significance and present meaning into focus'. The pertinent question here is 'what does the text speak about?' (Ricoeur, 1970). The fourth, phenomenological level of any text is the reading experience, and Ricouer's examination here focuses on the textual strategies within the text and the reader's mode of reception. The chief consideration here is with the experiential aspects of the text-reader relationship, with reading as an intersubjective and not a subjective experience. At this level the question being asked is 'what does this text say to me that is common to the reading experience of other readers?', an issue we will return to in Chapter 9. Finally, texts operate at an interpretational level. What is at issue here is the hidden tension between the text's autonomy and 'the assimilating force of the reader's appropriation' (Valdes, 1991). In order to comprehend a text, a reader always has to 'appropriate' it, i.e. work on it such that the reading becomes an understanding. The relevant question in this context is 'how has my world changed because of the reading of the text?' As Ricoeur (1970) reminds us:

> Written texts stand apart temporally and intentionally from the immediacy of dialogue. The written text is, above all, a composition, a strategy of communication that is subjected to a process of exteriorization, using a collective multifaceted, polysemic, and highly valorized system of cultural signs. (p. 45)

Given the formulating distinctions between talk and text we can turn now to a consideration of power relations in text.

Power relations in language: texts, discourses and ideology

There is little doubt that significant and major contributions to the study of the relationship between power and language have emerged from feminist critical theory and literary criticism. Selden (1985) argues that one of the fundamental starting points of modern feminism was Simone de Beauvoir's observation that whenever a woman tries to define herself, she starts by saying 'I am a woman' – no man would begin by defining himself on the basis of gender. More than anything this reveals the basic asymmetry between the terms 'masculine' and 'feminine' – man defines the human, not woman:

> If we accept Foucault's argument that what is 'true' depends on who controls discourse, then it is reasonable to believe that men's domination of discourses has trapped women inside a male 'truth' . . . from this point of view it makes sense for women writers to contest men's control of language rather than merely retreat into a ghetto of feminine discourse. (Selden, 1985, p. 131)

The control of discourse is what is at issue and care needs to be taken in avoiding a simplistic notion that language simply 'reflects' contemporary social relations and does not itself serve to (re)produce asymmetrical power relations. Ideology always plays a hidden role in language, one that post-structuralism has served to articulate. Moreover, we can never step outside language onto some neutral territory. With regard to the notion of text as discourse, there are at least three levels of 'language as text' on which we can consider the feminist critique of language: at the lexical level (words), the sentence level (grammar) and at the level of larger bodies of text and writing (documents, scripts, novels, and so on).

Beginning with the lexical level, in a comprehensive review of gender-related terms, Mills (1991) argues that historically, dictionaries have not simply listed words and definitions in a neutral way, but, rather, reflect male experience and serve to undermine women. She points out that more space is given to male items, sex-stereotyped examples are often used to illustrate examples, and, revealingly, there are many more insulting terms for women than there are for men. Mills charts the history and use of many words used to define and describe women. Typically, specific categories are used to 'define' women based on sexual status: women as edible (tart, crumpet, dish); women as animals (old bat, chic, bitch) and women as 'containers' (dish, bag, vessel). Her analysis of 'fluff', for example, notes:

> Fluff: The origins of fluff seem to be connected with flue, meaning softy downy material, and are thought to be an onomatopoeic modification of that word, imitating the action of puffing away some light substance. Since the 1790s fluff has meant light, feathery, downy, flocculent stuff. In the 1890s it came to be used figuratively with reference to personal character of intellect. At around this time fluff became a slang term for female pubic hair (see BEAVER). By 1903 the expression a little BIT of fluff was first Australian and subsequently US and UK slang for a young woman – presumably because she was considered, in Webster's definition of *fluff*, 'something essentially trivial (see TRIVIA) and lacking in importance or solid worth'.
> *Fluff* is also used in modern speech to denote an error, fault or blunder. Although there would seem to be no direct link, a view of woman as some sort of mistake or failed male has influenced Western thinking for centuries. Aristotle, for example, wrote: 'We should look upon the female state as being as it were a deformity . . . the female, in fact, is female on account of an inability of a sort, viz. it lacks the power to concoct semen.' (p. 94)

The aim in analysing words in this way is not only to show how women have been oppressed and subjugated by the use of language in text, but also to draw attention to the fact that language is constantly changing and we have a choice about how we are going to use our words. Although language can be a tool of oppression, 'it can also be a weapon in the struggle against patriarchy' (Mills, 1991, p. xvi).

But changing words so that they better reflect the aspirations and experiences of specific groups is not accomplished easily. And even where the specifically stereotyped words are changed (e.g. chairman to chairperson), it does not necessarily mean that attitudes and ideologies underpinning language use have changed. Campbell and Schram (1995), for example, examined the non-sexist language used in psychology textbooks, and noted that although nearly all recent books had adopted a non-sexist policy, there was little discussion of feminist approaches. Ehrlich and King (1994) analysed instances where words such as Ms (substitutions for Mrs and Miss), pronouns (generic use of *he* changed to *he/she*) and titles (chairperson) and found that very often the prevailing attitudes and values of a culture determine how these innovative, non-sexist terms get interpreted, in spite of their intended neutrality. They cite the findings of Dubois and Crouch (1987), who analysed announcements of academics changing jobs and found that chairperson indicated a woman, whereas a man is always a chairman:

Margaret P. Eby, *Chairperson* of Humanities at U. of Michigan at Dearbor, to dean of the College of Humanities and Fine Arts and Professor of Music at U. of North Iowa.

David W. Hamilton, Associate Professor of Anatomy at Harvard, to *Chairman* of Anatomy at U. of Minnesota.

(Ehrlich & King, 1994, p. 63)

Such examples highlight the significance of the relationship between power and language. In the 1970s, however, sociolinguists often focused on such relations (establishing correlations between language use and other social variables such as race and gender) on the assumption that language was somehow static, simply reflecting social categories. Critics of this view point out that language use is itself a social practice:

> While an individual's language use is an expression of social norms and relations, it can also function to resist or subvert these norms. . . . Instances of sexist language not only reflect sexist social practices, but also reproduce these practices. Conversely, non-sexist and feminist language reform is not merely a reflex of non-sexist social reform, but enacts reform in individual interactions. (Ehrlich & King, p. 72)

Given that words rarely appear in isolation, we can now consider our next level of analysis: the sentence. In her summary of *Womanwords*, Mills (1991) reminds us that Chomsky's analysis of language always emphasises a distinction between competence and performance (see Chapter 2). Performance of a language (as practice) is never neutral, whereas competence is always so. Competence refers to the knowledge of a grammar internalised by a speaker who has no consciousness of possessing such a skill: 'internalised language can never be sexist . . . there is a difference between the lexicon of a language which is never neutral and the basic grammar structure which is' (p. xiv). Radical feminist linguists contest this analysis, and the issues they raise bear upon current debates regarding political correctness. Penelope (1990), for example, provides an insightful analysis of English grammar, arguing that grammar as ideology serves to control women's relationship to language.

In effect, Penelope's (1990) critique rests on a careful reading of the relationship between theories of grammar and ideas in cognitive science. We noted earlier (Chapter 2) that theories of grammar (such as Chomsky's transformational grammar) rest on the assumption that the mind is a kind of recursion engine. And related to the 'mental scaffolding' which is the mind are deeply rooted conceptual metaphors (Lakoff & Johnson, 1980), themselves underpinning the linguistic structures required for grammatical competence. Penelope (1990) analyses the relationship between these ideas in cognitive science and formal grammars, arguing that such linguistic prescriptions are a 'protection racket' for maintaining mythical language purity. This prevents women from altering linguistic conventions that serve patriarchy. As an example, she notes that one of the principal conceptual metaphors is LANGUAGE IS A CONTAINER, while another is WOMAN IS A

CONTAINER, and where these merge into LANGUAGE IS A WOMAN, such metaphors 'reflect the correspondence between men's concerns with enforcing the purity of language and the purity of women' (p. 139).

This form of analysis has led to considerable debate, both within and beyond the language research community, thus reflecting contemporary concern over what has become known as 'political correctness' (Newfield, 1993; Saper, 1995). Understanding our third level of textual analysis (i.e. texts beyond the level of the sentence) can be helped by some discussion of this recent instance of the relationship between language and power. Feminist critical linguistics is often used by opponents of political correctness as a 'typical' example of the attack on 'free speech' being perpetuated by those who are deemed *politically correct* (Cox, 1994; Whitney & Wartella, 1992). The debate over political correctness serves as an interesting example of relationship between the role of ideology, power and language, particularly with regard to text and discourse.

The PC movement emerged in the mid-1980s out of a small group of Midwestern and Pacific coast American universities, where the term 'politically correct' began to be used where faculty and students wished to show sensitivity toward the increasing number of 'minority' groups entering the university system (Dennis, 1992). By the early 1990s political correctness began to be represented as an insidious movement to promote a left-wing/liberal political agenda on university campuses which marginalised the white, male-dominated mainstream in favour of minorities, multi-cultural and feminist sub-cultural groups (Whitney & Wartella, 1992). One reason for this was that a group of largely right-wing educators and popular media writers (Bernstein, 1990; D'Souza, 1991) who were concerned with changing administrative aspects of the American university system, latched on to the furore which surrounded the idea that traditional values, moral standing and the appreciation of 'great works' in education were under attack. In effect PC was 'constructed' by a small group of right-wing intellectuals writing their own summary essays in specialised political journals (e.g. *Newsweek*) and then attracting the attention of the mass media.

Political correctness as a 'movement' is probably something of a misnomer. What it represents is an attempt to incorporate into mainstream education (particularly higher education) certain key ideas which have emerged out of post-structuralism, critical theory and what is known as 'deconstructionism'. What this amalgam of theories and movements emphasise is that there is no such thing as 'objective truth', and reality is itself socially constructed through language. In a similar way to the 'extruding of versions of reality' produced by participants in conversation, texts reflect prevailing discourses and genres of literary form which themselves (re)produce particular ideological interpretations of reality. Language is never 'neutral' but always imbibes one or other set of ideological constructs, and unless we engage in an appropriate level of reflexive critical inquiry we will often not recognise the assumptions underpinning many of the texts we read (within education and elsewhere). Interestingly, D'Souza (1991), one of the most trenchant critics of political correctness, ridiculed the notion that we should have a 'revolution of the victims'. In other words it simply was not appropriate that minority groups (however defined) should impose their will on the curriculum of university courses by insisting that 'great works' were ideologically unsound. The debate over political correctness has now entered mainstream contemporary life (where even the President of the United States felt compelled to offer his own interpretation of the issue), providing us with a compelling example of the relationship between language and power.

Concluding comments

We have noted that the feminist position within contemporary literary criticism articulates how ideology and power are contested within domains where language is viewed as a 'formal object'. Similarly, expressions of the significance of power relations in talk have extended the research agenda of CA and have opened up a number of promising questions for psychologists interested in language (particularly in applied contexts). Viewing developments in language research in this way raises important questions for contemporary psycholinguistics, particularly given the continuing dominance of the cognitive approach. One key issue which arises is why there seems a considerable distance between the approaches commonly found in the psychology of language and developments in related fields with a shared interest in language (e.g. pragmatics and semiotics). Given that psychology is the scientific study of mental life and behaviour it seems somewhat surprising that psycholinguistics appears to be out of touch or even lagging behind current developments.

One reason for this current impasse is that psychology had a somewhat problematic history in establishing itself as a scientific discipline and understandably there has been little interest in engaging in the sociological and philosophical debates surrounding the discursive nature of science. Things have been difficult enough for the discipline without now appearing to contribute to the 'deconstruction' of science as social practice. Another reason is that some of the fundamental assumptions of a scientific psychology are undermined by reflexive critical inquiry. For example, critical theory argues that principles of universality and generalisability are themselves ideological constructs and rest upon the formulation (and production) of rhetorical texts. Arguably, however, the main reason for the approaches found within psycholinguistics is that the study of language has concentrated on a psychology of 'text' and not a psychology of language and communication. Lexical decision tasks, models of semantic memory, schema and script theory, syntactic comprehension, metaphor comprehension and other related areas of psycholinguistics are all critically concerned with words, sentences and texts – and not talk. There has been an over-concentration on structural aspects of text and the emphasis has been on that form of 'individuated' structuralism outlined by Chomsky. To understand reasons why other competing versions of 'structuralism' did not find a place within psycholinguistics we need to consider the influence of semiotics – the study of sign-systems.

8

Sign-Systems and Social Semiotics

When semiotics emerged as the 'science of signs and sign-systems' it appeared to offer the promise of a systematic, comprehensive and coherent study of communication processes. At a general level one purpose of communication is to ensure the continuity of ideas, experiences and knowledge from generation to generation expressed in symbols so that they can be transmitted across space and time. Semiotics provides a way of describing and explaining the processes and structures through which the 'meanings' of these experiences can be communicated, what Sebeok (1985) calls the 'time-binding' function of social communication: the human capacity for transcending the limitations of inherited characteristics through the use of language, number, gesture and other symbolic forms.

At the heart of structuralism (the movement of which semiotics forms a major part) was the scientific endeavour of discovering the codes, rules and systems which underpin all human social and cultural practices. Saussure, the founding father of semiotics, projected a discipline which had an exceptionally wide scope. He defines the main principles as being

> concerned with the formulation and encoding of messages by sources, the trans-
> mission of these messages through channels, the decoding and interpretation of
> these messages by destinations, and their signification. The entire transaction, or
> semiosis, takes place within a context to which the system is highly sensitive and
> which the system, in turn, affects. Any living entity, or its products, can be either
> message sources or destinations. Humans are unique in being able to process
> both verbal and averbal messages. (Saussure, 1974, p. 69)

One reason why Saussure's formulation influenced the study of language and linguistics to the extent it did was that it rested upon the material (physical) basis of sound. He argued that all sounds, and the key distinctions we make when hearing one rather than another sound, can be derived from a principle of openness/closure. His analysis of the parts of the speech system (articulatory mechanisms) responsible for the production and recognition of sound difference underpinned his conception of semiosis: the recognition of difference being the universal basis for any semiotic system. As Hodge and Kress (1988) note:

> sounds are labelled in terms of features that derive from that part of the vocal
> mechanism that is most characteristically involved in their production. For
> instance dentals like *d* or *t* are produced with the tongue touching the teeth:
> labials such as *b*, *p* are produced using lips. What is happening here is that the
> space of articulation is sub-divided and assigned meaning, and these become the
> basis for the subdivisions of the stream of sound. (p. 28)

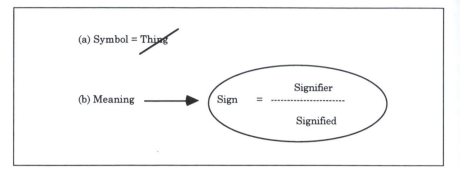

Figure 8.1 *Signs and symbols*

So, it is important to grasp the idea that any sound can only mean something against the backdrop of all other different possible sounds. And the sound for the word 'cow' only means something with reference to all those sounds that are not 'cow'. Again we have to remind ourselves that the notion of a symbol being equal to a real thing is simply mistaken (i.e. the word 'cow' is not magically connected to its referent – a real cow). The meaning of any sign is that indissoluble relationship between the signifier and the signified outlined by Saussure (see Figure 8.1).

As Selden (1985) argues, things have no place in the study of signs and the elements of language acquire meaning not as a result of some connection between words and things but only as part of a system of relations. We noted in Chapter 1 that the location of that system of relations (structure of the language) was quite different for Saussure and Chomsky. For Saussure, signification processes are collective, with linguistic structures and their meaning pre-existing any individual, i.e. located in the human collective consciousness. For Chomsky, the structural components of language had to rest upon the innate 'language learning' predispositions of the human mind, i.e. an individual's mind, the classical 'logocentric' position of Western philosophy. What they do share of course is the emphasis on a structuralist account of language: the possibilities inherent in a formal analysis of abstract structure, a science of signs and sign-systems

Although Saussure affirmed the social over the individual it can be argued that his emphasis on the social was exceptionally vague. Hodge and Kress (1988) point out that at every step of Saussure's formulation of the sign he seemed to exclude all those elements which could form the basis of a truly 'social semiosis'. They note that Saussure's basic strategy was to project a largely undifferentiated field and then gradually split each element into two, leading eventually to his emphasis on the signifier, as in Figure 8.2. A social semiotics, which emphasises signification processes rather than structure, would seek to incorporate all the italicised elements of Figure 8.2. Hodge and Kress (1988) argue that Saussure's first distinction was between language as a pure object of thought against all other systems external to it (even though they might have an interest, such as politics). Second, he

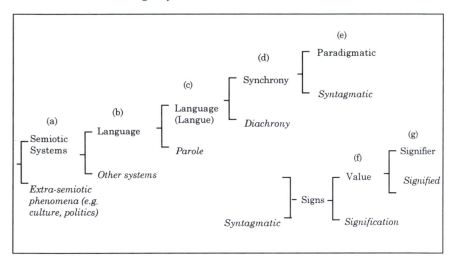

Figure 8.2 *Domains of a social semiotics (adapted from Hodge & Kress, 1988, p. 17)*

excluded other systems distinct from language (visual representations such as paintings), which he termed 'extra-linguistic'. At the next stage, he formulated the distinction between the abstract system which underlies the rules of speech (*langue*) and speech itself (*parole*). Speech itself he considered impossible to study systematically, an interesting thesis given the recent developments in CA. Again, this *langue/parole* distinction is echoed in the competence/performance categorisation of Chomsky's theory.

Moving to the next stage of the differentiation process, Hodge and Kress (1988) point out that Saussure favoured the synchronic study of language, i.e. the study of the system at a given point in time, rather than the diachronic – the analysis of language change. From here the synchronic was to be further delineated into the paradigmatic (language selection and association) and the syntagmatic, 'considerations of value (elements and their relations in a system) rather than signification' (p. 17). Favouring syntagmatic analysis, signs themselves were seen as having the double form we are familiar with, signifier (surface form) and signified (meaning), and although Saussure pointed to the importance of the signified and the indissoluble nature of 'signs as meaning', in practice he concentrated on the signifier. Hodge and Kress note:

> He affirmed the social over the individual, but only as an abstract, immobilized version of the social order, potentially threatened by actions of innumerable individuals. . . . The strength of this attempt to escape the world of processes [all those elements in italics] reveals his fascinated recognition of these forces, even if they appear in his theory only as negations. (p. 17)

A social semiotic analysis of signs would seek to include the missing elements of this progression: (a) culture, society and politics as intrinsic to semiotics (in Figure 8.2. above); (b) other semiotic systems alongside verbal language; (c) *parole*, the act of speaking; (d) diachrony, time, history, process and change; (f) the process of signification, the transactions between signifying systems and structures of reference; and (g) structures of the signified.

Signification process and sign-system production

The process of signification (the production of signs and sign-systems in a particular context) is one aspect that is accessible to a 'social semiotic' analysis. For example, consider the 'sign' depicted in (a) of Figure 8.3, and note that by itself it is a very ambiguous kind of sign (if it can be called a sign at all – not just two lines joined together or a slightly off centre right-angle). However, placed in context, as in (c) of Figure 8.3 then it is immediately recognisable as a sign meaning 'play' on a portable tape-recorder or 'walkman'. As an element in a system of relations (with other signs) the signifier $>$ is both recognisable and meaningful. In articulating the development of the signification process one needs to consider the emergence and history of a sign. In the late 1950s and early 1960s large tape-recording machines began to enter the domestic market. They were cumbersome, awkward to use and came with few sophisticated options. The Phillips SL, for example, had a large lever which was pushed to the right to indicate 'play', and used either with or without another button pressed down for recording (and note the observation that the 'red' of the record button on modern walkmen harks back to the early use of the colour red as an indicator that the machine is 'on'). Gradually conventions for the actions which could be carried out became established and 'fast-forward, 'back', 'play', 'pause', and so on, became the accepted words employed. The signs were also becoming conventionalised and, more often than not, were placed above or below the words attached to the buttons. Over time, and in line with both the miniaturisation of the products and the international markets they appealed to, the words began to disappear, leaving only the signs.

The signs were not randomly selected, however, as if metamorphisising out of the actions of each button. Note that double arrows for 'fast-forward' uses repetition and intensification so as to indicate speed. And 'backwards' would not be recognised at all were it not for the relationship between 'play' and 'fast forward' (i.e. to understand $\ll$ you need first to see the connection between $>$ and $\gg$ followed by noting that $\ll$ is the reverse of $\gg$). Further, the sign for 'pause' is arguably related to the 'stop' but with a piece missing out of the square – it is not quite stop, but neither is it 'play'. The social semiotics of these sign relationships also bears upon the placing of the whole system in and beyond the context of its original use. During the 1960s and 1970s when the signs were emerging they did so always in parallel either with words such as 'Play' or 'Fast Forward' or

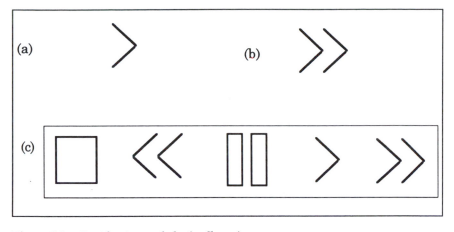

Figure 8.3 *Signification and the 'walkman'*

simply 'P' or 'FF'. By the mid-1980s, however, the words had disappeared, and the system stood on its own. Pick up a Sony Walkman tape-recorder made in the late 1980s and you will find no words, only these signs which form an immediately recognisable and conventional sign-system indicating actions and operations with this and related domains. Notice how the same set of five or six 'sign characters' (fast-forward, play, and so on) have transmuted into the world of video-recording and into computer graphics. A typical example of the latter can be found in 'multi-media' software called 'Macromind Director', where the operations panel for playing a short movie clip consists simply of the same character set – immediately recognisable to both naïve user and professional alike. It should also not escape our notice that many of the signs that we find in hi-fi systems and information technology contexts also find their expression (simulations and extensions) in other contexts, e.g. in the signs and icons in car dashboards or in the signs often found on washing-machines. There is a constant translation of signs from one context to another, particularly where those signs are indicative of well-established procedures that have their corollary in new and innovative domains.

Signification processes (the production and interpretation of signs) need to be distinguished from semiotic analysis, the traditional structural analysis of signs and sign-systems. Although analysis of this type has formed the principal basis for numerous areas of linguistic inquiry (e.g. transformational grammar), the attention remains syntagmatic – focused on the sign and its relations within any given abstract system. We can consider two different ways the analysis of signification processes has developed, the first emphasising ideological and social–cultural aspects of social semiotics (Hodge & Kress, 1988), the second in the extensions and refinements of Saussure's ideas in the work of the American semiotician Charles Peirce.

Ideology and social semiotics

Beginning with Hodge and Kress (1988), their argument, as we noted above, was that the social dimensions of semiotics are so intrinsic to the nature and function of signs that the systems in which they are embedded cannot be studied in isolation from their social–cultural context (e.g. the 'Walkman's signs' need to be read with reference to the development of the tape-recorder and subsequent innovations in video and computer graphics). Hodge and Kress (1988) outline their theory by noting that three key elements in communication are messages, texts and discourses:

> A message has directionality, a source, a goal and a purpose. It works on what is called the plane of representation or the 'mimetic' plane. . . . Text (from the latin *textus* – something woven together) is a message structure which has some sort of unity. . . . Discourse, on the contrary, is the social process in which texts are embedded.
>
> Texts are both the material realisation of systems of signs: – also the site where change continually takes place (that is, they are historical – not static). Both text and message signify the specific social relationships at the moment of their production or reproduction. (pp. 5–6)

The social processes they refer to consist of two elements: logonomic rules and ideological complexes. Logonomic rules are best viewed as 'higher-order' control mechanisms. Consider what is involved in understanding a joke, sarcasm or irony. In order to 'get the joke' or understand the sarcastic comment, often some 'second-level message' must be recognised and thus regulate the function of the message. Such higher-order control mechanisms are known as 'logonomic systems defined as

> a set of rules prescribing the conditions for production and reception of meanings which specify who can claim to initiate (produce, communicate) or know (receive or understand) meanings about what topics under what conditions and in what modalities (how, when and why). (Hodge & Kress, 1988, p. 4)

Hodge and Kress argue that logonomic rules are regulated or 'policed' by concrete agents (parents, teachers, employers, university lecturers) and at the same time they can be challenged and changed (i.e. the political correctness movement). Logonomic systems cannot be invisible or obscure, or they would not work. They become highly visible in politeness conventions, etiquette, industrial relations, and so on.

Working in conjunction with logonomic systems, ideological complexes are functionally related sets of contradictory versions of the world, coercively imposed by one social group on another on behalf of its own distinctive interests, or subversively offered by another social group in attempts at resistance in its own interests. Hodge and Kress (1988) argue that ideological complexes and logonomic systems are related function and content, with logonomic systems expressing ideological content by controlling one category of behaviour (the production of sign-systems), 'while

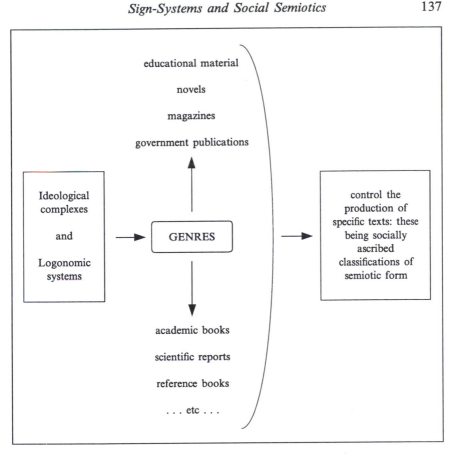

Figure 8.4 *Message, text and discourse*

the ideological complex as a whole projects a set of contradictions which both legitimate and ameliorate the premise of the domination' (p. 5). Their position can be summarised as in Figure 8.4.

Discourse(s) or 'genre(s)' are the social processes in which texts are constituted. They are informed by ideological complexes which utilise logonomic rules. Hence we do not simply read and process texts as if they are neutral objects; rather they are themselves constrained by discourse frames which promote, produce and serve one or other ideological view or version of the world. We need to be careful to recognise that this approach does not argue that we are somehow 'fixed' and constrained by discourses operating on us 'from above'. Rather we are active within such genres, constantly creating and re-creating whatever ideology they are serving. Williamson (1978) makes a similar point in her analysis of advertising, noting that ideology is always precisely that of which we are not aware. It becomes invisible because we are active in it; we constantly re-create it by our very use of this or that particular discourse in context. Hodge and Kress (1988) go on to analyse a number of different genres (including

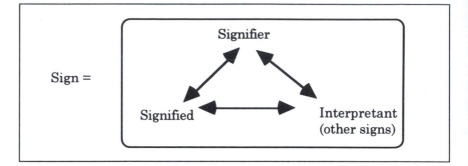

Figure 8.5 *Peirce's extend sign analysis*

advertising, comics and billboards) providing a detailed rationale for their account of signification processes as social practice.

Peircean semiotics

A second approach to the analysis of signification processes comes out of the work of Peirce, a mathematician and semiotician who extended Saussure's conception of the tripartite relation of sign = signifier/signified (see Figure 8.5). For Peirce (1935–66) the sign is not simply a relationship between the signifier (surface form) and signifier (its meaning), but also includes a third element, which makes clear that every sign determines an interpretant. To paraphrase Sebeok's (1994) analysis of this development, with the sign for the English noun 'horse', interpretants could include, 'gee-gee', 'pony', 'stallion', and even the word 'heroin'. Furthermore, there are no limits to the number, and form of interpretants' signs, and discourses on and of signs, which can overlay another sign. As Peirce (1935–66) notes, a sign is anything 'which determines something else (its interpretant) to refer to an object to which itself refers (its object) in the same way, the sign becoming a sign, and so on ad infinitum'. Sebeok (1994) makes the point that any paraphrase or extended discourse on any sign 'will enrich comprehension of the object it represents, as will also its interlingual translations and intersemiotic transmutations' (p. 13). Deconstructionist critics of language (e.g. Derrida, Foucault) have used this kind of analysis in support of their proposals that there are no 'truths' in written texts (unequivocal messages from originating authors), only signs, their interpretants (more signs) and the unlimited field of semiosis.

An additional important aspect of Peirce's semiotic theory was his classification of different aspects of signs. These are differentiated into iconic, indexical and symbolic signs. He was careful to emphasise that this classification did not describe three different types of sign, rather within any given sign one or other of the three aspects would be dominant. Iconic signs are signs which serve to resemble the object which it is said to represent. So, in the United Kingdom the road sign for 'falling rocks' shows a picture of a hillside with stones 'running down' one side, i.e. a close similarity to what would actually happen in a landslide beside the road. Eco (1983) suggests that the Star-Spangled Banner (the flag of the United States) is another good example of an iconic sign, where each of the fifty white stars in a single blue canton 'stands for' one of the fifty states in the present Union, whereas each of the thirteen stripes 'stands for' one of the colonies that originally formed the Union. He emphasises that the iconic relations can be grasped only by those already informed of the code, or convention (namely American history) being used. There are other aspects of the flag which are indexical and symbolic; the aspect that predominates is always a function of the context, again emphasising signification processes – the recognition of signs in context.

Indexical signs are signs where the signifier is contiguous with its signified. It points to an object or is a sample of it. So, the footprint Robinson Crusoe found in the sand was an index to him of some creature. A no-smoking sign with a cigarette crossed out would be indexical in the sense that the cigarette it represents stands for all cigarettes that could be smoked. Deictic terms are also 'indexical signs' in that they when I use the term 'I' the object I'm pointing to is me, whereas when the Pope uses the same term he is pointing to the object who represents the head of the Catholic church.

Finally, symbolic signs are all those aspects of signs which depend upon other signs (and related codes) for their recognition and interpretation. Every word in this book is a symbolic sign, given that it rests upon rules of grammar and discourse particular to the English language (another code). A symbolic sign is one whose relationship to the object it is said to represent is entirely arbitrary. In other words, it is only understandable with reference to a pre-existing social convention which specifies the way in which the sign 'stands for' that which it represents. Peirce also proposed that the three categories or aspects of the sign find their correspondence in logic where the iconic presupposes actuality (what is actually true), indexicality necessity (what is logically necessary) and the symbolic possibility (the hypothetical). Sebeok (1983) clarifies this observation, noting that the iconic is the modality where direct perception is very persuasive and 'actuality' is the key; indexicality emphasises cause–effect chains or 'contiguity' links (there is a close fit between sign and meaning but not a direct one); and with the symbolic, the relation of sign to object is based on other signs, 'although [this is] the lowest modality, it is interesting that it is said to involve the highest forms of thought' (p. 456).

Peirce's elaboration of the sign and his emphasis on the role of the interpretant (the overlaying of other signs and sign-systems) has been utilised by many semioticians and others in related disciplines (including art and architecture, film theory and cultural studies). Eco (1983) asks us, for example, to consider the physical labour involved in the production of sign-systems or the 'process of signification'. This ranges from the mere *recognition* of existing phenomena through their *ostension* (representativeness) to the production of *replicas* and the effort required for the *invention* of new expressions. In advertising Williamson (1978) has employed a semiotic analysis to show the relationship between signs and meanings in consumer products, whereas Fiske (1978) demonstrates how semiotics can be used in analysing television. In the remainder of this chapter we can consider the development of an applied social semiotics in three domains: photography, interface design and film.

Applied social semiotics: photography

John Berger (1972) proposed that 'photographs are records of things seen', and 'photography has no language of its own: there is no transformation, the only decision is the choice of moment to record and isolate' (p. 23). Semioticians such as Eco (1982), however, take exception to this, saying that if photography is to be likened to perception, this is not because the former is a 'natural' process but because the latter is also coded, adopting a constructivist account of visual processing. Tagg (1988) articulates why the analysis of photography is problematic when he comments:

> The photographer turns his or her camera on a world of objects already con-structed as a world of uses, values and meanings though in the perceptual process these may not appear as such but only as qualities discerned in a 'natural' recognition of 'what is there'. By more or less conscious adjustment of an infinite field of significant determinations ranging from the arrangement and lighting of this 'world of objects' to the mechanics and field of view of the camera and the sensitivity of the film, paper and chemical, the photographer abstracts from the distribution of reflected light from the objects to procure a pattern of light and dark on paper which can in no way be regarded as a replication of the 'given' subject. The pattern on paper is, in turn, the object of a perception – or reading – in which it is constituted as a meaningful image according to learned schemas. (p. 187)

The meaning of the photographic image is constructed from an interaction of these various schemes and codes. It is better to see it as a composite of signs, much more akin to a sentence or discourse than to a single word. Tagg (1988) again:

> In common too, with other language-like systems, photographs may be exhaust-ively analysed as projections of a limited number of rhetorical forms in which a society's values and beliefs are naturalised. (p. 188)

Photographs are not veridical representations of reality, despite appear-ances. They are material items produced by a certain elaborate mode of production and distributed, circulated and consumed within a given set of social relations. They are images made meaningful and understood within the very relations of their production and sited within a wider ideological complex. Consider the two photographs in Figure 8.6. Figure 8.6(a) is a very conventionalised form of the 'first day at school' photograph which follows particularly prescribed rules and conventions (how the child should pose, the position of the shot, and so on). In contrast Figure 8.6(b) is a

Figure 8.6(a)   *First day at school: milestones recorded (Anonymous)*

Figure 8.6(b)   *Family living-room (Sean Hudson)*

photograph of an everyday scene showing people interacting in their living-room. Here, however, the child is not displaying a certain pose, dressed in a special way or otherwise instructed to act in accordance with the photo-taking event.

Roland Barthes (1967), often described as a 'post-structuralist' critic, commented on the difference between language and iconic imagery, noting how particular this was in the case of photography:

> The linguistic sign bears an arbitrary relationship to its referent; the photographic image, it can be argued, does not. There is no law in nature which dictates that the linguistics sign 'tree' should be associated with the thing with which it is in fact associated: this is a matter of cultural convention. In the case of the photograph, the image is in a sense *caused* by its referent. A photo-sensitive emulsion necessarily registers the distribution of light to which it is exposed. The chiaroscuro of the photographic image replicates that precept to the exposed film: 'In every photograph there is the stupefying evidence of this-is-what-happened-and-how.' (p. 39)

In a similar fashion Burgin (1982) notes that the structure of representation in photography points towards the implicit reproduction of ideology. The photograph seems to present itself as something that cannot be argued with, 'an offer you can't refuse'. He notes those curious occasions where you might be shown a 'puzzle photograph' of the 'guess what this is variety'; once you discover what the object is, the picture is instantaneously transformed into a 'thing' and we cannot imagine how we did not see it in the first place. The point Burgin wants to emphasise, of course, is that it is only during the curious 'I wonder what that could be' phase that we might be made aware that we are selecting an image from a set of alternatives, in other words working to supply information that the picture is not providing for us. Normally this 'decoding' is so instantaneous and 'natural' that we are unaware that the reading of the photograph as 'sign' rests upon a discursive frame, a set of interpretants (related signs, images, our knowl-edge of other photographic conventions, and so on) which makes recognition possible. It is very difficult for us to comprehend the notion that the photograph does not represent the 'real' but instead is only another set of images (texts), whose production is embedded in all those actions and events which make up a signification process of this kind.

Applied social semiotics: interface design

A second area where there is an increasing interest in the application of semiotics is in interface design, i.e. the design of the signs, images and representations you are presented with when you switch on a personal computer. The meanings of the iconic signs presented at the interface have been examined by Rogers (1989), who provides one classification of the function and form of icons and aims to develop a 'grammar' of icon forms: one which maps onto the underlying system structure. She points out that a great deal of effort is being expended in what she calls 'iconic interfacing', noting, however, that this development is taking place in something of a vacuum:

> Unlike verbal language, in which there are a set of syntactic and semantic rules which provide us with a means of disambiguating the meaning of verbal language, pictorial language has, as yet, no equivalent set of rules underlying its comprehension. (p. 106)

Rogers lists a number of the pros and cons of using icons: advantages including providing an impression of 'easiness' (not forced to engage with the computer in some form of 'computer-speak') and the universal meaningfulness of icons; disadvantages including the lack of rules of design and the inherent danger of the ambiguous sign.

Leaving aside the problematic nature of assuming the 'universality' of sign recognition, the complexities of the 'graphical user interface' (GUI) design may benefit from a semiotic analysis. Consider first the equivalence (or even confusion) over whether iconic images presented on the screen indicate sign/actions or 'tool use'. Sinha (1988) provides a lucid account of Vygotsky's view of the distinction between a sign and a tool (arguably, Vygotsky is best described as a developmental semiotician):

> The basic analogy between sign and tool rests on the mediating function that characterises each of them. [However,] a most essential difference between sign and tool, and the basis for the real divergence of the two lines [of their development], is the different ways that they orient human behaviour. The tool's function is to serve as the conductor of human influence on the object of activity; it is externally oriented; it must lead to changes in objects. It is a means by which human activity aims at mastering . . . nature. The sign, on the other hand, changes nothing in the object of a psychological operation. It is a means of internal activity aimed at mastering oneself; this sign is internally oriented. (p. 95)

What is missing from this account is any sense that signs have their identity and meaning only in contexts of use. Yet it is precisely such pragmatic and structural aspects of signifiers that are mobilised in the semiotic organisation of the computer interaction (see also Reason & Forrester, 1991). The computer interaction is designed to be meaningful in relation to a planned functioning of the total human–computer system, and the meaningfulness of the interface is dependent upon the structuring of that foundation of pre-given semiotic possibilities. Consider 'signs' presented in the form of windows and menus, as in Figure 8.7, where windows are typically rectangular objects and menus (which can be 'pulled down') labelled with significant words associated with actions. While recognising that the GUI has made it possible for many non-technical computer users to find a gateway into the use of 'interactive' information technology, consider further the complexities of the representations involved. Windows have many moving parts and menus do not. For example you can close a window box, size it, use scroll bars, activate the 'drag' bar, change the sizing handle, and so on, but nobody has told you about what it means to have a white space on a screen. And so, while you can change the box frame and reveal more paper, the question remains: where is the

Figure 8.7　*Windows and menus at the interface (System 6.0.7 ©1990 Apple Computer Inc. All Rights Reserved. Used with permission)*

information which is not yet shown? When the window comes to the front, where does the information come from? Similarly, where is the information occluded by the menu which drops down? Is it on top? (In fact it has to be asked what IT is and whether it can be said to be ON TOP.) The screen invokes what we may term a 'virtual metaphysics' of a kind familiar from the crazy – yet semio-logical – physics of the children's cartoon. In such a world, it seems legitimate to ask questions such as: where is the flame when the candle is blown out?

Consider how a new user might interpret a 'window' and what she might think can be done with it. The window divides the screen into regions which have an inside and an outside, and usually a boundary frame divides these parts. (The frame itself may be further visually differentiated into scroll bars, title bar, sizing gadgets, and so on.) The semiotic field invoked by the metaphor tempts us to think of the frame bounding a view onto something beyond the frame. The 'screen' apparently has a phenomenological depth: there are two 'levels' – the 'surface' and the 'beyond'. The window allows us to see what lies beyond it: a list of files and applications, perhaps, 'on' a 'sheet' which can be seen 'through' the window. It is this scenario which makes sense of the action of scroll bars, of course, and thereby incidentally contributes to the ambiguity of the 'direction arrows' on the bars: do they point in the direction in which we wish to look next, or in the direction in which we wish to move the sheet beyond the window?

The phenomenological depth expressed in the window's name (which orients the user to a set of expectations of possibility) is partially confirmed by its operation. There are important – if superficially minor – dislocations

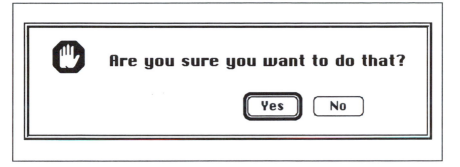

Figure 8.8 *Warning images at the screen interface*

with respect to the prior behaviour of 'ordinary' windows, however. How do you influence the amount of the scene 'beyond' that revealed by the window? Not – as the habits of perspective would suggest – by the viewer going nearer to or further away from the window, but by altering the size of the window itself. Although the window metaphor invites a carry-over of relevant experiences of window-related attitudes and understandings from the mundane world to that of the interface, it does so in a way which requires a progressive 'de-materialisation', as it were, of the actual ground which seems to support the initial usefulness and intelligibility of the metaphor. The concept 'window' must undergo a very rapid metamorphosis of signification if it is to grasp the nature of the developing interface.

Alternatively, consider another common 'sign' encountered when using a computer, as in Figure 8.8. Although the actions implicit in the recognition of this sign might appear obvious, there are a number of noteworthy aspects to the 'reading' of the sign. First, there are at least three things the hand might be doing, welcoming, saying 'hello' or saying 'stop'. Second, the little mark on the bottom of the hand indicates American design. In contrast to European hands found in road or information signs, American hands tend to be larger or chubbier (maybe indexing the economic superiority of the better fed culture!). Third, the foreground/background of the hand indicates that the sign is transmuted from the American road traffic sign for STOP. Leaving aside the other signification processes presupposed by the language in the sign itself, it is clear that even a simple supposedly unambiguous sign requires some understanding of its production in order to give it an appropriate reading.

Applied social semiotics: film

The first attempts by semioticians to turn their attention to film and film criticism were greeted with rather extreme reactions:

semiotics was a procrustean enterprise comparable to painting by numbers, at once unwittingly absurd and insidiously political, practised by possessed sectarians, pod-people, and overdressed ladies bedecked in bangles and baubles, whose general demeanour had the poised vigilance of a lobotomised ferret. (Lapsley & Westlake, 1988, p. 33)

Semiotics (as the scientific study of signs and signification processes) heralded the end of all traditional aesthetics. Ideas of art as organic unity were discarded and replaced by the supposition that all meanings and aesthetic effects were explicable in terms of determining structures and mechanisms. Art was open to scientific analysis. And so was film.

Following developments by Metz, Pasolini and others, film theorists were particularly influenced by the work of the psychoanalyst semiotician Jacques Lacan. Lacan argued that Saussure and his followers had over-emphasised the 'signified' at the expense of the 'signifier'. Sturrock (1986) notes that Lacan was intent on removing the illusion that the signifier (expression) answers to the function of representing the signified (meaning or content). Ultimately there may only be signifiers (the 'meanings' that signifiers point to turn out themselves to be other signifiers), and so on, and so on, thus a permanent slippage of meaning and an infinite possibility of interpretation. This implies that there is a continual sliding of signifieds under signifiers as these enter into new relationships. Meaning is not at all the stable relationship between signifier and signified presumed by Saussure. Selden (1985) asks us to consider what happens when we use a dictionary to find a meaning (signified) of a word (signifier):

> [In fact] the dictionary confirms only the relentless deferment of meaning: not only do we find for every signifier several signifieds (a 'crib' signifies a manger, a child's bed, a hut, a job, a mine-shaft lining, a plagiarism, a literal translation, discarded cards at cribbage), but each of the signifieds becomes yet another signifier which can be traced in the dictionary with its own array of signifieds ('bed' signifies a place for sleeping, a garden plot, a layer of oysters, channel of a river, a stratum). The process continues interminably, as the signifiers lead a chameleon-like existence, changing their colours with each new context. (p. 73)

What stops the continuous slide and momentarily fixes meaning is the punctuation of the signifying chain by the action of the subject, expressed by Lacan as in Figure 8.9.

On this basis film theorists asserted that film is a language appearing to render the real transparently but actually secreting an ideology. The task therefore was to create a new language, enabling men and women to think what had previously been unthinkable. Lapsley and Westlake (1988) make the point that meaning is produced by the subject in this process of punctuation; but, equally, the subject is produced by the meanings available in the signifying chain. For the subject this is such by virtue of a self-conception that is only available within discourse:

> The desire of the subject engenders varying interpretations of the unfolding text; the text offers in return the condition of subjectivity. For Lacan there is, therefore, an unceasing dialectic of the subject and meaning, an idea that would recur in various guises within film theory. (p. 108)

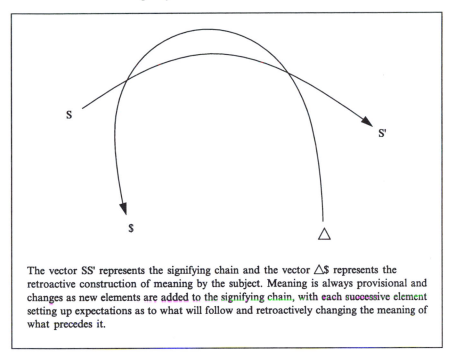

The vector SS' represents the signifying chain and the vector △$ represents the retroactive construction of meaning by the subject. Meaning is always provisional and changes as new elements are added to the signifying chain, with each successive element setting up expectations as to what will follow and retroactively changing the meaning of what precedes it.

Figure 8.9 *Lacan's development of the sign (adapted from Lapsley & Westlake, 1988)*

Arguably semiotics has had the greatest influence in film within the study of narrative. Narrative itself has been defined as the devices, strategies and conventions governing the organisation of a story (fictional or factual) into sequence. Within a general consensus that narrative is a crucially important form and paradigm of thought and language, the diversity of the views on narrative exemplifies a growing pluralism. Definitions have included *a reference to what is not actually present* and *the representation of an imaginary reality*. Narrative is said to depend on the metaphorical imagination and is produced through what Ricoeur (1976) calls the 'predicative assimilation', which

> 'grasps together' and integrates into one whole and complete story multiple and scattered events, thereby schematizing the *intelligible signification* attached to the narrative taken as a whole. (p. 185)

Narrative has been described as a meta-code, a human universal on the basis of which transcultural messages about the nature of a shared reality can be transmitted (White, 1980), and Lyotard (1984) describes post-modernism as an 'incredulity towards metanarratives' (truth and objectivity, the logocentric subject, and so on – i.e. all those 'stories' considered as the essential backdrop of cultural life). The study of narrative has a long history, and was originally viewed as a branch of rhetoric. Aristotle argued

that mere episodic stories were supplanted by narratives organised thematically to convey an idea through plot. Contemporary narratology can be
subdivided into abstract narratology (e.g. the structural analysis of myth,
the semiotics of narrative) and textual narratology (e.g. the discourse of
stories). Pavel (1985) defines narratology itself as the integrated study of all
levels of narrative phenomena, and recognises the problems associated with
the rapid development of a field which has seen the proliferation of many
competing schools. However, central to many conceptions of narrative is
the distinction between plot (any arrangement of incidents) and story (mere
raw material awaiting the organising principles of an interpreter).

The work of narrative cinema is primarily directed to the effacement
of all signs of its production. Consider the sub-system of the apparatus of
look and identification in the spectator's identification with the camera.
Although this is rigorously constructed, the rules for doing so have been
assimilated into sets of conventions of film-making. Among those identified
by Lapsley and Westlake (1988):

1 The provision of a master or establishing shot, enabling the spectator
   to orientate himself or herself with respect to each new shot in the
   sequence.
2 The 180° rule, ensuring that the spectator always finds the same
   characters in the same part of the screen, i.e. matching 'screen space'
   and 'narrative space'.
3 The 30° rule, which prevents the spectator experiencing a jump in space
   and permits a smooth continuity between shots.
4 The orchestration of actor's movements so that reframing and camera
   movement do not draw attention to themselves.

As they put it:

> The function of these taken for granted procedures is to achieve a coherent
> narrative space and the maintenance of perspective; their apparent innocence
> masks their conventionality, and hence their ideological complicity and effectivity
> . . . narrative cinema offers the illusion of contradiction resolved when in reality
> it yields nothing of the sort. (p. 155)

The main point to come out of the semiotic analysis of narrative in
cinema is that it is only possible to read 'signs' if you comprehend the
narrative context in which they exist or are revealed. Narrative contexts can
only be understood with regard to the set of social practices, procedures
and techniques which underpin them. Imagine you know about traffic lights
and in a strange country see a cluster of signs at a road junction. You don't
wait to be told what each sign means – you don't decode the 'icons' that
the signs present; rather, because you know the set of actions/states that are
relevant and expected (stop, wait, go, filter right, and so on), in other words
in the 'narrative field' of road junctions, you seek to identify the most
probably appropriate sign for each semiotic function that you suppose to
exist.

Concluding comments

Understanding the nature of signs and sign-systems is an essential part of studying language as a communication code (or codes). There remains some debate over whether semiotics is part of linguistics or linguistics a sub-species of semiotics (Sebeok, 1994). Sebeok's review of various expert opinions on the issue concludes that linguistics is a 'structurally autonomous' part of semiotics which itself includes all forms of verbal and non-verbal signification. However, we need to remember that Saussure's original formulations of semiotics (as structuralism) rested upon the phonological articulation of sound coding (phoneme as lexeme – and thus the word as a sign). Applying semiotics to the analysis of the 'sign/word' is both realisable and often appropriate. It is much more difficult to extend or apply a semiological analysis to the level of the written text. Ricoeur (1970) notes that there is no semiotics of the sentence, although he argues that we can adapt Peirce's tripartite conception of 'sign–object–interpretant' to the level of the text:

> In the new triangle, the object is the text itself; the sign is the depth semantics disclosed by structural analysis; and the series of interpretants is the chain of interpretations produced by the interpreting community and incorporated into the dynamics of the text. (p. 63)

The mention of depth semantics, structural analysis and 'chains of interpretations' provides us with an ideal way to introduce the next two chapters on reading and writing. Hopefully, this introduction to semiotics has provided a background against which to place many of the issues which surround our understanding of the processes involved in these two activities.

9

The Role of the Reader
in Text Interpretation

The most important goal of reading research in the psychology of language is to understand the comprehension processes involved in the act of reading. Over the last twenty years there has been a considerable amount of reading research and the aim of this chapter is to provide a general overview of the key topics. Of course, psychology is not the only area researching reading and to ignore developments in areas such as literary criticism and literary theory would be a disservice to anyone with an interest in the topic. Concentrating solely on the *reading* process can also misrepresent the significance of the study of reading for the psycholinguistic analysis of text. We noted earlier the problems associated with failing to conceptually distinguish **talk** from **text**. Texts exhibit their own structure, can be analysed completely separately from any notion of an intending author or ideal reader, and take a multiplicity of forms. If we want to argue that the cognitive processes utilised when reading the ingredients on the back of a packet of biscuits are the same as when reading Joyce's *Finnegans Wake*, then a purely psychological account of the reading process may be all we require. If not, then we need to consider additional perspectives which may help inform us of what it is to understand a piece of written text.

Psychological approaches to the study of reading

The psychology of reading can be divided into three areas. The first is concerned primarily with eye-movements, looking in detail at the relationship between eye-movement patterns (recordings of where people fixate their eyes as they scan reading material) and reading comprehension processes. The second area subsumes a range of models and ideas about reading, where some theorists tend to focus on what might be built up from the processing of individual words, while others concentrate on the constructions that readers impose upon texts as they read. The third area is concerned with reading as a task and the purposes it might fulfil, e.g. how people adopt one strategy for difficult reading material, another when reading a magazine or newspaper. In what follows it would be helpful to keep in mind that psycholinguistic studies of reading assume the core constructs of the information processing paradigm, i.e. reading will

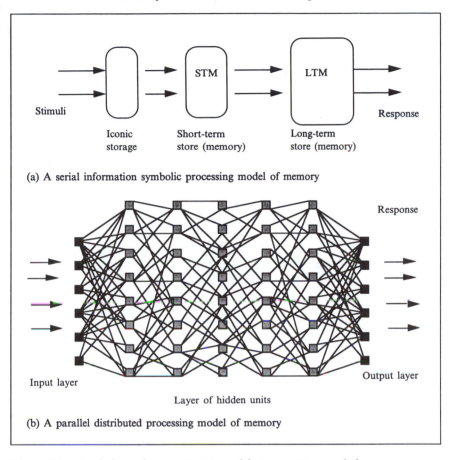

(a) A serial information symbolic processing model of memory

(b) A parallel distributed processing model of memory

Figure 9.1 *Symbolic and connectionist models in cognitive psychology*

eventually be understood once we can uncover the various cognitive stages involved in moving from the 'input' of the information (via eye-movements), through short-term storage processes implicit in processing sentences, to full comprehension and understanding of what is meant by the text. However, although the two dominant perspectives within cognitive psychology (the symbolic and connectionist) share the view that the mind is a computational entity, their proposals regarding the nature of mental processes differ considerably, as can be seen in their contrasting views on the nature of memory (as in Figure 9.1).

Figure 9.1(a) is an 'idealised' example of a SYMBOLIC processing view of memory, a perspective which informs many cognitive models of reading. Information reaches our system (e.g. the cells which are activated on our retina) and the first pre-attentive stage would involve some kind of iconic store or buffer. Note, we would not be aware of this in any conscious way. The next stage of the process involves our short-term memory, a place which, although it has a limited capacity, can be utilised in particular ways if we wish to transfer information into longer-term memory (i.e. remember it for a longer period). This latter stage, our long-term memory (sometimes referred to as semantic memory), holds all the information which we have attained over the many years that we have been alive. There are numerous models which hold to this general view of memory, albeit in different ways (e.g. Atkinson & Shiffrin, 1971; Collins & Quillian, 1973). Cognition is a set of discrete mental states and information processing involves the manipulation of symbols (see also the comments on methodological solipsism in Chapter 2).

In contrast the CONNECTIONIST or parallel distributed view (Figure 9.1(b)) proposes that we do not process information in a serial symbolic fashion, but rather are constantly processing information from parallel sources. In this conception, memory (or any other related cognitive system) is not to be found located in a particular store, but is much better understood as a dynamic 'neuronal-mind' event. Memory (or any other cognitive processes) is to be found in the particular pattern of neuronal excitation taking place at any given point in time. Cognition is not 'in a place' but is always a neuronal activity. The connectionist account adopts the analogy of brain-style neuronal interactions (i.e. the fact that we have brains which are made up of millions of interconnected neurones which can be viewed as 'on–off' switches) and proposes that our cognitive system works in a very similar way. This approach to cognition is best understood as 'neurophysiologically inspired' rather than there being any direct corre-spondence between the cognitive system and real brains. The model of mind implicit in the connectionist outlook is akin to 'brain as representation'. In contemporary studies of reading (particularly word recognition studies[1]) the divergence between these two approaches is becoming more pronounced (e.g. Seidenberg, Plaut, Petersen, McClelland & McKrae, 1994).

Eye-movements and reading processes

Before considering psychological theories of reading which concentrate on eye-movement patterns, it would be useful to review one or two of the methods employed. One favoured technique is comparatively simple and involves presenting text on specially constructed computer screens to readers. The reader's pupil and corneal reflections are recorded in an unobtrusive fashion by closely positioned television cameras. Monitoring systems are employed so that the reader's point of regard is computed every 10 seconds or so and data reduction techniques convert the observations per second into fixations and then gazes on each word (see Thibadeau, Just & Carpenter, 1982). Another method has been more commonly termed the 'moving window' technique (McConkie, 1979). While the system is very similar to the one mentioned above, it is more sophisticated in that it can be arranged so that text is presented legibly at the point of fixation (in this case normally one line at a time) but degraded in various ways at different angles about the fixation point. As the eyes move about the screen, so too does the window of legible text on the display. This method has allowed very specific proposals to be made concerning factors which subjects use as cues to aid the reading process.

A third technique is concerned with isolating and separating out those elements of the eye-movement process which affect reading per se. In other words, what happens when you remove the need to make eye-movements at all? The rapid sequential visual presentation (RSVP) method presents the subject with a single word at a time, in the centrally placed foveal region of fixation (i.e. directly in front of the person reading). The subject normally reads one word and presses a key on the computer keyboard when he/she is ready to move on to the next word (Joula, Ward & MacNamara, 1982). It is then possible to examine various factors which influence reading speed, comprehension, and so on.

When we examine the relationship between the perception of the visual details which make up the printed word or words and the nature of the eye-movements in reading, two major areas of debate arise: first what is perceived during a fixation; and, second, what is perceived across fixations in reading (Underwood, 1985)? At a general level McConkie (1983) defines the perceptual span as the region around the centre of vision within which some aspects of the visual detail of interest are used in reading or affect the reading process. This rather vague definition is broken down into three components: (a) the momentary span, defined as the region of text attended to at some point of fixation; (b) the individual fixation span, consisting of the region included in at least one momentary span; and (c) the perceptual span, the area which includes all the individual fixation spans. Rayner (1978) and Underwood and McConkie (1981) have shown that information about specific letters can be acquired no further than ten spaces to the right of fixation and McConkie (1979) reports that distinctions among lower-case letters cannot be made more than six letters to the right, i.e. for readers reading from left to right.

However, Well (1983) is critical of the notion of 'perceptual span' and suggests that there seems little reason to expect that measures of perceptual span and mean saccade length (the length of a saccadic movement) should be closely related. Rayner and Pollatsek (1981) have shown that saccade length is influenced not only by available information on the present fixation (i.e. the size of the window) but also by the information available on the preceding fixation. They argue that saccade length may reflect the region within which enough information is acquired for words to be identified, given the additional support of the linguistic context. Rayner and Pollatsek (1981) stress that perceptual span cannot be linked to a region of 'perceptibility' in the visual information processing sense, and their results demonstrate that perceptual span as McConkie (1981, 1983) defines it extends to a region where partial information is acquired.

In other words, the visual information acquired on the current fixation may not be sufficient for identification of a word in the parafovea or periphery, but will nevertheless 'prime' or decrease the activation threshold of the internal representation of the word. This will mean that identification of the word can be more easily achieved when additional information is acquired on the next fixation. Whatever the fine detail of the perceptual processes involved, the concept of 'perceptual span' as defined by McConkie (1983) does not seem to be a particularly helpful heuristic.

One of the key issues in the research is the effect of 'context' on eye-movement patterns, context here being the words, phrases and paragraphs which surround the current word being read. Carpenter and Just (1983) have set out a detailed theoretical model of the general characteristics of reading based on two assumptions about cognitive processing. First, the 'immediacy assumption' states that a reader tries to interpret each word of a text immediately on encountering it. Rather than wait until a number of words have been encountered, serial and parallel processes are operating on each processed word, such as encoding the word, accessing a meaning, assigning it to its referent and determining its status in the sentence and the discourse (Just & Carpenter, 1980). Second, the 'eye–mind' assumption states that the reader continues to fixate a word until all the cognitive processes activated by that word have been completed (in light of some as yet unknown criterion). The eye–mind assumption does not preclude the possibility that the cognitive system considers only the word being currently fixated. A basic tenet of the model is that there is a direct relationship between the length of the duration of any current fixation (on a word) and the degree of information processing being carried out.

A major criticism centres on the idea of 'immediacy' and 'eye–mind' synchronicity. McConkie, Underwood, Zola and Wolverton (1985) point out that some basic physiological considerations have not been adequately taken into account and that it is simply unwarranted to take the position that there is a direct relationship between the amount of time spent fixating a word and the degree of processing involved with that word, although Pollatsek and Rayner (1990) offer a rejoinder to this view. Notwithstanding the ongoing controversy in this area, there remains a considerable gap between the fine-detailed level of the eye-movement research literature and other research areas of reading. Although the whole approach might appear ecologically curious, it helps to keep in mind that the aim is to spell out in very specific detail the relationship between eye-movement and reading comprehension. The results from eye-movement research have yet to be incorporated by the more general models of reading.

Psychological models of reading

Models of what is 'going on' inside people's heads when they read have appeared in a wide range of disciplines: linguistics, artificial intelligence, cognitive psychology, educational psychology, psycholinguistics, and so on. However, the range of models is as diverse as the number of disciplines which have an interest in the phenomenon. If one was to adopt a 'bird's eye view' of the currently popular models in the psychology of language, two categories would be apparent. On the one hand, we can identify fairly general models which attempt to give an overall picture of the process, from one or other theoretical perspective (Gough, 1972; Rumelhart, 1977; Stanovitch, 1980). In contrast to this, we have models which look in more detail at one or other cognitive process related to reading and comprehension (e.g. attentional processes – Anderson & Pearson, 1984a), often leading to the suggestion that one or other process has particular significance for reading and therefore should form the basis of more concisely formulated models of the activity (Kintsch, 1988). There are also a number of connectionist models of reading beginning to appear (e.g. Sharkey, 1990); however, as they have yet to broaden their concerns beyond the comprehension of words (or at best short sentences), they will not be discussed here.

'Bottom-up' models

It is a reasonable starting point to propose that in order to comprehend the meaning of a text a reader has to have processed each one of the individual sentences that make it up. In turn this will depend upon having correctly understood the clauses and phrases of the sentences (sub-parts of the sentence). Correspondingly this will depend on recognising the words which make up such units, which of course relies upon recognising the component letters. Considered in this way, it seems the processes involved in reading should be organised hierarchically with the attainment of any particular level subsuming the execution of lower subordinate levels. What's more, the opposite processing assumption is not necessarily true. One can understand or recognise letters words, and sentences in isolation; however, it is hard to imagine comprehending a text without first putting all the constituent parts together. The reader starts from the 'bottom' with individual letter segments and builds up through the words, sentences and paragraphs to the full meaning of the text.

Gough's (1972) model is a typical example of a bottom-up theory of reading (we might note that contemporary connectionist models are essentially 'bottom-up' as well – Jacobs & Grainger, 1994). Starting with eye-fixations and from an information processing 'flow' conception, Gough outlines the process whereby meaning is derived from the visual input. Eye-fixation results contribute to the formation of an iconic image from that part of the page on which the eye focuses. It is hypothesised that the iconic image persists for a brief period of time after the external stimulus has been removed (Sperling, 1963), has a reasonably large capacity (up to eighteen letters), and is thought to be in a categorical form. Gough (1972) proposes that 'we read letter by letter, serially from left to right, and that the letters in the icon emerge serially, one every 10 to 20 msec into some form of character register' (p. 353).

To explain the transition from character register to lexicon Gough favours the proposal that readers map print onto a string of systematic phonemes, rather than actual speech. These systematic phonemes are abstract representations of speech that are related to sound but not the sounds themselves (Chomsky & Halle, 1965). After the mapping, words in a sentence are then processed left to right. If processing takes place in this fashion, many words would have ambiguous meanings at the time they are first processed and would therefore have an inappropriate meaning attached to them. Gough (1972) suggests that this is the case and that

> lexical search would appear to be a parallel process, with the race going to the swift. When the first entry is located its contents are accepted as the reading of the word until it proves incompatible with subsequent data. (p. 39)

The lexical entries are assumed to be stored in primary memory until they can be organised into a larger unit. Hence, primary memory is seen as the necessary storage system for the comprehension device. Adopting a Chomskian perspective, on the basis of syntactic and semantic rules the comprehension device arrives at the deep structure of the word string in primary memory. Once the deep structure is extracted, the semantic content is moved to 'The Place Where Sentences Go When They Are Understood' (TPWSGWTAU); the contents of primary memory are then cleared and new items can be entered. Although there is some support for the 'bottom-up' model at the level of the word (Gough, 1966), evidence at the level of the sentence or paragraph is much more equivocal. The relationship between 'data-driven' input and the comprehension of meaning remains speculative, and, if anything, lacking in imagination.

'Top-down' models

Top-down conceptions of reading assume that a reader is actively involved in hypothesis testing as he/she moves through any given text. Proficient reading consists in 'constructing meaning from text with the least amount of time and effort, selectively using the fewest and most productive cues to construct meaning' (Goodman & Gollasch, 1980, p. 10). Intuitively it might appear that this position is (again) quite reasonable. We are often conscious as skilled readers that we are paying absolutely no attention to the 'letter by letter' level of analysis when we are engrossed in comprehending subtle arguments in a piece of prose. Adams (1982) has pointed out that there is widespread empirical evidence that skilled readers are characterised by their greater sensitivity to a variety of more or less subtle higher-order cues. For example, comparisons are made between the reader's awareness of syntactic as against 'text-world' constraints (e.g. de Beaugrande, 1980). The fact that coherent text contains many sources of redundancy suggests that the necessity of processing graphemic detail (the particular typographical elements that make up a letter or word) will be significantly reduced.

Smith's (1971, 1973) 'top-down' model of reading relies very much on the concept of redundancy. Redundancy is present whenever information exists from more than one source, and the probability of making decisions about a particular factor is enhanced by these additional elements. By asserting that the brain cannot process all the visual information in a page quick enough to allow ease of comprehension, he suggests that reading is accelerated not by increasing the rate of eye-fixations, but by reducing the dependency on visual information through making use of meaning (1971, p. 42). Reading involves looking for meaning, not merely specific words. Smith (1971) argues that due to the sensitivity to semantic and syntactic redundancy afforded by sentences, the good reader develops hypotheses about incoming words and is then able to confirm the identity of a word by sampling only a few features of the visual display of a new word. However, there is now a firm body of evidence which calls into question the notion of 'feature-detectors' (Pomerantz, 1981), or at least the conception of 'feature–letter' facilitation that this 'top-down' theory rests upon. In this instance there is a failure to explain how expectations and hypotheses interrelate with letter and word processing, in other words a solely 'top-down' account seems as unrealisable as a 'bottom-up' theory of reading.

Adams (1982) has considered various strands of evidence for both 'top-down' and 'bottom-up' theories of reading, with reference to predications for individual differences across good and poor readers. This area in particular could be seen as a testing ground for the validity of various theoretical positions, especially as there is a significant amount of evidence demonstrating that the differences in abilities at the level of letter and word processing are the single best class of discriminators between good and poor readers (Greasser, Hoffman & Clark, 1980; Stanovitch, 1980).

According to 'top-down' theorists, poor readers rely heavily on context, and this should be considered a strength, not a weakness (Smith, 1973). In contrast, earlier 'bottom-up' theories provided a rational structure for teachers using instructional remedial programmes (Cromer, 1970). One should start at the bottom with individual letter recognition and work upwards through the higher levels. However, it is arguable that although poorer readers' awareness of context may be a starting point for remedial reading schemes (a 'top-down' argument), the fact that they need to rely on context at all indicates that they have not processed the graphemic level of detail in the way that good readers are able to and unconscious of. Reading programmes based on one or other of these models suffer significantly through the one-sidedness of their conceptualisation of the reading process. The top-down or higher-order models have failed to take into account the demands made upon the reader by the text itself, and the bottom-up or data-driven models have ignored the role of higher-order processes which the reader brings to the text. Each perspective tells only part of the story. With this we move to alternative models which have attempted to integrate both conceptions, known commonly as interactive or schema-theoretic models.

Interactive or schema-theoretic models

Common to interactive or schema-theoretic models is the idea that concept-driven aspects of reading interrelate with each other during the reading process (Stanovitch, 1980). No one process is dominant, and, additionally, the 'whole is more than the sum of the parts', especially regarding the flexibility of the proposed mechanism. In attempting to explain the ongoing interactions between top-down and bottom-up processes, schema theories rest on certain assumptions which do have problems of their own (Adams, 1982). One is the notion of flexible interaction itself, another the claim that cognition is schema-based, and a third the emphasis upon cognition being of 'limited capacity'.

From the outset the reader's cognitive processing system is assumed to be organised in such a way that the output of one level of processing is the input for the next. In a typically 'bottom-up' sense, information extracted from the page is automatically processed upwards from visual detail onto increasingly comprehensive levels of interpretation. At the same time and in parallel, 'top-down' processes are in operation and the mind is compulsively searching for information to satisfy partially activated higher-order knowledge complexes, priming the lower-level complexes corresponding to their components. It becomes academic how the process starts once reading proceeds.

The schema assumption arises from the conception that perception consists in representing or organising information in terms of previously acquired knowledge. This is the case for all levels of analysis, from fine detail sensory features (e.g. recognising parts of objects) right through to complex social interaction. It is also assumed that a single complex of knowledge and processes underlies all cognitive activities. In other words knowledge is categorised in relation to the circumstances to which is relates: e.g. the only knowledge unique to reading are those elements specifically related to the printed medium. Below (or above?) the specific level of knowledge, there is the more general representational structure, a more diffuse abstract system (Rumelhart, 1977). However, in light of the fact there is a potentially very rich knowledge base involved in comprehension, schema-theoretic models have adopted the idea of the limited-capacity processor responsible for establishing the interpretative goals of the system. By allocating attention to particular problem areas (and ignoring other potentially rich sources of information), the system determines whether, and how, the text will be understood.

A schema theory is fundamentally a theory about how knowledge is represented, and how that representational structure influences the use of that knowledge. According to most schema theories, all knowledge is stored in discrete units, which are the schemata. The process of comprehension is identical to the process of selecting and verifying a conceptual schema. A schema is an abstract representation of a generalised concept of a situation and is said to account for a situation whenever the situation can be taken as an instance of the concept represented by the schema (Rumelhart, 1977).

Schema-directed processing works in the following way. When an event occurs at the sensory level (early visual processing of a letter) this automatically activates certain 'low-level' schemata (e.g. feature detectors of some form), which in turn activate (in a data-driven fashion) certain of the 'higher-level' schemata, normally the most likely or probable ones associated with the lower-level schemata. These higher-level schemata would then initiate conceptually driven processing by activating the sub-schemata not already activated in an attempt to evaluate its 'goodness of fit'. If we ask how a relevant schema suggests itself, then presumably we start off with the fact that the initial 'bottom-up' processing of referenced input letters and words leads to a suggestion for an initial hypothesis. From this readers begin to construct a schema (or schemata) for what is going on in a story. In turn this schema will provide the context for incoming data to be tested against, and where the match fits, appropriate 'slots' in the schema will be fitted. We can also consider the case where the unexpected happens.

Bransford and Johnson (1972), in an often cited study, asked readers to identify the activity being described via a long list of particular actions, and found that those subjects who were not given the appropriate title ('washing clothes') had great difficulty in understanding what the passage was about in contrast to those provided with the title. Merely providing an appropriate subject title was enough for the formation of the schema, and the 'filling of the slots' (the actions to be carried out) was suddenly very appropriate. However, while there are successful applications of schema theory to certain levels of text comprehension (Anderson & Pearson, 1984b), at the level of explicit empirical predictions, the interactive theories pose their own set of problems. For example, there is the assumed relationship between the comprehension of discourse, on the one hand, and the comprehension of text, on the other. While it is reasonable to argue that at some fundamental level comprehension and understanding will involve processes basic to both talk and text, there are innumerable examples in this area where concepts from linguistics, discourse analysis and text analysis have been transferred into the reading research paradigm without any formal argument being offered for the particular developments involved.

To give an example, Morgan and Sellner (1980) point out that Rumelhart's (1975) paper on story grammars and text linguistics (which became the basis for his ideas on 'schemata') is fundamentally flawed. His conception of text comprehension makes the mistake of applying a formal analysis (based on sentence parsing ideas) to the level of 'coherence of content' within texts. In light of the fact that such an analysis produces an identifiable pattern, Rumelhart (1975) went on to assume that this 'story grammar' is a significant contributory factor influencing how readers obtain 'meaning' from written text. Morgan and Sellner (1980) argue cogently that linguistic analysis which places great reliance on phenomena such as coherence markers (e.g. referring pronouns – see Halliday & Hasan, 1977) cannot explain or even relate the 'coherence' thus identified with 'meaning assimilation' processes in the reader's head. Lexical markers do not cause the pattern of coherence in texts. They are merely an effect arising out of the more abstract coherent nature of narrative in the first place.

Summary of cognitive approaches to reading

It would appear, then, that research into reading within psychology is a very complex and multi-layered research paradigm approachable from many different angles, with no cohesive picture emerging. On the one hand, we have the fine-detailed approach from eye-movement research, or the closely related (at least methodologically) bottom-up paradigm, where there are attempts to precisely define each stage in the process piece by piece. While this methodologically rigorous approach has certain advantages, it suffers from the criticism that it tells us very little about everyday reading processes. Few consistently replicable studies in these areas have moved beyond the level of the letter and the word, and even at this level of detail the models can be extremely complex (Carr & Pollatsek, 1985).

In contrast a number of studies have demonstrated various levels of 'top-down' and interactive reading processes. For example, individual letters are recognised faster when they are embedded in words, and words are more perceptible when contained in meaningful sentences (rather than mean-ingless phrases). It has also been shown that, irrespective of syntactic complexity, sentences which integrate semantic relations more coherently are assimilated more easily (Haviland & Clark, 1974; Huggins & Adams, 1980) and the speed with which a sentence is read depends on the nature of the surrounding text (Garrod & Sanford, 1990). Possibly all that can be said for now is that there appears a considerable gap between the various levels of analysis directed at uncovering the cognitive processes involved in reading. It is very difficult to see how the parts fit together in any coherent fashion. While it is clear that we may be asking too much looking for a theoretical framework encompassing the wide variety of processes which underlie reading, it is somewhat disconcerting to realise that the disparities between the various outlooks are so great, and the empirical evidence for many of the models rather sparse and inconclusive.

Reading as a skill and strategies of reading

Within the view of reading as a skill there are various levels of analysis possible (cf. Yussen, Mathews & Hiebert, 1982), and indeed the models already described can be seen as addressing the lower-level skills of letter recognition, word recognition, and so forth, which are characterised by the automaticity associated with skilled behaviour. We can also see how the idea of a learned, flexible skill would relate to the content of some of the models described earlier. For example, the learning process can be seen as the acquisition of relevant schemata and sub-schemata, with increasing skill being characterised by the ability to select sub-schemata appropriate to the specific task.

If reading is purposive, or goal-directed, it follows that the goal must be elaborated into some form of plan for action, or strategy. It is the execution of this plan which is observable as reading behaviour, giving rise to some outcome, and it is the outcome which the researcher must attempt to measure or evaluate. Viewing reading in terms of purpose, strategy and outcome is evidenced in the work of Laurie Thomas and his associates (cf. Harri-Augstein, Smith & Thomas, 1982). Thomas also adds 'review' as a fourth stage and sees the review as providing feedback for the modification of the purpose and strategy. If reading is seen as a skill, then the strategy one adopts should be related to the purpose in order to secure the desired outcome. At a gross level, this can be seen in the different approaches which the average reader takes towards, say, textbooks and magazines. At a more detailed level, if the purpose is to gain a general impression of the text, then a 'skimming' is appropriate; if specific information is required, then a 'scanning' procedure might be appropriate; if a detailed critique of the author's views is required, neither of these strategies alone would be sufficient. It is perhaps the strategy level of the reading process which receives least attention within education, and if we wish to understand reading as something more than 'searching for meaning', then we need to look outside the boundaries of the psychology of reading.

Critical theory and reading

When considering reading and the role of the reader in text interpretation we cannot confine ourselves to a strictly psychological *process* perspective. Over the last thirty years there has been a significant and growing interest in reading within literary criticism, linguistics, philosophy and critical theory. Contemporary interest in 'post-structuralism' and deconstruction-ism can be traced to the critical analysis of the text (and reader interpret-ation) outlined by thinkers such as Barthes, Derrida, Foucault and Eco. To paraphrase Selden (1985), earlier structuralist critics had set out to master the text and uncover its secrets, only to be superseded by post-structuralist criticism which asserted that the 'author' was dead and that to maintain that any given text could encapsulate a single intentional message (from the author to the reader) was an untenable proposition. If readers have to act upon texts so as to 'get the meaning', then the text itself can never be self-formulated. Many texts can have a multiple number of potential readings, as literary criticism in the latter part of the twentieth century has shown.

In contrast to a psychological perspective which focuses on the individual who is doing the reading, contemporary literary theory, criticism and semiotics begin with the analysis of the text. Furthermore, while a psychological approach focuses on how people 'read for meaning', literary theory and post-structuralism ask under what conditions is any 'reading' possible, i.e. a focus on a 'reading' such that the possibility and potential for meaning can be recognised. Central to the debates within literary theories of reading is whether or not the text determines the nature of the reading or whether the reader brings to the reading situation a number of codes of interpretation, which then interpenetrate the 'text-world', resulting in a particular reading or understanding. Livingstone (1990) notes that reader-oriented theories in literary criticism view texts not as repositories of meaning but as sets of devices which guide the negotiation of meaning by the reader. And it is not only the role of the reader which is controversial in post-structuralist criticism, but also the status of the author.

Roland Barthes was one of the most trenchant critics of the idealised notion of authorship and origin. He rejected the whole idea that the author is the origin of the text, the principal authority for its interpretation. As Selden notes (1985):

> The death of the author is already inherent in structuralism, which treats individual utterances (paroles) as the products of impersonal systems (langues). What is new in Barthes is the idea that readers are free to open and close the text's signifying process without respect to the signified. (p. 75)

These apparently radical notions that texts are free-floating multiple elements, that readers can have quite different interpretations from any the author intended, and that originality itself is a fictional or ideological construct can be traced to the analytical methodology of structural linguistics. The discovery that language as a system of signification which can function independently of the actual persons who are doing the enunciating indicates, to paraphrase Kearney (1988), that the author is never more than the instance writing, just as *I* is nothing other than the instance saying *I*. The modern notion of the book is replaced with the postmodern notion of the text, where the latter is an impersonalised writing process absent of authorship. To quote Barthes:

> A text is a multidimensional space . . . in which a variety of writings, none of them original, blend and clash, [the writer's] only power is to mix writings, to counter the one with the other, in such a way as never to rest on any of them. Did he wish to express himself, he ought at least to know that the inner 'think' he thinks to 'translate' is itself only a ready-formed dictionary, its words only explainable through other words, and so on indefinitely. (quoted in Kearney, 1988, p. 276)

Other critics take a less radical stance regarding authorship, arguing instead that, when writing, an author attempts to foresee a 'Model Reader', one who shares the same sets of assumptions and codes which make an appropriate reading realisable. Eco (1979) argues that narrative texts can be categorised as either 'open' or 'closed' as far as reader interpretation is concerned. He compares texts such as Superman comics or the James Bond novels and notes that such stories are open to all, equally understandable because they are aimed at arousing a precise response in the reader; their purpose is to pull the reader along a predetermined path, 'carefully displaying their effects so as to arouse pity or fear, excitement or depression at the due place and at the right moment. Every step of the story elicits just the expectation that its further course will satisfy' (p. 8). Such texts he classifies as closed.

In contrast, the level of competence presupposed in reading texts such as Joyce's *Finnegans Wake* or *Ulysses* is of a different nature altogether. Here the 'Model Reader' has to be able to master quite different codes and enters into the co-construction of an interpretation itself. Such texts Eco defines as open and notes that the process of interpretation is not incidental to the text, but is itself a structural element of the comprehension process. An open text does not, however, mean that you can use it any way desired; it cannot afford any interpretation:

> The 'ideal reader' of *Finnegans Wake* cannot be a Greek reader of the second century B.C. or an illiterate man of Aran. The reader is strictly defined by the lexical and the syntactical organisation of the text: the text is nothing else but the semantic–pragmatic production of its own Model Reader. (Eco, 1979, p. 10)

In a review of contemporary literary theories Selden (1985) notes that there are at least seven distinct reader-oriented perspectives (the phenomenological, reception theory, theories of the 'implied reader', literary competence theory, feminist theory, to name a few), and notes that, whatever else we might think about the radical formulations offered, it is no longer possible to consider the meaning of a text without considering the reader's contribution to it. This is a contribution not simply to the 'construction of meaning' but to the developing response of the reader as the reading proceeds. For example, Bleich's (1978) reader-response subjective criticism was developed from classroom studies of how readers 'responded' to texts such that their response helped articulate the meaning they would engender from them. In other words he distinguishes between the readers' 'response', on the one hand, and meaning interpretation, on the other. The latter is the domain of the psychology of reading – what any given content is said to mean – while a post-structuralist account demands an analysis of both the 'response' and the meaning obtained, together providing a method for highlighting how 'readings' come about. In a sense, whereas the psychologist is interested in what the content means, the reader-oriented critic is interested in the relationship between form and content: an understanding of the conditions which must be in place (e.g. subjective codes and systems of thought) so that a reading of meaning is possible at all.

This last point also hints at why the psychology of reading has largely side-stepped or ignored many developments within the study of language over the last twenty to thirty years. Post-structuralism and deconstructionism have had considerable influence on cultural studies, sociology, social anthropology, linguistics and semiotics precisely because there is a central concern with the analysis and criticism of the relationship between form and content. Reader-oriented theories can take as their 'texts' not only reading material, but also film, music, systems of symbol and myth, advertising and television, anywhere where there are texts and messages to be decoded and analysed. Understanding the conditions which make semiosis possible at all is a project that encompasses meaning in all guises. And understandably, where a deconstructionist critique of text seeks to articulate the 'literary' nature of experimentation and scientific discourse itself (e.g. Althusser, 1990), experimental psycholinguists are as likely to respond with ridicule as with disbelief. This is a rather unfortunate development as structuralist and post-structuralist theories of reading can provide a rich source of ideas and concepts germane to the contemporary study of the psychology of reading, an issue highlighted by Flowers (1987) in her analysis of the reader–writer relationship.

Concluding comments

This overview of reading is necessarily selective, with the concomitant danger of ignoring many important developments in the area. There are, however, a number of things we can note. We have seen that within the psychology of reading eye-movement research concerns itself with very specific reactions to small samples of text; models of reading attempt to establish the nature of the cognitive processes involved in reading; and the view of reading as a skill has concentrated on questions of learner effectiveness and purpose. One theme which runs through these three sub-areas is that of the schema. The main reason why this concept is popular is that it enables a consistent view to be taken across the range of phenomena involved in the psychology of reading. As such, it provides a coherent basis for a wide variety of experimental research; however, there remains a suspicion (my own) that the only thing schema research has succeeded in is telling me what to do when washing clothes or eating in a restaurant (see Bransford & Johnson, 1972; Schank & Abelson, 1977). The psychology of reading, however, continues to concentrate in the 'content' of meaning, maintaining the status of authorial intentionality, i.e. the author's message is in the text and the role of the reader in text interpretation is to decode its content. In contrast, contemporary literary theory demands an analysis of the relationship between recognising and responding to the text as 'a text' and the (potentially infinite) interpretations of meaning realisable. With this understanding of the gap between these two approaches, we can turn to the other side of the 'textual' equation and the role of the writer in text generation.

Note

1. For reasons of space a review of word recognition in reading is not included in what follows. The conception of a mental lexicon or 'dictionary in the head' has been proposed in

psychological research ever since Cattell (1885) and Huey's (1908) early work into letter/word context effects. Numerous papers have subsequently reported the basic data of this area, that letters are recognised faster if they are embedded in words (compared to non-words), repetition of words (familiarity) decreases this 'recognition threshold', and sentence context has an influence on the probability of recognising particular target words. The experiments in this area typically involve presenting single or pairs of words to subjects for very short periods of time (normally somewhere between 50 and 400 milliseconds). With reference to eye movement research, although there are a number of models of the word recognition process there is still some considerable way to go before understanding how these relate to more general models of reading (Bolata, Flores d'Arcais & Rayner, 1990; Kintsch & van Dijk, 1978; Rumelhart, 1977).

10

Writing and the Construction of Narrative Text

Living, as we do, in a 'literate' culture, we often have difficulty in thinking about language without thinking about the written word. The signs and symbols we know as letters and words are so much part of our culture that it takes a considerable leap of the imagination to go back to what our earliest experience of language was, i.e. as sound. As children our task (in acquiring language) was all about learning how to make sounds such that other people responded to them as meaningful utterances. Only when our noises were heard by others as being justifiable attempts at communication did we enter and become part of the 'discursive' social world. Moreover, it was a long time before we were presented with the problem of how this stream of sounds could be represented by making signs on paper or some other appropriate 'technology' (e.g. a child's blackboard). Learning to be 'literate' turned out to be a very different thing from learning to be 'literal'. The Russian developmental psychologist and semiotician, Lev Vygotsky (1962) emphasised the abstract nature of written language when he commented:

> Written language presupposes . . . a high degree of abstractness. It is a language without intonation, without musical elements, without expressiveness, without any phonation. It is a language that lacks the essential property of spoken language, the phonetic substance. (p. 224)

Notwithstanding earlier comments regarding the talk/text distinction, we can begin by inquiring into the relationship between writing and thinking. It is now commonplace for educationalists to show concern about the rise of the 'video culture' and the demise of literary skills (reading, spelling, composition). The introduction of information technologies such as television, video, multi-media, and so on, has paralleled a reported decline in spelling and punctuation abilities leading to calls for a return to the 'three Rs' (reading, writing and arithmetic) and a certain distrust and antipathy towards perceiving new technology as an equivalent information medium to the written word. Of course, this is not the first occasion for educationalists to voice distrust and disquiet over the introduction of a new technology for information transmission. During the fourth century BC with the early development of writing systems Greek rhetoricians such as Plato were concerned that if the new invention called writing became popular then people would no longer take the trouble to learn the complex mnemonics used to aid memory (e.g. for learning extended verses, stories, epic poems, and so on). Finnegan (1989) comments on Plato's report of an Egyptian king's response to the writing of letters:

> This discovery of yours will create forgetfulness in the learner's souls, because they will not use their memories; they will trust to the external written characters and not remember of themselves (Phaedrus). (quoted in Hare & Russell, 1970, p. 184)

Plato recognised that using writing systems would change the nature of the rhetorical devices used to persuade and argue (i.e. between oratory and written disputation and argument). In other words, although there was an obvious pressing need for the development of systems which overcame the limitation of talk (particularly in that speech is normally bound to the situation of its occurrence), writing would itself create a whole new set of problems, and mean the loss of sophisticated memory skills.

Trying to imagine the study of language before the invention of writing is again difficult, if not impossible. Harris (1989) notes that it was the invention of writing that made speech *speech* and language *language*. Before the invention of writing there was no distinction, only speech (sound), and while the oral tradition made 'texts' out of speech acts (the 'texts' and stories considered essential for any society being preserved across generations), language as a structural object did not yet exist. The key to understanding the transformation of talk into text, and thus how writing restructures thought, is through what Harris calls the 'autoglottic inquiry'. This examines the nature of communication with regard to the 'autoglottic space', the prising open of a conceptual space between the sentence and the utterance. Into this space, within the Western tradition, the syllogism is inserted (Socrates is a man . . . all men are human . . . Socrates must be human). Without the 'autoglottic space' the development of logic would have been impossible.

So, on the one hand, we need to recognise that the invention of writing underpins the basis of language as a formal object (as a structural entity). The ability to use signs and symbols in a domain where they can be 'decontextualised', i.e removed from the discursive constraints of talk and interaction, makes possible a whole range of sign-system activities (using symbols to stand for classes of objects, entities and their relations with each other as in calculus; symbol transmission over space and time; linguistic re-representation in different language systems, and so on). At the same time, writing, as a technological procedure for representing phonemes (individual speech sounds and the construction of alphabetic writing), can encapsulate subtleties of meaning and representation in exceptionally open, unstructured and innovative forms (e.g. poetry).

Summarising at least three reasons why writing is important, Harris (1989) argues, first, that writing is crucial because it 'presupposes the validity of unsponsored language' (p. 100). When we say something we immediately 'sponsor' the utterance spoken and we are accountable for it.

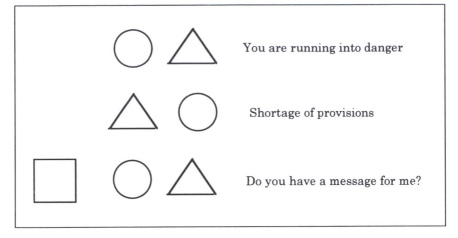

Figure 10.1   *A minimal 'double articulation' language – the seaman's code*

Not so the written word: sentences remain autoglottic abstractions. Second, the creation of an autoglottic space depends on the fact that written words have a physical existence which is independent of their author's existence. Third, writing offers a form of unsponsored language which is not constrained to limited categories of talk as social practice. It is simply impossible to predict the many different ways a text could be used in the future. Harris concludes that in a primary oral culture there are no genuinely auto-logical forms of verbal knowledge because there is no technology by means of which words and their relationships can be decontextualised at will. Writing constitutes such a technology.

It can be argued, then, that what helps legitimate the distinction between talk and text is that the first is a sign-system (sound differentiation in context as a dynamic activity) that immediately symbolises meaning. Even if you do not understand what I say in a conversation, then an explanation and an account can be demanded and given. In contrast, writing is a sign-system that symbolises another sign-system, an approximation to speech, in other words on the same side as discourse but of a very different form. Understanding how writing researchers consider the relationship between speech and writing can help articulate why writing is often considered indicative of what it is to be human and what constitutes a 'civilised' culture.

Writing can also be viewed as a tool employed to build other tools (letters and words to construct paragraphs and texts, never mind ideas). Any system of signs is said to be 'double articulated' where it has two levels of organisation: a first level with a sense-determinate function, such as morphemes (minimal grammatical units), words and sentences; and a second level with a sense-discriminative function (distinctive features such as phonemes and syllables). Holensten (1980) cites the case of the traditional seaman's code (see Figure 10.1) which Buhler (1965) described as a minimal double articulation language. The only function of the signs in this system is to distinguish the complex signals from each other where they occur in different positions. As Holensten (1980) notes, signs that had a sense-determinative function in their original usage, such as natural numbers, can become sense-discriminative, as in the case of bus numbers signifying different routes through the city. Here the sole function of the difference between the number 23 bus and the number 93 is to discriminate between the different journeys. Having a number 3 in the second position does not mean that they share some special quality or whatever. In the case of written language, tools already available with a sense-determinative function (spoken language) are now converted into tools with a sense-discriminative function, although we must take care to note that the characterisation of sound differences into graphemic distinctions (letter shapes) is not one-to-one for most alphabets. For anthropologists, double articulation in language is the mark of being human, and Jakobson (1973) emphasises the cognitive abilities implicit in human language use:

> The creation and use of signs that are not intended to designate non-semiotic entities (things outside the sign-system), but rather to produce other signs, presupposes a cognitive competence, the ability to produce tools to produce other tools. (p. 58)

Presupposing cognitive competencies implicit in human language use should again remind us of the assumed correspondence between speech and writing (talk and text). Typically, writing is often seen as secondary to speech, what Scinto (1986) calls the phonocentric folk theory of language. In contrast the Prague school of linguistics took the view that spoken and written forms were both instantiations of langue (see Chapter 8 for an outline of Saussure's *langue/parole* distinction). To paraphrase Scinto, written and spoken language are equivalent systems with respect to structure and function, 'each fulfilling specific communicative and social functions within a given language community' (p. 22). The specific communicative differences between talk and text are a recurring theme of this book.

Investigating writing by studying the development of writing skills

Studying the development of a psychological attribute can provide insights into the nature of any given phenomenon. Developmental psycholinguists have attempted to carefully map out how children's writing skills develop, and in doing so provide us with certain ideas about the psychology of writing. One thing we might note is that although the child prodigy is well documented in areas such as musical ability, chess and mathematics, the equivalent has yet to be found in literature or writing, reminding us that in learning to write the child has to acquire a particular kind of interpretative role. Learning to write is not just a case of learning to approximate or translate what is said into what is written, but requires an inculcation into different 'logonomic rules' and ideological codes relevant for the production of genres of writing style.

The first thing to note is that the processes involved in the recognition of writing (being able to recognise that a mark or inscription is a piece of writing) are not the same as those required for production. One of the earliest, and most significant, problems for the aspiring child writer is learning the correspondence between the sounds of speech (talk) and the signs on the page (the alphabet). Notwithstanding the observation that some languages appear rather more complex in this respect compared to others,[1] in English there is no consistency between the particular phonemic (sound) distinction being made and the written letter or letter combination. For example, although the sound of the letter combination a-c-h in *ache* is the same as a-k in *cake*, the words look quite different.

A corresponding task for children is that they have to learn very specific visio-motor skills (with a high degree of co-ordination) so as to produce a visible representation of language – e.g. learn the pattern for *b* and then over time generalise this pattern for many different contexts with various writing instruments (b, b, **b** or ℔). Furthermore, learning the individual letters is not enough: they must be combined in such a way that they represent certain sounds in the conventional fashion (compare, sh; ch; ou; ea; ie, and so on). The child's awareness of the difficulties of sound–letter correspondence is seen in the study of one boy (Paul Bissex) who learned to write before going to school. This was one of the first case studies of such a child (see Nystrand, 1986, for a similar study of pre-school girl), and a characteristic of his writing was the lack of spaces or gaps between the letters he wrote, as in the following (from Bissex, 1980):

Paul's attempt	*Meaning*
EFUDOTSELEIWELGAU- APRZET	'If you don't be silly, I will give you a present'
EFUKANOPNKAZIWIL- GEVAUAKANOPENR	'If you can open cans then I will give you a can opener'

This was then followed by a stage in his writing where he used dots for gaps in the speech sounds, as in the following:

SHAP.ING.LETS	Shopping list
5000. BATLZ.AV.WESKY	5,000 bottles of whiskey
AND.100.BATLZ.AV.BER	and 100 bottles of beer
AND.5000.BAGZ.AV.DOG.FOD	and 5,000 bags of dog food

After this, what emerges is a relatively complete orthography with appropriate conventions for upper- and lower-case lettering, full stops, and so on. However, the importance of learning conventions and styles appropriate to the construction of written texts appears crucial to the child's writing skills. In her analysis of Samantha's developing writing abilities, Himley (1986) notes that the notion of genre is crucial, here defining genre as a conventional way to realise a particular kind of meaning potential. For this child the impetus to write came from the social context (peers, school), which helped determine a genre (the 'book'), which in turn informed and defined particular textual options. Noting that development in writing does not occur in a single direct line, the developmental discontinuities in the process resemble 'spirals' of development, where:

> Her interpretation of that genre, in conjunction with her expressive intentionality, results in her conceptualising and negotiating various semiotic choice points . . . she moves from texts that 'look like' certain genres to texts that 'say something' and then to texts that mean solely within the resources of written language. (p. 157)

The transition from making 'things' (books where actions can be conducted) to saying something with those things (drawing, scribbling, writing) to constructing texts in highly conventionalised genres takes many years. The processes involved remain largely unknown, although developmental psychologists have emphasised the significance of the child's cognitive development. Both Piaget (1952) and Vygotsky (1978) have stressed the importance of the child being able to recognise the context specific nature of the 'written world'. Writing has also been linked to the development of abstract conceptualisation abilities. The argument is that learning to master the skills of writing involves the ability to engage with a decontextualised realm (unlike speech), a set of abilities which include both 'lower-order' skills, such as the automation of handwriting and spelling, and 'higher-order' competencies, such as problem-solving strategies and manipulation of abstract thought. Martlew (1983), for instance, comments that:

> A high level of abstract conceptualisation is involved in writing which entails the individual in translating both experience of the world and imaginary events into autonomous text. The writer must restructure his thinking to meet the demands of convention and explicitness demanded in writing, for without this, the meaning intended would not necessarily be the meaning communicated. Spoken language, as a shared, negotiated enterprise, does not require this objective awareness. Speakers do not need to operate on experience in a formal and abstract manner. (p. 271)

While proposals about abstract conceptualisation find some support in studies of writing development (e.g. Scardamalia, 1981), there are those who argue that the criteria underpinning whether a text is 'highly abstract' or indicative of 'higher-order' conceptualisation processes is much more a question of discourse genre and literary style (e.g. Hodge & Kress, 1988). In other words there is always a background context for the act of writing, a discursive frame where styles or genres of writing are produced and recognised as appropriate (or not). This is as true for writing a note to the milkman as composing a poem for a literary magazine. With this in mind we can turn to how the process of writing has been studied.

Cognitive models of writing

Compare reading with writing research in the psychology of language and one immediate observation is that there are many more studies of the former. In part this is due to methodological factors – it is somewhat easier to study reading (e.g. eye-movement research) and have more rigorous control over the variables being examined. It is only in the recent past (with the influence of more sophisticated computer technology – see below) that studies of writing and related composition processes have increased.

The Collins and Gentner (1980) cognitive framework theory of writing serves as a good example of how writing research in psychology is approached (see Figure 10.2). They define writing as the process of generating and editing text within a variety of constraints, which take three forms: structural, content and purpose. Structural constraints are defined by conventions for good sentence, paragraph or text/document forms; content constraints derive from the ideas which have to be expressed and how they are related to each other; and purpose constraints are determined by the goals of the writer and the model he/she has of the reader.

While this kind of overview can help articulate different aspects involved in the production of written texts, it appears to be more a recipe guide to writing, i.e. conceived as a problem-solving space where form and content can be separated out in some way and dealt with independently. Psychological studies of the writing processes have tried to utilise models of this type when examining problem-solving strategies, text generation, and so on. Kelley (1988), for example, focuses on attentional processes in writing and takes the view that the limited-capacity nature of our attentional processing has a direct bearing upon the cognitive processes involved in reading. His study considered the efficiency of the writing process and quality of the written product (text) and asked how these are influenced by 'pre-writing' and composing a rough first draft. Employing dependent measures which included processing time (how long to read/write), cognitive effort (as this applies to planning, translating and reviewing ideas) and a secondary-task reaction time,[2] Kelley carried out two experiments, the difference being that in the second the subjects were asked to produce either a rough or polished draft, and indicate a 'mental outline' strategy (under one of the conditions). The results indicated that preparing a written outline (compared to not doing so) led to 'higher-quality documents', yet whether people were asked to produce a rough or polished draft made no difference (on any of the measures). Furthermore, a 'mental outline' was as good as a written outline (suggesting that a written outline does not act as a memory aid), and both mental and written outline conditions eased attentional overload by allowing the writer time to focus on translating ideas into text.

Similar studies have been conducted by Hayes and Flowers (1986), who argue that sound writing instruction should draw upon a clear understanding of the organisation of the cognitive processes underlying the act of

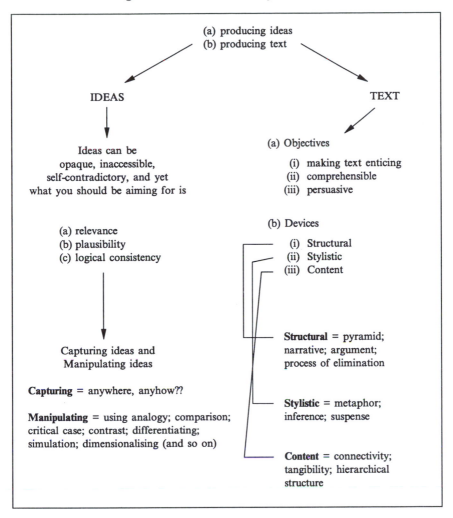

Figure 10.2 *Collins and Gentner's (1980) distinction between content and form*

writing. They suggest that writing is goal-directed, hierarchically organised, and that good writers employ three major processes to accomplish their goals: planning, sentence generation and revision. These processes are, of course, heavily interwoven because commonly writing is performed in parts and the writing process applied recursively. With regard to planning, Hayes and Flowers rely on the schema idea favoured in reading research. They argue that writers need to possess schema-based knowledge of writing strategies (e.g. they say writers will need to draw upon a range of textual conventions and genre patterns). Most importantly, they point out that planning, extending and reformulating goals takes place not only before writing begins, but as it proceeds. In general they stress that what enhances the production of written texts is knowing how to define the writing task with appropriate and manageable goals, having a high level of procedural knowledge (of writing) to draw on, and being able to monitor and direct the writing process.

There remains some difficulty, however, in adopting a cognitive account of writing. One problem is the conceptual distance between the fine-grained analysis of mental states and processes employed in cognitive psychology and the actual act of writing (a fairly gross motor skill difficult to investigate with the information processing measures normally employed in studies of attention, memory or areas of reading). Another is that while linguistics possesses methods and procedures for the structural analysis of text (e.g. de Beaugrande, 1980), where the aim is to tap into the writer's comprehension, these can become exceptionally cumbersome and complex (Kintsch & van Dijk, 1983). This can also help explain why there has been much less research on the psychology of writing compared to reading.

Within the psychology of reading and writing it is clear that the favoured model underlying story representation is the schema. Similarly, within literary criticism and linguistics, there is much concern over the central position given to narrative, arguably another name for story schema. The novelist A.S. Byatt talks of the 'great human need for narrative', and certainly when considering the psychology of writing, narrative analysis cannot be overlooked given the narratalogical nature of text construction (beginning–plot/problem–resolution–ending).

Narrative and writing

As an analytic methodological tool, narrative is of increasing interest in a diverse number of social science disciplines (sociology, linguistics, social anthropology), reflecting the growing willingness of social science disciplines to share methodologies. As we noted in Chapter 8, narrative itself has been defined as the devices, strategies and conventions governing the organisation of a story (fictional or factual) into sequence.

The study of narrative has a long history, and was originally viewed as a branch of rhetoric. Aristotle argued that mere episodic stories were supplanted by narratives organised thematically to convey an idea through plot. Narrative treatments of justice gradually converged in philosophic inquiries into the nature, and finally the theory, of justice – an analytical mode that reached its classical culmination in Plato's dialogues (Havelock, 1983). Feldman (1991) argues that in becoming conscious of making stories, 'the early Greeks quite literally invented invention, and with it the link between narrative and what is not. . . . Without this concept we cannot observe the intricate connectedness of narrativity to reflectivity' (p.124). Swearingern (1990) notes that the parallelism between various forms of narrative (oral, tacit, universal, developmental) has led to the study of the relation of narrative and logical modes of thought, and the suggestion that

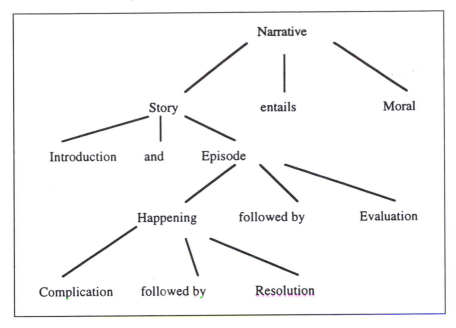

Figure 10.3 *Van Dijk's (1976) narrative grammar*

propositions can be defined as mental templates, sometimes characterised as stories, at other times argument.

Reiterating the points made earlier (p. 147) contemporary narratology is subdivided into abstract narratology (e.g. the structural analysis of myth, the semiotics of narrative) and textual narratology (e.g. the discourse of stories). Pavel (1985) defines narratology itself as the integrated study of all levels of narrative phenomena, and recognises the problems associated with the rapid development of a field which has seen the proliferation of many competing schools. However, central to many conceptions of narrative is the distinction between plot (any arrangement of incidents) and story (mere raw material awaiting the organising principles of an interpreter). The early studies of literary narrative focused upon the structural components of myth and folk-tale (e.g. Propp, 1968), defining an abstract narratology, extended in some cases along lines familiar to transformational grammarians. Van Dijk (1976), for example, emphasises the relationship between narrative structure and moral or evaluative criteria (see Figure 10.3).

Textual narratology, in contrast, has concentrated on the discourse of stories. Genette (1972), for example, distinguishes between (a) the narrative itself, (b) narrative content and (c) narration, the act of narrative production. Within critical theory and communication studies narrative analysis examines textual and literary styles, including those peculiar to scientific and technical texts. Toolan (1988) makes the point that the emphasis on scientific inquiry as an ongoing revisable narrative is uncontested within linguistics and the philosophy of science. He also notes that a great deal of the teaching of science within education rests upon utilising narrative as a way of introducing ideas (e.g. the concepts of fuel, energy and work might be introduced in a primary school by telling stories about having breakfast before setting out for the day), again reminding us that narratology is a key discursive practice for both talk and text.

Arguably, of course, the texts most of us write are only very rarely stories, in the sense originally developed by narratologists. Our writing experience is most often non-fictional (writing letters, assignments at school and college, notes to the milkman, an advert in the local paper, and so on). However, studies of writing within linguistics and English language have again tended to focus on composition and criticism, and rarely on the practice and process of writing. However, there has been a recent and growing interest in writing (and reading) within the electronic domain (Boulter, 1989; Lanham, 1993; Pea, 1985). The increase, ease and availability of personal computers and word processing has led to the introduction of information systems which call into question many cherished beliefs regarding authorship, reading and the author–reader relationship. This is particularly the case with what have become known as hypertext and hypermedia systems.

Hypertext, hypermedia and the author–reader relationship

A useful way to begin to understand the notion of hypertext is by considering that when we read a text or book we normally start at the beginning and move in a serial fashion through it until finished. Unless we are reading a dictionary, encyclopaedia or textbook, we are unlikely to begin reading at any point whatsoever. The fact that a computer is not limited to presenting information in a serial fashion was recognised by computer scientists during the 1940s (Bush, 1945). Theoretically information can be made available in any way imaginable, and computer designers normally define hypertext systems as electronic environments which make possible innovative forms of information presentation. In contrast a computer user might describe a hypertext system as a computer environment where you can get to any other point from the place where you first started (and back again). Figure 10.4 provides a general idea of the difference between a hypertext system and the 'technology' of the book.

In a hypertext system pages, text, documents, can be accessed (and left) from any point and linked together by either the originating author or a reader. In effect readers can become (re-)authors and the question of originality becomes interesting and problematic. Certainly, within the contemporary educational world and the emergence of hypertext (hypermedia[3]), the rhetoric of potential and possibility far outweighs evidence of caution, which is itself surprising given that many problems in the study of reading, writing and comprehending hypertext documents remain unsolved.

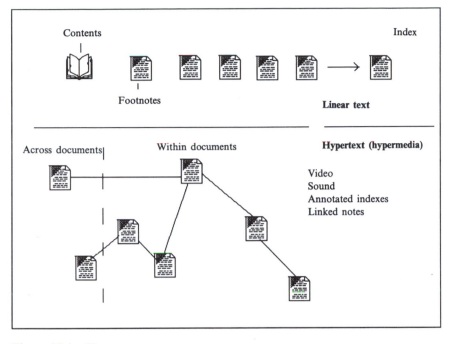

Figure 10.4 *Hypertext systems*

Consider, for example, Landow (1992), who suggests that hypertext is fundamentally an 'intertextual system' which may or may not fulfil the claims made by structuralists and post-structuralists regarding the nature of the author–reader relationship. He talks of 'moving readers and writers into a new writing space' and comments that structuralists and post-structuralists have long described thinking and writing in terms of

> exteriorized, in-process generation of meaning, the belief in which does so much to weaken traditional conceptions of self and author. Hypertext fiction forces us to extend this description of meaning-generation to the reader's construction of narrative. It forces us to recognize that the active author–reader fabricates text and meaning from 'another's' text in the same way that each speaker constructs individual sentences and entire discusses from 'another's' grammar, vocabulary and syntax. (p. 117)

In a similar vein, Boulter (1989) comments that because the hypertext reader is confronting structural possibilities provided by the hypertext author, this enhances his/her awareness of the author's simultaneous presence in, yet absence from, the text. Again the rhetoric of potential and possibility is clear:

> the computer promises to redefine the relationship between author, reader and writing space. Word processing, which looks back to the medium of print, only hints at what the computer can do. More sophisticated programs for 'hypertext' and 'hypermedia' can now present text as an evolving structure, the sum of hierarchical and associative connections among verbal and pictorial elements.

> Unlike printing, which lends fixity and monumentality to the text, electronic writing is a radically unstable and impermanent form, in which the text exists only from moment to moment and in which the reader joins with the writer in constituting the text. (p. 131)

There are a smaller number of commentators who adopt a more sceptical approach to the potential of hypertext, and the implications of its adoption in educational contexts (Brown, 1989; Doland, 1989; Rasking, 1987). Doland (1989) asks whether hypertext programs (here meaning specific forms of hypertexts instantiated as courseware) should somehow be pedagogically neutral (i.e. in a fashion to which educational textbooks aspire). Beyond the issue of whether books ever attain such an ideal, it is clear that a hypertext/hypermedia document may be very powerful and persuasive indeed; there is, Doland notes, very little possibility of achieving hermeneutic neutrality:

> Hypertext is basically an interpretative act: that is to say, it possesses its own meaning and impresses its own meaning upon texts. As a rhetoric tool hypertext involves both power and danger. (p. 10)

Hypertext and hypermedia documents are (more than other forms of media) peculiarly open to interpretative 'freighting'. This is a term used by Doland and others to highlight the observation that for a naïve user of an educational hypertext a relationship or link between two nodes of information creates an assertion about reality:

> simply to create a linkage is to create meaning . . . [and] . . . without special awareness of the cognitive factors implicit in massively accessible bodies of knowledge as hypertext might create, a great deal of intellectual intoxication might result. (p. 11)

There are few detailed formulations of the author–reader relationship in hypermedia, and what follows rests in part on work by Flowers (1987) and her proposals regarding the 'mental network of meaning'. Flowers comments on the different perspectives in the study of discourse (cognitive, new critical, cultural, and so on), and makes the point that 'cognitive and cultural perspectives on discourse can richly complement one another since each operates from the major premise of reading and writing as constructive acts' (p. 114).

Although she emphasises that the way these very different views of reading ('cognitive vs cultural') interrelate is problematic, they nevertheless focus upon the dynamic nature of reading and writing. The individual's active constructive processes play the leading role. Flowers summarises the forces impinging upon the cognition of the writer as in Figure 10.5(a). Both reader and writer are operating within a framework demarcated between 'external' background framing forces (which would include discourse conventions, specific social contexts and the particular language used) and constructively activated more 'internal' forces brought into place by reader and writer during their mental efforts. Flowers comments that this separation reflects the difference between the information a writer could

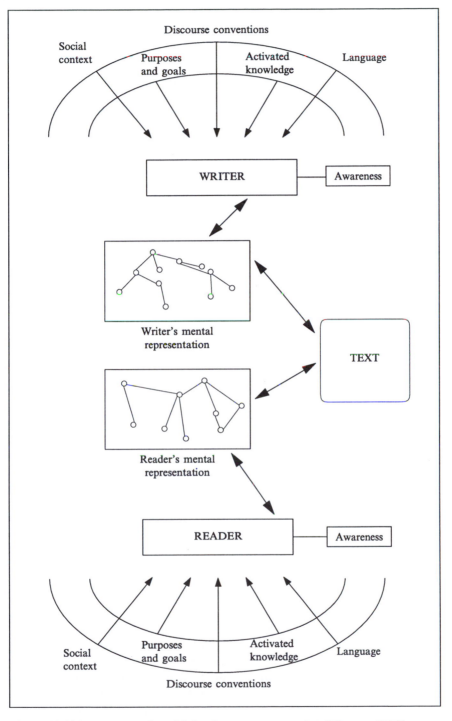

Figure 10.5(a) *Conceptual model for discourse construction (Flowers, 1987)*

respond to, and that which is 'actively represented in the writer's mind in a given performance' (p. 110). The writers' and readers' mental representations are conceived as very similar to mental representation models found in cognitive psychology (e.g. Anderson, 1983; Kintsch & van Dijk, 1978). While utilising this general framework, Flowers (1987) is careful to note that such representations are not directly accessible to the investigator, but are built and rebuilt during the process of writing, and the text itself is 'simply one instantiation of that mental network of meaning' (p. 111).

The somewhat marginalised box 'awareness' in Figure 10.5(a) is there to remind us that readers and writers are only sometimes aware of the negotiated path between these external and internal structures and forces. Flowers (1987) argues that 'blissful ignorance can describe the philosophical stance of readers who assume that they are reading the text objectively perceiving an unmediated version of the "author's" meaning' (p. 112). Interestingly, Flowers' emphasis on the active construction of a mental representation as reading proceeds, amounting to an instantiated mental text interdependent with the reader's own background knowledge and the 'text-world', corresponds to some degree with Ricoeur's (1970) notion of appropriation. Flowers' article concludes:

> these points of active cognition, these sites of struggle with the text, are often connected to aspects of reading that theorists and teachers also find interesting: they involve those parts of the text that the readers find exciting or problematic: they help predict a person's success or failure in comprehending the text; and they help us trace the path by which individual readers construct the texts they read and recall. (p. 128)

Such metaphors of navigation, and active constructive processes implicate the 'hypertextual' aesthetic of the reader–writer relationship, a recognisable dimension of literature since Sterne's *Tristram Shandy*.[4] For now, we can turn to Figure 10.5(b) and extend Flowers' (1987) model of the reader–writer relationship, and the suggestion that hypertext and hypermedia environments have a certain potential for bridging the gap between text and talk. The 'lines of force' impinging on the reader–writer relationship remain as they are, notwithstanding the proviso that the electronic environment has evolved its own particular set of conventions and social practices for communication (Nickerson, 1994; Sharples, 1993). The writer is now better conceived of as a social semiotician, i.e. an author who will utilise a range of text, images, video material, or whatever, in a fashion which will seek to enhance serendipity and a sense of making available potential (rather than actual) structures. Doland (1989) reminds us that hypertexts can be exceptionally limiting environments, providing the reader with only one or two possible 'readings' of the text (go this way now because this is the correct way to interpret this document). But one key question is how do you provide indications within any hypermedia environment that a whole range of structures are possible and realisable?

Here, I would like to extend Landow's (1992) emphasis on dia-lexias, which he introduces as 'lexialogical dialogues' which construct or produce

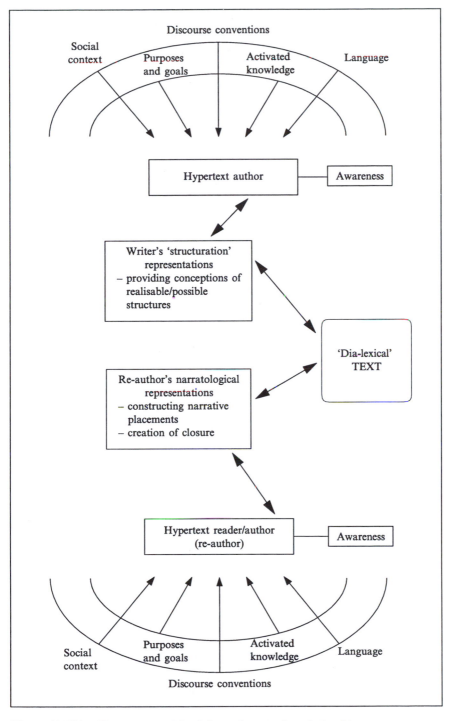

Figure 10.5(b) *Hypertext model of the author–reader relationship*

an interactive 'narratalogical comprehension'. Landow and his colleagues at Brown University have conducted extensive studies on the use of hypertext in literary domains (Landow, 1989, 1992). What is interesting here is that, where users of such environments are instructed simply to browse and investigate, they can produce little sense of coherence and order until they recognise realisable conditions of narrative closure (i.e. endings imply beginnings and so on). Arguably, lexialogical dialogues which facilitate 'narratalogical comprehension' cannot be based upon 'conversational' dialogic conceptions given the characteristics of talk outlined earlier. Rather, 'dia-lexical' hypertexts (hypermedia texts) would be better formulated on Ricoeur's conception of transformed interpretation. Valdes (1991) makes the point that a key aspect of literature is that it is 'written discourse with the capacity to redescribe the world for its readers', and further:

> Literary criticism is the transformation of interpretation into a dynamic dialectic between the distanciation of the text and the appropriation of the reader. By 'distanciation' Ricoeur means the semantic autonomy of the text, which stands removed from its unknown multiple readers. By 'appropriation' he means the process of making one's own what was not. 'The dialectic of distanciation and appropriation is the last word in the absence of absolute knowledge. (p. 44)

Hypertexts articulate a sense of semantic autonomy (distanciation) which was more opaque within traditional text. Authorship of hypertext documents (media) will rest as much on being able to provide for what is not yet realised as on what is already provided structurally. The process of 'appropriation' will be related to the restructuring possibilities made available to the hypertext reader. And so, the third aspect of Figure 10.5(b) above that should be emphasised is the role of re-authorship in hypermedia. Whatever else studies of learning in hypertext environments have shown, where provision is made for a user to impose or construct his/her own structural representations, then comprehension is enhanced (McAleese, 1989; McKnight, Dillon & Richardson, 1992).

Concluding comments

To write is to create text, and the study of writing has focused on the text as object rather than the act of writing as process. There is, of course, a curious ambivalence about the act of writing. As I write this sentence I am also the first reader, which itself should remind us that the author–reader relationship remains a problematic issue for linguistic criticism (and contemporary computer science). In contrast the psychology of writing has held to the traditional view that the author 'packages up' the ideas he/she has in the text in such as way that the reader will be able to 'get the message' without having to pay too much attention to the medium it is expressed in (the text). In the study of writing and reading we find the clearest evidence that the debates and issues which have engaged contemporary linguistics and critical theory have been ignored or misunderstood by psycholinguists. There is a considerable gap between the ideas and concepts which inform cognitive approaches to the study of text and those found within other disciplines (including linguistics, sociolinguistics, critical theory, psychoanalysis and social anthropology). Understanding why this impasse has reached a critical point (if it has) is the topic of the following and final chapter.

Notes

1. In Japanese *Kanji* the child has to learn over six thousand distinct characters, compared to the fifty-two for English.

2. This last measure entails asking a subject to respond to a secondary task (e.g. how many numbers are in sequence) while he/she is involved in the primary task of writing. The assumption is that if you are deeply engrossed (increased cognitive effort), then it will take you longer to respond to this secondary task than if you are only writing in a more superficial way. The time taken to respond thus indicates cognitive engagement.

3. Hypermedia might be defined in a shorthand form as 'a general interactive media integrating text, graphics, audio and video in a computer-based or television-based environment'. The definitions 'hypermedia' and 'hypertext' are used here interchangeably. People reading hypertext documents are often provided with links or interconnections which permit novel methods of 'navigating' information.

4. In *Tristram Shandy*, unconventionally, the hero doesn't appear until near the end of the book, and throughout the reader is constantly provided with asides, pointers to other information and various other 'routes' into and out of the text.

11

Postmodern Psychology and Language: Discourse Analysis and Social Psychology

We have now covered a range of topics on language of relevance to the psychologist interested in communication processes and procedures. At the outset one aim in providing the alliterative 'thinking–talk–text' theme was to emphasise the distinction between language as a structure, which lends itself to formal analysis, and the process of communication, i.e. all those sign-producing behaviours which are of particular interest to the psycholinguist. Communicating can clearly take many forms (verbal and non-verbal) and it is important for the student of language to recognise various distinctions between communication and language. There is little to be gained from the study of Chomsky's work if you are interested in talk, and conversely considerable difficulty in employing an ethnomethodological account of formal semantics. Chomsky's (1957) transformational grammar rests upon a particularly formal account of language, and although it has implications for theories of cognition and mind it is avowedly structuralist in the original sense – language remains a 'formal object'. Although talk might seem the most transparent and unproblematic medium of communication, we have seen that the ethnomethodologically inspired CA perspective can also lend itself to structural analysis, albeit of a somewhat different form.

For many students of language it is hard to see how such diverse topics fit into an overall framework focusing on the psychology of language. Thus the second aim of the 'thinking–talk–text' theme is to provide a 'trajectory' of topic focus, beginning as if 'inside the head', moving outwards into the study of everyday talk and behaviour, and then finally onto the study of text, the repository of sign-systems and text-producing activities which antedate our entry into the social world. The third aim has been to provide the student with insights into the points of contact, integration and potential conflict between psychology and neighbouring disciplines with an interest in language. We noted that psycholinguistics itself emerged from an individualistic interpretation of structuralism married with experimental methodology (linguistics and psychology). The study of deixis opened up a way of bridging the cognitive with the social in the understanding of everyday terms of reference, but also drew attention to the insights of social anthropologists, sociolinguists and those working in pragmatics. Likewise when we turned to the study of talk it became clear that social psychological accounts of non-verbal behaviour have been superseded by CA, itself now seeking to incorporate, or at least respond to, the criticisms of feminist and cross-cultural theory.

When we come to the analysis of reading and writing, arguably we find the greatest disparity between psycholinguistic and alternative approaches, e.g. in the somewhat curious gap between cognitive theories of reading and reader-oriented perspectives in literary criticism. Although both schools are addressing the same problem, within each domain you will find little reference to the other. Social science theorists have commented on the resistance within psychology to contemporary issues within sociology, critical theory and postmodern thought (e.g. Rose, 1990), and although this is understandable in certain sub-themes of the discipline (e.g. experimental methodology or neuropsychology), it is more difficult to understand when the focus is on language and communication. The remainder of this chapter will examine why the psychology of language has yet to embrace the 'postmodern' turn evidenced in many (if not all) related areas of language study covered in this book. In service of this aim, we will look in some detail at the discourse analysis movement within social psychology, an example of how the study of language can move beyond the rather formalist limitations of traditional psycholinguistics.

Postmodernism and postmodern psychology

Defining postmodernism is almost as problematic as identifying when (and why) modernism as a cultural project ended. Postmodernism can be viewed as a crisis within philosophy and the human sciences reflecting a loss of faith in the entire project of modernity and its belief in progress, reason and the power of human consciousness. It is also an umbrella term encompassing post-structuralism, deconstructionism, semiosis and intertextuality (see Appignanesi & Garrett (1995) for an amusing introduction to postmodernism). Whatever else, it is not a doctrine or political movement but more an orientation or attitude towards the whole idea of critical inquiry and intellectual life. Kvale (1992) provides us with a number of defining characteristics of postmodernism, summarised as in Table 11.1.

As a metaphysics or orienting philosophical attitude, postmodernity is compared with modernity in at least four ways. First, while modernity took as axiomatic the notion of progress through increasing scientific knowledge, postmodernity eschews such assumptions, focusing instead upon social practice and the role of context in institutional life:

> Postmodern society consists less of totalities to be ruled by preconceived models than by decentralisation to heteregenous local contexts characterized by flexibility and change. . . . There is a critique of the modernist search for foundational forms and belief in a linear progress through more knowledge. (Kvale, 1992, p. 2)

Second, in contrast to the modernist emphasis on studying the external reality 'out there', postmodernity focuses on the interdependent nature of language and being. All perspectives or interpretations of 'the real' are

Table 11.1 *Postmodern metaphysics*

Modernity	Postmodernity
1 Belief in emancipation and progress through more knowledge and scientific progress	1 Decentralised local contexts characterised by flexibility and change
2 Reality independent of observer	2 Language as constituting the structures of a perspectival social reality
3 Objectivity/subjectivity distinction	3 Hyperreality of self-referential signs
4 Universal social laws and the individual self	4 Interaction of local networks

predicated on the culturally bound presuppositions which underpin language as social practice. In turn, the objectivity/subjectivity distinction central to Kantian formulations of language and thought begins to break down. Instead the call is to embrace forms of reflexive critical inquiry, aware of the limitations and potentialities of playing one rather than another 'language game' (Wittgenstein, 1953). Signifieds cannot exist 'out there' in the world, our perception of reality is always refracted back through the 'hyperreality' of self-referential signs. Finally, the idea of being able to discover and identify universal social laws alongside the epistemic subject-self is misguided, replaced now by an emphasis on the role of localised social networks and a value-constituting social science (Lather, 1992). The psychology of and on the 'subject' is to be replaced by a psychology for the person, a psychology informed by an analysis of power and ideology:

> Postmodern thought has involved an expansion of reason, it has gone beyond the cognitive and scientific domains to permeate those of ethics and aesthetics as well; it has analysed the nexus of power and knowledge, in particular the de-individualizing of power into anonymous structures. (Kvale, 1992, p. 3)

The metaphysical comparison highlighted in Table 11.1 can be extended to psychology itself. Summarising Gergen's (1992) analysis of postmodern psychology, there are at least five domains where a comparison can be instructive (see Table 11.2). The first contrast reminds us (as before) of the socially constituted nature of scientific practice. Within the philosophy of science, Kuhn (1970) argued cogently that we do not develop science painstakingly through increments to knowledge but do so by a change in perspective. Gergen (1992) points out that criticisms of this kind shifted the centre of gravity in science away from foundationalism, leaving the 'problem of knowledge' waiting to be solved. The second comparison highlights the significance of articulating a distinct subject matter within psychology. A postmodern psychology could ultimately lead to a vanishing subject matter. In other words if the status of the individuated subject is no

Table 11.2   *Psychological constructs*

Modernist psychology	Postmodernist psychology
1 Belief in a knowable world	1 Truth as perspective (following Kuhn and Feyerabend)
2 Basic subject matter within discipline boundaries of psychology	2 Vanishing subject matter given that discourse about the world operates largely on the basis of social processes – in turn crystallised in terms of various theoretical rules and options
3 Universal principles/laws	3 Critical self-reflection as essential aspect of the postmodern approach – investigators must take account of the historical circumstances of their inquiry
4 Empirical method – truth through method ideologically neutral and impersonal	4 Marginalisation of method – method loses its central position
5 Scientific progress	5 The idea of scientific truth is rendered intelligible by virtue of its literary or narrative character (a literary achievement)

longer a central focus of the discipline, areas associated with cognitive and biological psychology may form a signficant part of an emerging cognitive or neuroscience discipline, with other social, developmental and associated applied domains becoming part of health sciences.

Underpinning modernist psychology, of course, is the belief in generalisable laws and principles. The contrast with a psychology which insists on the importance of reflexive critical inquiry could not be more striking. The laboratory experiment itself now needs to be understood as a particular set of social practices conducted in a specific place and time, where results are only understandable with regard to the set of institutional procedures in play in that context. No longer is it defensible to assert the neutral status of the scientific method (comparison 4); indeed the notion of scientific truth itself has to be understood in part as a literary achievement:

> Thus, as the language guides the formation of our accounts, so does it construct an array of putative objects. One may never exit the language to give a true and accurate portrayal of what is the case. Understanding of the world is thus a product not of the world as it is, but of textual history [and] if our language conventions are, in turn, dependent on social processes, and these processes carry with them various ideological or value biases, then all scientific writing and all out attempts at objectivity are essentially value-saturated products of social agreement. (Gergen, 1992, p. 22)

Whether a distinctive postmodern psychology will emerge from an amalgam of social psychologists, psycholinguists and feminist psychology is as yet unknown. Kvale (1992) argues that the postmodern 'death of the subject/author' is tantamount to the death of psychology, and, given that psychology was the privileged way for modernity to understand humanity, 'a postmodern age may also mean a post-psychology age' (p. 54). More positively, Gergen (1992) suggests that the psychologist will be in a unique position to bring the psychological and the cultural closer together. Whatever else, the psychology of language has yet to respond or even enter into the debate regarding the discursive nature of contemporary psychology, somewhat surprising given the post-structuralist proposal that there is no language to describe what is given independent of all language. Descombes (1986) notes:

> All language describes a given relative to the language used, and therefore what we are given is always the gift of language. To describe the constitution of our experience we must turn to our language, not to the intentional operations of consciousness. (p. 70)

In other words there is a fundamental problem in the gap between biology and language and it could be the dialectical nature of 'discourse in action' which serves as a partial solution. With this in mind we can consider the extent to which the recent emergence of the discourse-analytic movement within social psychology answers some of the issues raised by a psychology of language focused upon thinking, talk and text.

Discourse analysis and social psychology: language as social action

For students of language the first important thing to note about discourse analysis is that the term itself means two quite different things within linguistics and social psychology. As one part of the field of pragmatics, discourse analysis is a set of methods for examining coherence and structure in extended texts. Levinson (1983) defines discourse analysis as

> essentially a series of attempts to extend the techniques so successful in linguistics, beyond the unit of the sentence. The procedures employed (often implicitly) are essentially the following: (a) the isolation of a set of basic categories or units of discourse, (b) the formulation of a set of concatenation rules stated over those categories, delimiting well-formed sequences of categories (coherent discourses) from ill-formed sequences (incoherent categories). (p. 286)

This methodology of text analysis has been used within linguistics for studies of legal documents, literary texts and classroom discourse (e.g. Sinclair & Coulthard, 1975), although criticisms of the approach have been raised (see Levinson, 1983).

Within social psychology and the social psychology of language, discourse analysis, although in part borrowing from linguistics, can be defined as a functionally oriented approach to the analysis of text and talk. This is an approach to the study of language use which can be seen as part of the 'language-dominant' view of language outlined in Chapter 2. Edwards and Potter (1992) trace the origins of discourse analysis or the discursive psychological approach to Wittgenstein's (1953) philosophy of language, the sociology of knowledge as social practice and the developments within ethnomethodology, semiotics and post-structuralism. They outline five defining features of the discourse-analytic approach as follows (somewhat abridged here):

1: Discourse analysis (DA) is primarily concerned with naturally occurring talk and text (the latter often focusing on transcriptions of the former)
2: Rather than focusing on linguistic structures DA concentrates on the content of talk, with the social organization of it's subject matter.
3: DA concentrates on talk as social action, with an emphasis on the construction of 'versions of events' by participants, the use of rhetorical devices and the importance of variability (in such) as a function of context and use.
4: DA is interested in the rhetorical (argumentative) organization of everyday talk and thinking. In particular DA is interested in understanding the way rhetoric is employed to support and repress alternative accounts of social life and everyday behaviour.
5: DA seeks to address the issue of cognitivism in psychological inquiry, particularly the criteria which underpin ascriptions of life and mind, 'with examining discourse for how cognitive issues of knowledge and belief, fact and error, truth and explanation are dealt with. (p. 29)

Discourse analysis is interested in how people use knowledge of the past in the present. It is also the study of how everyday versions of events (including persons, things, states of affairs) are constructed and occasioned in talk and text:

> From a discursive perspective it (language) exists as a domain of social action, of communication and culture, whose relations to an external world of event, and to an internal world of cognitions, are a function of the social and communicative actions that talk is designed for. (Edwards et al., 1992, p. 442)

and discourse analysis is:

> essentially a theoretical orientation in which versions of mind and reality, including event reports, are explicable in terms of principles of report construction, as situated discursive action, prior to any status they may have as clues to the nature of the world, or to the workings of mind. Specific versions of events (and other things) are seen as socially produced outcomes, or accomplishments, of discourse, rather than as neutral inputs to psychological processes, or as cognitive states that versions reveal. (Edwards et al., 1992, p. 443)

Before going on to consider noteworthy responses to the emergence of discursive psychology, the significance of rhetoric as a background framing assumption should be emphasised. The relationship between rhetoric, argument and discourse (talk and text) has been an important part of Western thought since the early Greeks. Rhetoric can be defined as the theory and practice of eloquence (either spoken or written), in other words the whole art of using language to persuade others. Since the fourth century BC rhetoric was considered a faculty or an ability and Aristotle developed the relationship between the rhetorical concept of persuasion and the logical concept of the probable. Welch (1990) notes that rhetoric as a discursive skill was seriously diminished with the rise of scientism and Cartesian rationalism, 'the ability to do something became radically subordinated to whatness, or "content"' (p. 94). However, for social scientists interested in language, the kind of proof appropriate to studying human behaviour has less to do with the logical necessity of mathematics and much more to do with what seems likely to be the case.

Thus, an argument that can properly be called rhetoric has to take into account both the extent to which the issue under discussion seems to be true and the persuasive effectiveness it might have. This in turn depends on the relationship between speaker or listener (and writer and reader). Within social psychology Billig (1987) highlights the significance of classical rhetoric and argumentation, noting that many of the processes of thinking are modelled upon those of argumentation. Billig (1990) also notes that postmodernism conceives of science as an intrinsically rhetorical or persuasive activity, where 'a rhetorical analysis of science is not so much an exposé, but an analysis which looks at the way that scientists argue and discuss their scientific cases' (p. 50).

An important rhetorical device in the discursive practice of science is the use of metaphor. Metaphor has been described as the rhetorical process by which discourses unleash the power that certain fictions have to redescribe reality (Ricoeur, 1978). The language of psychology is replete with metaphorical devices of this nature. The 'information processing' metaphor, for example, conceives of the mind as being a system where inputs (stimuli from the environment) undergo 'processing' before resulting in 'outputs' in the form of behaviour. The person as scientist, engaging in everyday activities of hypothesis testing and refutation, was the enduring metaphor of Kelley's (1963) personal construct theory in personality research. Psychoanalysis and cognitive dissonance employ the metaphor of equilibrium to good effect and the recent emergence of connectionism within cognitive psychology can be viewed as a 'brain as representation' metaphor of mind.

One issue for discursive psychology, then, is to highlight the models and metaphors used by psychologists in the rhetoric which motivates their theory construction and compare these with the models and metaphors used by those who make up the subject population under investigation. We noted above that one of the defining characteristics of the discursive-analytic approach was to articulate the implicit assumptions in the dominant cognitivism of contemporary psychology. It should come as no surprise that when discourse analysts turned their attention to the study of memory (particularly remembering), this engendered a fairly heated response from cognitive psychology.

The social context of memory: a primary site of dispute between cognitive psychologists and discourse analysts

Alongside topics such as perception, attention and learning, memory would appear to be one topic within psychology that by definition must be 'cognitive'. Notwithstanding the post-structuralist critique of the relationship between language and the world, our experience of what it is to remember aligned with our possessing our own individual memories appears to guarantee the cognitivist basis of memory. Within cognitive psychology there have been three main approaches to the study of memory: serial information processing multi-store models (Atkinson & Shiffrin, 1971), working memory models (Baddeley, 1986) and parallel distributed connectionist models (McClelland & Rumelhart, 1986), and in large part all have shared certain assumptions about the relationship between categories, concepts and language (the cognition-dominant view – see Chapter 1).

During the early 1980s inspired by calls for a more ecologically valid approach to the study of memory (Neisser, 1982), there was a move to establish studies of memory in real-world contexts (rather than the laboratory). Subsequently studies within memory research focused on applied issues such as eye-witness testimony (Christie & Ellis, 1981), gerontology (Rabbitt, 1992), memory for events (Baddeley, 1990) and autobiographical memory (Kopelman, Wilson & Baddeley, 1990). However, although such studies paid more attention to the workings of everyday memory, discourse analysts argued that such studies continued to deal with language in much the same way as in experimental laboratory-based research. Language continued to be seen as a transparent medium for examining the relationship between cognition and the real world.

In their book *Discursive Psychology*, Edwards and Potter (1992) outline their critique of memory research, noting that in both the information processing and ecological memory theories the researcher is subject to the same fundamental problem i.e. what really happened? Both perspectives require that the objective world is unproblematically known by the psychologist, in some different way from the people involved in the experiments, so that the psychologist can claim to know to what extent the 'subject', whether perceiving, comprehending or remembering, got it (whatever event is being recalled) right. Looking in detail at a study carried out by Neisser (1982) on the testimony cited by John Dean during the Watergate hearings, Edwards and Potter (1992) argue that the types of memory identified (verbatim, gist and repisodic) remain as much the textual constructions of the researcher as they are the cognitive attributes of the individual involved. Their argument is that actual rememberings are always particular realisations of event-stories from an infinite number of possible interpretations.

Outlining the discourse-analytic approach to the study of memory Edwards et al. (1992) call for a redefinition of the concept. Rather than presupposing this or that complex memory structure within the individual, attention should be focused on accounts and reports of past events, as they occur spontaneously in discourse. The study of memory should move from the individual to the social. In one noteworthy study of how parents seem to instruct their children 'how to remember', Edwards and Middleton (1986) highlighted the significance of the conversational context for constructing accounts of events and identities. With regard to method, Edwards et al. (1992) call for a close analysis of actual reports, descriptions and versions of events in terms of content, sequential planning and rhetorical organisation. As for theory, discourse analysis they suggest is a broad amalgamation of discourse analysis (the linguistic version identified above), conversational analysis, ethnomethodology, linguistic philosophy, rhetoric and the sociology of science.

Not suprisingly the majority of cognitive psychologists consider the discursive perspective on memory research misguided, misconceived and certainly methodologically flawed. A peer commentary on a summary review of discursive psychology (Baddeley et al., 1992) suggests that discourse analysts should read more cognitive psychology, and that discourse analysis could never tell us anything about memory ('we are practical, not philosophical' – Hitch, 1992), and is, in fact, not psychology at all (Neisser, 1992). Social psychologists also take exception to discourse analysts' emphasis on context, action and talk, arguing that we must always be able to examine the motives or intentions of the speaker (Abrams & Hogg, 1990), clearly seeking to maintain the status of the 'epistemic subject'. Given the cognition-dominant view of language found in contemporary psycholinguistics, only recently has there been some interest in the emergence of discursive psychology. Such observations lend themselves to a summary evaluation of a psychology of language which emphasises the significance of communication.

Prospects for a postmodern psychology of language

The emergence of discourse analysis can serve as a 'test-case' for considering whether the psychology of language should move beyond those topics and issues which lend themselves to the cognition-dominant view of language. Again we can return to the three forms of communication central to the topics we have covered in our deliberations: thinking (self-communication), talk and text. At the present time discourse analysis does not directly contribute to theoretical issues concerning the relationship between language and thinking. That is, although the concern with rhetoric and argumentation (Billig, 1987) highlights the cultural basis for expressions of rationality in our thinking, the question of thinking itself is largely side-stepped. We noted in Chapter 2 that cognitive psycholinguistics (whether of the symbolic or the connectionist variety) holds dear to those key assumptions of cognition and categorisation outlined by Kant. Language is always going to 'hook onto' thinking in some as yet unspecified way, and such a view maintains the significance and importance of the individuating subject, as Sinha (1988) argues.

Outside of psychology the study of language is influenced as much by the language-dominant view expressed by Wittgenstein (1953) and the social constructionists as by the cognitive account. We saw how structuralism itself originally emphasised the collective over the individual; however, it was understandable that psychology as the scientific study of mental life and behaviour favoured the Chomskian individualistic interpretation out of which psycholinguistics emerged. Linguistics, sociology, social anthropology and critical theory contributed to, and were influenced by, continuing (now post-structuralist) developments in language. In fact it was this source of ideas combined with dissatisfactions within social psychology which led to the emergence of discursive psychology. The question of thinking is now replaced by the problematics of text, discourse and a deconstruction of those criteria and social practices which must be in place before you can claim that any 'thinking' or cognitive life exists within an individual.

Understanding why this issue may be unresolvable might become clearer if you ask yourself the question: where did the syntax that's in my head come from? A cognitivist has little choice but assume that our mind does consist of propositional attitudes, mental states, innate predispositions and all associated *cogito* for comprehending language structure. A social constructionist will argue will that the structure of language exists 'out there' in the collective conscious of the culture, expressed in the myriad of social practices and institutions which underpin language as social action. In fact the whole notion of syntactic structure is a particular language game within a specific cultural context, one of a number of Western cultural ideas amenable to deconstruction. Discourse analysts do not hold to an extreme version of this approach, we might note:

> it can sensibly be argued that whatever people say, they must have some sort of underlying cognitive machinery . . . the discursive action model is not designed to deny all sorts of cognitive organization. Rather it questions some major assumptions and procedures through which particular kinds of underlying cognitions are traditionally identified. (Edwards & Potter, 1992, p. 157)

When we move from thinking to talk, discourse analysts provide one way of bridging the gap between psychological and ethnomethodological approaches to conversation. The emphasis on looking in detail at what people actually do, and then construct models and methods for understanding their representations of the world has been used advantageously in many applied contexts (e.g. Gilbert & Mulkay, 1984; Griffin, 1986; Scheppele, 1994). However, it can be argued that although discourse analysts utilise central constructs of the ethnomethodological perspective (particularly accountability and agency), they appear to resist a wholehearted commitment to the idea that it is always (and only) the participants themselves who provide the criteria and orienting formulations of rational behaviour during conversational conduct (see Chapter 6). Moreover, although discourse analysts are sensitive to the problems of transcription (conventions for 'translating' naturally occurring talk into written text) and recognise that differences between talk and text are often glossed over in cognitive approaches to language, there remains evidence of a tendency to conflate the two. The theoretical distinctions outlined in Chapter 7 may provide a partial solution to this problem.

Within traditional psycholinguistics there remains little evidence that the post-structuralist critique of the 'text' has had any enduring influence. In a sense contemporary research either ignores the issue altogether or responds in a way not dissimilar to the Oxford academics' final response to Derrida pictured in Steve Bell's amusing comic strip (see Figure 11.1). Within discourse analysis there has been work deconstructing the role of educational texts within social psychology so as to highlight prevalent (largely logocentric) assumptions of that branch of the discipline (e.g. Stringer, 1990). Elswhere in psychology, we noted the considerable distance between psychological approaches to the study of reading and writing and contemporary ideas in other areas of language study. Although some have attempted a rapprochement or at least attempted to recognise the points of contact (Flowers, 1987), within psychology the text remains a largely unproblematic entity, simply a set of sentences which somehow encapsulates the unambiguous meaning intended by the originating author. Interestingly the increasing use of information technology has recast the problem of the author–reader relationship (Landow, 1992, and see Chapter 10) and encouraged those with applied problems in this domain to seek answers from ethnomethodology and semiotics (Andersen, 1994; Luff, Gilbert & Frolich, 1991).

The question remains whether the psychology of language should seek to extend its domain of inquiry so as to encompass topics which fall somewhat outside of the remit of the cognitivist orientation. One answer might simply be that it should not, and instead (cognitive) psycholinguistics should become further embedded within cognitive science, that confluence of interdisciplinary topics that share a commitment to modelling cognition and knowledge processes as formal abstract systems. Language within such an enterprise remains a formal object.

If, however, the psychology of language is fundamentally concerned with communication processes, then there is much to be said for considering a range of theoretical orientations and models. Investigating what thinking is (or might be) can only be undertaken with a recognition of its interdependence with language (whether verbal or averbal). We saw in Chapter 3 that theories of meaning remain rather restricted unless they consider the function of language – considerations of meaning demand an examination of communication. Likewise, deictic comprehension is interdependent with language use, and we noted that even grammatical constraints may be motivated by social forces (Brown & Levinson, 1978). Analysing how people communicate with each other demands an analysis of the richness of conversation and interaction beyond the parameters of the information processing metaphor. A cognition-dominant view of language is certainly at odds with the ethnomethodological orientation of conversational analysis,

Figure 11.1 *Controversy over the text!*

although we might note that this has not prevented applied psychologists welcoming the approach (Luff et al., 1990).

When we turn to the complexities of the text and other systems for encoding discourse, there are a number of rich conceptual frameworks within semiotics which the psycholinguist can utilise. Within reading research the contrast between the modernist perspective of cognitive psychology and the post-structuralist orientation of critical theory is striking. The psychology of reading remains somewhat resistant to the idea that the reader's contribution to comprehension is not just an 'add-on' but central to our understanding of text, and critical theory could supplement psychological approaches. Casting a somewhat positive eye over these developments, a distinct psychosemiotics of language may emerge from a combination of psychological methodology and semiotic theory. As we noted, language research employs a whole range of methodologies, and there could be considerable benefits in moving the emphasis away from the hypothetico-deductive approach of cognitive psycholinguistics. A psychology of language which combines methodological diversity with a commitment to engaging in reflexive critical inquiry (i.e. seeking to articulate the role of background theoretical assumptions as a parallel theme to any investigation) would extend the boundaries of the discipline and accommodate the interests of the cognition- and language-dominant perspectives. Otherwise, contemporary psycholinguistics may be in danger of having little to offer those within psychology who remain concerned with understanding language as communication.

References

Abkarian, G.G. (1982). Comprehension of deictic locatives: the object behind it. *Journal of Psycholinguistic Research, 11*, 229–245.

Abrams, D.A., & Hogg, M.A. (1990). The context of discourse: Let's not throw out the baby with the bathwater. *Philosophical Psychology, 3*, 219–225.

Adams, M.J. (1982). Models of reading. In J.F. Le-Ny & W. Kintsch (Eds.), *Language and comprehension.* Amsterdam: North-Holland.

Agha, A. (1994). Honorofication. *Annual Review of Anthropology, 23*, 277–302.

Allwood, J., Andersson, L.G., & Dahl, O. (1977). *Logic in linguistics.* Cambridge: Cambridge University Press.

Althusser, L. (1990). *Philosophy and spontaneous philosophy of the scientists* (B. Brewster, Trans.). London: Verso.

Andersen, P.B. (1994). Towards an aesthetics of hypertext systems: A semiotic approach. In N. Streitz, A. Rizk & J. Andere (Eds.), *Hypertext: Concepts, systems and applications.* Proceedings of the First European Conference on Hypertext, INRIA, France. Cambridge: Cambridge University Press.

Anderson, J.R. (1983). *The architecture of cognition.* Cambridge, MA: Harvard University Press.

Anderson, R.C., & Pearson, P. (1984a). Reading comprehension and word knowledge. In B.A. Hutson (Ed.), *Advances in reading/language research.* Greenwith, CT: JAI Press.

Anderson, R.C., & Pearson, P.D. (1984b). A schema-theoretic view of basic processes in reading comprehension (Tech. Rep. No. 306). Urbana-Champaign: University of Illinois, Center for the Study of Reading.

Appignanesi, R., & Garrett, C. (1995). *Postmodernism for beginners.* Cambridge: Icon Books.

Argyle, M. (1975). *Bodily communication.* London: Methuen.

Armstrong, D.F., Stokoe, W.C., & Wilcox, S.E. (1994). Signs of the origin of syntax. *Current Anthropology, 35*, 349–368.

Atkinson, J.M., & Drew, P. (1979). *Order in court.* London: Macmillan.

Atkinson, R.C., & Shiffrin, R.M. (1971). The control of short term memory. *Scientific American, 224*, 82–90.

Austin, J.L. (1961). *Philosophical papers.* Oxford: Clarendon Press.

Austin, J.L. (1962). *How to do things with words.* Oxford: Clarendon Press.

Baddeley, A.D. (1986). *Working memory.* New York: Oxford University Press.

Baddeley, A. (1990). *Human memory: Theory and practice.* London: Lawrence Erlbaum Associates.

Baddeley, A. (1992). Peer commentary on *Discursive Social Psychology. Psychologist, 5*, 447–452.

Baddeley, A., Banaji, M., Barclay, C.R., Cohen, G., Hitch, G., Hyman, I.E., Neisser, U., Robinson, J.A., Roediger, H.L., & Wheeler (1992). Peer commentaries on Edwards, Potter and Middleton. *Psychologist, 5*, 447–455.

Barthes, R. (1967). *Elements of sociology* (A. Lavers & C. Smith, Trans.). London: Cape.

Barthes, R. (1977). The death of the author. In *Image–Music–Text* (S. Heath, Trans.). London: Fontana.

Barthes, R. (1985). *A lover's discourse* (R. Howard, Trans.). Harmondsworth: Penguin.

Beattie, G. (1983). *Talk: An analysis of speech and non-verbal behaviour in conversation.* Milton Keynes: Open University Press.

Beattie, G.W., & Beattie, C.A. (1981). Postural congruence in a naturalistic setting. *Semiotica*, *35*, 41–55.

Berger, J. (1972). *Ways of seeing*. Harmondsworth: Penguin.

Berger, P.L., & Luckman, T. (1967). *The social construction of reality: A treatise in the sociology of knowledge*. London: Allen Lane.

Bernstein, R. (1990, 23 August). The rising hegemony of the politically correct. *New York Times*, p. 4.

Billig, M. (1987). *Arguing and thinking: A rhetorical approach to social psychology*. Cambridge: Cambridge University Press.

Billig, M. (1990). Rhetoric of social psychology. In I. Parker & J. Shotter (Eds.), *Deconstructing social psychology*. London: Routledge.

Birdwhistell, E.L. (1970). *Kinesics and context*. Philadelphia: University of Pennsylvania Press.

Bissex, G. (1980). *Gnys at wrk: A child learns to write and read*. Cambridge, MA: Harvard University Press.

Bleich, D. (1978). *Subjective criticism*. Baltimore and London: Johns Hopkins University Press.

Bloor, D. (1983). *Wittgenstein: A social theory of knowledge*. London: Macmillan.

Bolata, D.A., Flores d'Arcias, G.B., & Rayner, K. (Eds.). (1990). *Comprehension processes in reading*. Hove: Lawrence Erlbaum Associates.

Boulter, J.D. (1989). Beyond word processing. The computer as a new writing space. *Language and Communication*, *9*, 129–142.

Bransford, J.D., & Johnson, M.K. (1972). Contextual prerequisities for understanding: Some investigations of comprehension and recall. *Journal of Verbal Learning and Verbal Behaviour*, *11*, 717–726.

Brener, R. (1983). Learning the deictic meaning of third person pronouns. *Journal of Psycholinguistic Research*, *12*, 235–262.

Brown, P. (1994). The ins and ons of Tzeltal locative expressions: The semantics of static descriptions of location. *Linguistics*, *32*, 743–790.

Brown, P., & Levinson, S. (1978). Universals in language use: Politeness phenomena. In E.N. Goody (Ed.), *Questions and politeness: Strategies in social interaction*. Cambridge: Cambridge University Press.

Brown, P.J. (1989). *Assessing the quality of hypertext documents*. Occasional paper, University of Kent, Computing Laboratory.

Brown, R. (1986). *Social psychology: The second edition*. London: Collier Macmillan.

Brown, R., & Gillman, A. (1960). The pronouns of power and solidarity. In T. Sebeok (Ed.), *Style in language*. Cambridge: Cambridge University Press.

Bruner, J.S. (1975). The ontogenesis of speech acts. *Journal of Child Language*, *2*, 1–19.

Buhler, F. (1965). *Sprachtheorie*. Stuttgart: Fisher.

Burgin, V. (Ed.). (1982). *Thinking photography*. London: Macmillan.

Burgoon, J.K. (1991). Relational message interpretations of touch, conversational distance, and posture. *Journal of Nonverbal Behaviour*, *15*, 233–259.

Bush, V. (1945, July). As we may think. *Atlantic Monthly*, *176*, 101–108.

Cameron, D. (1989, March). *Rules, power and communication*. Paper presented at the 'Conversation, Discourse, Conflict' Conference, Trinity College, Dublin.

Campbell, R., & Schram, P.J. (1995). Feminist research methods: A content-analysis of psychology and social-science textbooks. *Psychology of Women Quarterly*, *19*, 85–106.

Carlson-Radvansky, L.A., & Irwin, D.A. (1993). Frames of reference in vision and language: Where is above? *Cognition*, *46*, 223–244.

Carpenter, P.A., & Just, M.A. (1983). What your eyes do while your mind is reading. In K. Rayner (Ed.), *Eye movements in reading perceptual and language processes*. New York: Academic Press.

Carr, T.H., & Pollatsek, A. (1985). Recognizing printed words: A look at current models. In D. Besner, T.G. Waller & G.E. MacKinnon (Eds.), *Reading research: Advances in theory and practice* (Vol. 5). New York: Academic Press.

Carter, A.T. (1984). The acquisition of social deixis: children's usages of kin terms in Maharashtra, India. *Journal of Child Language*, *11*, 179–201.

Cattell, J.M. (1885). The inertia of the eye and the brain. *Brain*, *8*, 295–312.

Charney, R. (1979). Speech roles and the development of personal pronouns. *Journal of Child Language*, *7*, 3–69.

Chiat, S. (1981). Context-specificity and the generalizations in the acquisition of pronominal distinctions. *Journal of Child Language*, *8*, 76–91.

Choi, S., & Bowerman, M. (1991). Learning to express motion events in English and Korean. The influence of language-specific lexicalisations. *Cognition*, *41*, 83–121.

Chomsky, N. (1957). *Syntactic structures*. Gravenhage: Mouton.

Chomsky, N. (1959). A review of *Verbal behavior*. *Language*, *35*, 26–58.

Chomsky, N. (1965). *Aspects of the theory of syntax*. Cambridge: MIT Press.

Chomsky, N., & Halle, M. (1965). Some controversial questions in phonological theory. *Journal of Linguistics*, *1*, 97–138.

Christie, D.F.M., & Ellis, H.D. (1981). Photofit constuctions versus verbal descriptions of faces. *Journal of Applied Psychology*, *66*, 358–363.

Clark, E.V., & Sengul, C.J. (1978). Strategies in the acquisition of deixis. *Journal of Child Language*, *6*, 69–80.

Clark, H.H., & Carlson, T.B. (1981). Context for comprehension. In J. Long & A. Baddeley (Eds.), *Attention and performance IX*. Hillsdale, NJ: Lawrence Erlbaum Associates.

Clark, H.H., & Marshall, C.R. (1981). Definite reference and mutual knowledge. In A.K. Joshi, I. Sag & B. Webber (Eds.), *Elements of discourse understanding*. Cambridge: Cambridge University Press.

Clark, H.H., & Schaefer, E.F. (1987). Concealing one's meaning from overhearers. *Journal of Memory and Language*, *26*, 209–225.

Collins, A., & Gentner, D. (1980). A framework for a cognitive theory of writing. In L.W. Gregg & E.R. Steinberg (Eds.), *Cognitive processes in writing*. Hillsdale, NJ: Lawrence Erlbaum Associates.

Collins, A.M., & Quillian, M.R. (1973). Experiments on semantic memory and language comprehension. In L.W. Gregg (Ed.), *Cognition in learning and memory*. New York: Wiley.

Collins, R. (1988). Theoretical continuities in Goffman's work. In P. Drew & A. Wooton (Eds.), *Ervin Goffman: Exploring the interaction order*. Cambridge: Polity Press.

Collis, G. (1990, March). *In (the) front of the car: Complex prepositions and noun phrases*. Paper presented at the 1990 Child Language Seminar, University of Kent, Canterbury.

Coupland, J., Robinson, J.D., & Coupland, N. (1994). Frame negotiation in doctor–elderly patient consultations. *Discourse & Society*, *5*, 89–124.

Cox, C. (1994). Political correctness and freedom of speech in British universities. *Minerva*, *32*, 193–195.

Craig, H.K., & Washington, J.A. (1986). Children's turn-taking behaviours: Sociolinguistic interactions. *Journal of Pragmatics*, *10*, 173–197.

Crawford, C.B. (1994). Effects of sex and sex roles on same sex touch. *Perceptual and Motor Skills*, *78*, 391–394.

Cromer, W. (1970). The difference model: A new explanation for some reading difficulties. *Journal of Educational Psychology*, *61*, 471–483.

Dale, P.S. (1976). *Language development: Structure and function* (2nd ed.). New York: Holt, Rinehart & Winston.

Darwin, C. (1872). *The expression of the emotions in man and animals*. London: Murray.

de Beaugrande, R. (1980). *Text, discourse and process*. Norwood, NJ: Ablex Publishing.

DeBernardi, J. (1994). Social aspects of language use. In T. Ingold (Ed.), *Companion encyclopedia of anthropology*. London: Routledge.

Dennis, E.E. (1992). Freedom of expression, the university and the media. *Journal of Communication*, *42*, 73–94.

Derrida, J. (1977). Signature event context. *Glyph*, *1*, 172–197.

Descombes, A. (1986). *Objects of all sorts: A philosophical grammar* (L. Scott-Fox & J. Harding, Trans.). Oxford: Basil Blackwell.

de Villiers, P.A., & de Villiers, G. (1979). *Early language*. London: Fontana.

Doland, V.M. 1989. Hypermedia as an interpretive act. *Hypermedia*, *1*, 6–33.

Donaldson, M. (1978). *Children's minds*. London: Fontana.

Dore, J. (1979). Feeling, form and intention. In R.M. Golinkoff (Ed.), *The transition from pre-linguistic to linguistic communication*. Hillsdale, NJ: Lawrence Erlbaum Associates.

Drew, P., & Heritage, J. (1992). Analyzing talk at work: An introduction. In P. Drew & J. Heritage (Eds.), *Talk at work: Interaction in institutional settings*. Cambridge: Cambridge University Press.

D'Souza, D. (1991, September). Illiberal education: The politics of race and sex on campus. *Atlantic Monthly*, 51–58.

Dubois, B.L., & Crouch, I. (1987). Linguistic discruption. In J. Penfield (Ed.), *Women and language in transition*. Albany: State University of New York Press.

Dunn, J., & Shatz, M. (1989). Becoming a conversationalist despite (or because of) having an older sibling. *Child Development*, *60*, 399–410.

Eco, U. (1979). *The role of the reader. Explorations in the semiotics of texts*. London: Hutchinson.

Eco, U. (1982). Critique of the image. In V. Burgin (Ed.), *Thinking photography*. London: Macmillan.

Eco, U. (1983). Producing signs. In U. Eco & T.E. Sebeok (Eds.), *The sign of three: Dupin, Holmes and Pierce*. Indiana: Indiana University Press.

Edwards, P., & Middleton, D. (1986). Joint remembering: constructing an account of shared experience through conversational discourse. *Discourse Processes*, *9*, 423–59.

Edwards, D., & Potter, J. (Eds.). (1992). *Discursive psychology*. London: Sage.

Edwards, D., Potter, J., & Middleton, D. (1992). Toward a discursive psychology of remembering. *Psychologist*, *5*, 441–447.

Ehrlich, S., & King, R. (1994). Feminist meanings and the (de)politicization of the lexicon. *Language in Society*, *23*, 59–76.

Ekman, P. (1973). *Darwin and facial expression: A century of research in review*. New York: Academic Press.

Ekman, P. (1992). Facial expressions of emotion: New findings, new questions. *Psychological Science*, *3*, 34–38.

Ekman, P., Sorenson, E.R., & Friesen, W.V. (1969). Pan-cultural elements in facial displays of emotion. *Science*, *164*, 86–88.

Enrico, J. (1985). The fire as conduit to the other world: A Note on Haida deixis and Haida belief. *International Journal of American Linguistics*, *4*, 400–402.

Ervin-Tripp, S., & Mitchell-Kernan, C. (Eds.). (1977). *Child discourse*. New York and London: Academic Press.

Farris, C.S. (1992). Chinese preschool codeswitching: Mandarin baby-talk and the voice of authority. *Journal of Multilingual and Multicultural Development*, *13*, 187–213.

Feldman, C. (1991). Oral metalanguage. In D. Olson & N. Torrance, (Eds.), *Literacy and orality*. Cambridge: Cambridge University Press.

Feldman, C., & Bruner, J. (1987). Varieties of perspective: An overview. In J. Russell (Ed.), *Philisophical Perspectives on Developmental Psychology*. Oxford: Basil Blackwell.

Fillmore, C.J. (1971). Towards a theory of deixis. *The PCCLLU Papers*, Department of Linguistics, University of Hawaii, *3.4*, 219–241.

Fillmore, C.J. (1975). *Santa Cruz Lectures on Deixis*, 1971. Mimeo, Indiana University Linguistics Club.

Finnegan, R. (1989). Information technology. *Language and Communication*, *9*, 146–163.

Fisher, I.E. (1976). Dropping remarks and the Barbadian audience. *American Ethnologist*, *3*, 227–242.

Fisher, J.D., Ryttine, M., & Hesling, R. (1976). Hands touching hands: Affective and evaluative effects on an interpersonal touch. *Sociometry*, *39*, 416–421.

Fisher, S., & Todd, A.D. (Eds.). (1983). *The social organization of doctor–patient communication*. Washington, DC: Center for Applied Linguistics.

Fiske, J. (1978). *Reading television*. London: Methuen.

Fitzpatrick, M.A., & Ritchie, L.D. (1994). Communication schemata within the family: Multiple perspectives on family-interaction. *Human Communication Research*, *20*, 275–301.

Flowers, L.S. (1987). Cognition and the construction of discourse. *Poetics, 16*, 109–130.

Fodor, J. (1983). *The modularity of mind.* Cambridge, MA: MIT Press.

Forrester, M.A. (1988). Young children's polyadic conversation monitoring skills. *First Language, 8*, 201–226.

Forrester, M.A. (1989). Adult-to-child group addressing speech in the pre-school. *Child Language, Teaching and Therapy, 5*, 64–78.

Forrester, M.A. (1992). *The development of young children's social cognitive skills.* Hove: Lawrence Erlbaum Associates.

Fortesque, M. (1984). *West Greenlandic Eskimo.* London: Croom Helm.

Fox, D.S. (1980). *Teacher–child discourse interaction and the language of pre-school learning impaired children.* Doctoral dissertation, Teachers College, Columbia University.

Frawley, W. (1992). *Linguistic semantics.* Hillsdale, NJ: Hove: Lawrence Erlbaum Associates.

Frege, G. (1952). On sense and reference. In P.T. Geach & M. Black (Eds.), *Translations from the philosophical writings of Gottlob Frege.* Oxford: Blackwell.

Gallaher, P.E. (1992). Individual differences in nonverbal behavior: Dimensions of style. *Journal of Personality and Social Psychology, 63*, 133–145.

Garnham, A. (1985). *Psycholinguistics: Central topics.* London: Methuen.

Garrod, S., Freudenthal, D., & Boyle, E. (1994). The role of different types of anaphor in the online resolution of sentences in a discourse. *Journal of Memory and Language, 33*, 39–68.

Garrod, S., & Sanford, A. (1990). Referential processes in reading: Focusing on roles and individuals. In D.A. Bolata, G.B Flores d'Arcias & K. Rayner (Eds.), *Comprehension processes in reading.* Hove: Lawrence Erlbaum Associates.

Garvey, C., & Berninger, S. (1981). Timing and turn-taking in children's conversation. *Discourse Processes, 4*, 27–57.

Geerhardt, B. (1995). *Code switching within the same language in and out of pretend play.* Unpublished citation, Childes Bulletin Board.

Genette, G. (1972). *Figures III.* Paris: Seuil.

Gergen, K.J. (1992). Toward a postmodern psychology. In S. Kvale (Ed.), *Psychology and postmodernism.* London: Sage.

Gibson, J.J. (1966). *The senses considered as perceptual systems.* Boston: Houghton-Mifflin.

Gibson, J.J. (1979). *The ecological approach to visual perception.* Boston: Houghton-Mifflin.

Giddens, A. (1988). Goffman as a systematic social theorist. In P. Drew & A. Wooton (Eds.), *Goffman: Exploring the interaction order.* Cambridge: Polity Press.

Gilbert, G.N., & Mulkay, M. (1984). *Opening Pandora's box.* Cambridge: Cambridge University Press.

Giles, H. (1979). *Language and social psychology.* Oxford: Basil Blackwell.

Goffman, E. (1976). Replies and responses. *Language in Society, 5*, 257–313.

Goffman, E. (1979). *Gender advertisements.* London: Macmillan.

Goffman, E. (1981). *Forms of talk.* Oxford: Basil Blackwell.

Goldberg, J. (1990). Interrupting the discourse on interruptions. *Journal of Pragmatics, 14*, 883–903.

Golinkoff, R.M. (1983). The pre-verbal negotiation of failed messages: Insights into the transition period. In R.M. Golinkoff (Eds.), *The transition from pre-linguistic to linguistic communication.* Hillsdale, NJ: Lawrence Erlbaum Associates.

Goodell, E.W., & Sachs, J. (1992). Direct and indirect speech in English-speaking children's retold narratives. *Discourse Processes, 15*, 395–422.

Goodman, K.S., & Gollasch, Y.M. (1980). Learning to read is natural. In L.B. Resnick & P.A. Weaver (Eds.), *Theory and practice of early reading* (Vol. 1). Hillsdale, NJ: Lawrence Erlbaum Associates.

Goodwin, C. (1981). *Conversational organization: Interaction between speakers and hearers.* London: Academic Press.

Gough, P.B. (1966). The verification of sentences: The effects of delay of evidence and sentence length. *Journal of Verbal Learning and Verbal Behavior, 5*, 492–496.

Gough, P.B. (1972). One second of reading. In J.F. Kavanagh & I.G. Mattingly (Eds.), *Language by ear and by eye.* Cambridge, MA: MIT Press.

Graddol, D., Cheshire, J., & Swann, J. (1987). *Describing language*. Milton Keynes: Open University Press.

Greasser, A.C., Hoffman, N.L., & Clark, L.F. (1980). Structural components of reading time. *Journal of Verbal Learning and Verbal Behaviour, 19*, 135–151.

Greene, J. (1986). *Language understanding: A cognitive approach*. Milton Keynes: Open University Press.

Grice, H.P. (1957). Meaning. *Philosophical Review, 66*, 377–388. Reprinted (1971) in D. Steinberg & L. Jakobovits (Eds.), *Semantics: An interdisciplinary reader*. Cambridge: Cambridge University Press.

Grice, H.P. (1975). Logic and conversation. In P. Cole & J.L. Morgan (Eds.), *Syntax and Semantics. Vol. 3: Speech Acts*. New York: Academic Press.

Grice, H.P. (1982). Meaning revisited. In N. Smith (Ed.), *Mutual knowledge*. London: Academic Press.

Griffin, C. (1986). Qualitative methods and femal experience: A study of young women from school to the job market. In S. Wilkinson (Ed.), *Feminist social psychology: Developing theory and practice*. Open University Press, Buckingham.

Gupta, M.A., & Schork, N.J. (1995). Touch deprivation has an adverse effect on body-image: Some preliminary observations. *International Journal of Eating Disorders, 17*, 185–189.

Hall, E.T. (1963). A system for the notation of proxemic behavior. *American Anthropologist, 65*, 1003–1026.

Hall, J.A., & Brainwald, K.H. (1981). Gender cues in conversation. *Journal of Personality and Social Psychology, 40*, 99–110.

Halliday, M.A.K. (1975). *Learning how to mean: Explorations in the development of language development*. London: Edward Arnold.

Halliday, M.A.K. (1978). *Language as social semiotic: The social interpretation of language and meaning*. Baltimore: University Park Press.

Halliday, M.A.K., & Hasan, R. (1977). *Cohesion in English*. London: Longman.

Halmari, H., & Smith, W. (1994). Code switching and register shift: Evidence from Finnish–English child bilingual conversation. *Journal of Pragmatics, 21*, 427–445.

Hampton, J.A. (1988). Overextension of conjunctive concepts: Evidence for a unitary model of conept typicality and class inclusion. *Journal of Experimental Psychology: Learning, Memory and Cognition, 14*, 12–32.

Hare, R.M., & Russell, D.A. (Eds.). (1970). *The dialogues of Plato* (B. Jowett, Trans.). London: Sphere.

Haremustin, R.T. (1994). Discourses in the mirrored: A postmodern analysis of therapy. *Family Processes, 33*, 19–35.

Harré, R. (1993). *The Discursive Turn*. London: Sage.

Harri-Augstein, T., Smith, P., & Thomas, L. (1982). Reading and learning. *Scottish Educational Review, 15*, 148–152.

Harris, R. (1983). Language and speech. In R. Harris (Ed.), *Approaches to language*. Oxford: Oxford University Press.

Harris, R (1989). How does writing restructure thought? *Language and Communication, 9*(2/3), 99–106.

Haukiouja, T. (1993). Pointing in sign language and gesture: An alternative interpretation. *Language and Communication, 13*, 19–25.

Havelock, E. (1983). *The Greek concept of justice*. Cambridge, MA: Harvard University Press.

Haviland, S.E., & Clark, H.H. (1974). What's new? Acquiring new information as a process of comprehension. *Journal of Verbal Learning and Verbal Behaviour, 13*, 512–521.

Hayes, J.R., & Flowers, L.S. (1986). Writing research and the writer. *American Psychologist, 41*(10), 1106–1113.

Hickerson, N.P. (1980). *Linguistic anthropology*. New York: Holt, Rinehart & Winston.

Himley, M. (1986). Genre as generative: One perspective on one child's early writing growth. In M. Nystrand (Ed.), *The structure of written communication*. London: Academic Press.

Hitch, G.J. (1992). Why isn't discourse analysis more popular in the study of memory? *The Psychologist, 15*, 449–450.

Hodge, R., & Kress, G. (1988). *Social semiotics.* Cambridge: Polity Press.

Holensten, E. (1980). Double articulation in language. In F. Coulmas & K. Ehlich (Eds.), *Writing in focus.* New York: Mouton.

Hollos, M. (1977). The comprehension and use of social rules in pronoun selection by Hungarian children. In S. Ervin-Tripp & C. Mitchell-Kernan (Eds.), *Child discourse.* New York and London: Academic Press.

Holmes, J. (1983). The structure of teacher's directives. In J.C. Richards & R.W. Schmidt (1983). (Eds.), *Language and communication.* London: Longman.

Holmes, J. (1992). *An introduction to sociolinguistics.* London: Longman.

Howe, C. (1993). *Language learning: A special case for developmental psychology?* Hove: Lawrence Erlbaum Associates.

Huey, E.B. (1908). *The psychology and pedagogy of reading.* Cambridge, MA: MIT Press. (Reprinted 1968.)

Huggins, A.W., & Adams, M.J. (1980). The growth of children's sight vocabulary. *Reading Research Quarterly, 20,* 262–281.

Humphrey-Jones, C. (1986). Make, made-do and mend: The role of the hearer in misunderstandings. In G. McGregor (Ed.), *Language for hearers* (Language and Communication Library, Vol. 8). Oxford: Pergamon Press.

Jackendoff, R (1987). *Consciousness and the computational mind.* Cambridge, MA: MIT Press.

Jacobs, A.M., & Grainger, J. (1994). Models of visual word recognition – sampling the state of the art. *Journal of Experimental Psychology – Human Perception and Performance, 20*(6), 1311–1334.

Jakobson, R. (1973). *Main trends in the science of language.* New York: Harper Torchbooks.

Jarvella, R.J., & Klein, W. (1982). *Speech, place and action: Studies in deixis and related topics.* London: Wiley.

Jefferson, G. (1975). Sequential aspects of storytelling in conversation. In J. Schenkein (Ed.), *Studies in the organisation of conversational interaction.* New York: Academic Press.

Jefferson, G., & Schegloff, E.A. (1975). *Sketch: Some orderly aspects of overlap in natural conversation.* Paper delivered at the December 1975 meetings of the American Anthropological Association, mimeo, Department of Sociology, University of California, Los Angeles.

Johnson, D.M. (1994). Who is We? Constructing communities in United States–Mexico border discourse. *Discourse & Society, 5,* 207–231.

Joula, J.F., Ward, N., & McNamara, T. (1982). Visual search and reading rapid, serial presentations of letter strings, words and text. *Journal of Experimental Psychology: General, 111,* 208–227.

Just, M.A., & Carpenter, P.A. (1980). A theory of reading: From eye fixations to comprehension. *Psychological Review, 87,* 329–354.

Kalma, A. (1992). Gazing in triads: A powerful signal of floor apportionment. *British Journal of Social Psychology, 31,* 21–39.

Karmiloff-Smith, A. (1983). *A functional approach to child language: A study of determiners and reference.* Cambridge: Cambridge University Press.

Katz, J. (1981). *Language and other abstract objects.* Totowa, NJ: Roman and Littlefield.

Kearney, R. (1988). *The parodic imagination.* London: Hutchinson.

Kelley, G.A. (1963). *A theory of personality: The psychology of personal constructs.* New York: Norton.

Kelley, R.T. (1988). Attentional overload and writing performance: Effects of rough draft and outline strategies. *Journal of Experimental Psychology: Learning, Memory and Cognition, 14*(2), 355–365.

Kendon, A. (1967). Some functions of gaze direction in social interaction. *Acta Psychologica, 26,* 22–63.

Kendon, A. (1995). Gestures as illocutionary and discourse structure markers in southern Italian conversation. *Journal of Pragmatics, 23,* 247–279.

Kenner, A.N., & Katsimaglis, G. (1993). Gender differences in proxemics: Taxi seat choice. *Psychological Reports, 72,* 625–626.

Kintsch, W., & van Dijk, T.A. (1978). Towards a model of discourse comprehension and production. *Psychological Review, 85,* 363–394.

Kintsch, W., & van Dijk, T.A. (1983). *Discourse comprehension.* New York: Academic Press.

Kintsch, W. (1988). The role of knowledge in discourse comprehension: A construction–integration model. *Psychological Review, 95,* 163–182.

Kopelman, M., Wilson, B., & Baddeley, A. (1990). *The autobiographical memory interview.* Bury St Edmunds: Thames Valley Test Company.

Kuhn, T.S. (1970). *The structure of scientific revolutions* (2nd ed.). University of Chicago Press.

Kvale, S. (Ed.). (1992). *Psychology and postmodernism.* London: Sage.

Lacan, J. (1977). *Écrits: A selection* (A. Sheridan, Trans.). London: Tavistock Publications.

Lachman, R., Lachman, J.L., & Butterfield, E.C. (1979). *Cognitive psychology and information processing: An introduction.* Hillsdale, NJ: Lawrence Erlbaum Associates.

Lain, L.B., & Harwood, P.J. (1992). Mug shots and reader attitudes toward people in the news. *Journalism Quarterly, 69,* 293–300.

Lakoff, G. (1987). *Women, fire, and dangerous things: What categories reveal about the mind.* Chicago and London: University of Chicago Press.

Lakoff, G., & Johnson, M. (1980). *Metaphors we live by.* Chicago: University of Chicago Press.

Landow, G.P. (1989). Hypertext in literary education, criticism and scholarship. *Computers in the Humanities, 23,* 173–198.

Landow, G.P. (1992). *Hypertext: The convergence of contemporary critical theory and technology.* Baltimore: Johns Hopkins University Press.

Langer, M. (1988). *Merleau-Ponty's phenomenology of perception: A guide and commentary.* London: Macmillan.

Lanham, R. (1993). *The electronic word.* Chicago: University of Chicago Press.

Lapsley, R., & Westlake, M. (1988). *Film theory: An introduction.* Manchester: Manchester University Press.

Lather, P. (1992). Postmodernism and the human sciences. In S. Kvale (Ed.), *Psychology and postmodernism.* London: Sage.

Levinson, S.C. (1983). *Pragmatics.* Cambridge: Cambridge University Press.

Lévi-Strauss, C. (1963). *Structural anthropology* (C. Jacobson & B. Grundfest Schoepf, Trans.). New York: Basic Books.

Levy, E.T., & McNeill, D. (1992). Speech, gesture and discourse. *Discourse Processes, 15,* 277–301.

Lindsay, P.H., & Norman, D.A. (1972). *Human information processing: An introduction to psychology.* New York: Academic Press.

Livingston, M., & Hubel, D. (1988). Segregation of form, color, movement and depth. *Science, 240,* 740–749.

Livingstone, S. (1990). *Making sense of television: The psychology of audience participation.* New York: Pergamon Press.

Luff, P., Gilbert N., & Frohlich D. (Eds.). (1990). *Computers and conversation.* London: Academic Press.

Luria, A.R. (1973). *The working brain.* Harmondsworth: Penguin.

Lutz, C. (1983). Parental goals, ethnopsychology and the development of emotional meaning. *Ethos, 11,* 246–263.

Lynn, M., & Mynier, K. (1993). Effect of server posture on restaurant tipping. *Journal of Applied Social Psychology, 23,* 678–685.

Lyons, J. (1977). Deixis and anaphora. In T. Myers (Ed.), *The development of conversation and discourse.* Edinburgh: Edinburgh University Press.

Lyotard, J. (1984). *The post-modern condition: A report on knowledge* (G. Bennington & B. Massumi, Trans.). Manchester: Manchester University Press.

Makritsilipakou, M. (1994). Interruption revisited: Affiliative vs disaffiliative intervention. *Journal of Pragmatics, 21,* 401–426.

Marr, D. (1982). *Vision: A computational investigation into the human representation and processing of visual information.* New York: W.H. Freeman.

Marschark, M. (1994). Gesture and sign. *Applied Psycholinguistics, 15*, 209–236.

Martlew, M. (1983). The development of writing: Communication and cognition. In F. Coulmas & K. Ehlich (Eds.), *Writing in focus.* (Trends in Linguistics). Berlin: Mouton.

Matsumoto, D. (1992). More evidence for the universality of a contempt expression. *Motivation and Emotion, 16*, 363–368.

Maynard, D.W. (1980). Placement of topic change in conversation. *Semiotica, 30*, 263–290.

McAleese, R. (1989). *Hypertext: Theory into practice.* Oxford: Blackwell Scientific, Intellect.

McClelland, J.L., & Rumelhart, D.E. (1986). *Parallel distributed processing: Psychological and biological models* (Vol. II). Cambridge: MIT Press.

McConkie, G.W. (1979). On the role and control of eye movements in reading. In P.A. Kolers, M.E. Wrolstad & H. Bouma (Eds.), *Processing of visible language.* New York: Plenum Press.

McConkie, G.W. (1981). Evaluating and reporting data quality in eye movement research. *Behaviour Research Methods and Instrumentation, 13*, 97–106.

McConkie, G.W. (1983). Eye movements and perception during reading. In K. Rayner (Ed.), *Eye movements in reading: Perceptual and language processes.* London: Academic Press.

McConkie, G.W., Underwood, N.R., Zola, D., & Wolverton, G.S. (1985). Some temporal characteristics of processing during reading. *Journal of experimental psychology: Human perception and performance, 11*, 168–186.

McGregor, G. (1983). Listener's comments on conversation. *Language and Communication, 3*, 271–304.

McKnight, C., Dillon, A., & Richardson, J. (1992). *Hypertext: A psychological perspective.* Cambridge: Cambridge University Press.

McNeill, D. (1985). So you think gestures are nonverbal? *Psychological Review, 92*, 351–371.

McNeill, D., Cassell, J., & Levy, E.T. (1993). Abstract deixis. *Semiotica, 95*, 5–19.

McNeill, D., & Levy, E.T. (1993). Cohesion and gesture. *Discourse Processes, 16*, 363–386.

Merleau-Ponty, M. (1962). *Phenomenology of perception* (C. Smith, Trans.). London: Routledge and Kegan Paul.

Mills, J. (1991). *Womanwords: A vocabulary of culture and patriarchal society.* London: Virago.

Mishler, E. (1984). *The discourse of medicine: Dialectics of medical interviews.* Norwood, NJ: Ablex Publishing.

Montepare, J.M., & Vega, C. (1988). Women's vocal reactions to intimate and casual male friends. *Personality and Social Psychology Bulletin, 14*, 103–113.

Montepare, J.M., Steinberg, J., & Rosenberg, B. (1992). Characteristics of vocal communication between young adults and their parents and grandparents. *Communication Research, 19*, 479–492.

Morgan, J., & Sellner, M. (1980). Discourse and linguistic theory. In R. Spiro, B. Bruce & W. Brewer (Eds.), *Theoretical issues in reading comprehension.* Hillsdale, NJ: Lawrence Erlbaum Associates.

Motley, M.T. (1993). Facial affect and verbal context in conversation: Facial expression as interjection. *Human Communication Research, 20*, 3–40.

Murata, K. (1994). Intrusive or cooperative: A cross-cultural study of interruption. *Journal of Pragmatics, 21*, 385–400.

Murray, S.O., & Covelli, L.H. (1988). Women and men speaking at the same time. *Journal of Pragmatics, 12*, 103–111.

Neisser, U. (1982). *Memory observed: Remembering in natural contexts.* Oxford: W.H. Freeman.

Neisser, U. (1992). The psychology of memory and the sociolinguistics of remembering. *The Psychologist, 15*, 451–452.

Neuman, W.L. (1993). *Social research methods: Qualitative and quantitative approaches* (2nd ed.). London: Sage.

Newfield, C. (1993). What was political correctness, race, the right, and managerial democracy in the humanities? *Critical Inquiry, 19*, 308–336.

Nguyen, T., Heslin, R., & Nguyen, M.L. (1975). Meanings of touch: Sex differences. *Journal of Communication*, Summer, 92–103.

Nickerson, R.S. (1994). Electronic bulletin boards: A case study of computer-mediated communication. *Interacting with Computers, 6,* 117–134.

Nofsinger, R.E. (1991). *Everyday conversation.* London: Sage.

Nystrand, M. (Ed.). (1986). *The structure of written communication.* New York: Academic Press.

Ortony, A., Slack, J., & Stock, O. (Eds.). (1992). *Communication from an artificial intelligence perspective.* Berlin: Springer-Verlag.

Oshima-Takane, Y. (1988). Children learn from speech not addressed to them: The case of personal pronouns. *Journal of Child Language, 15,* 95–108.

Parker-Rhodes, F. (1978). *Inferential semantics.* Hemel-Hempstead: Harvester-Wheatsheaf.

Pathas, G. (1995). *Conversational analysis.* London: Sage.

Pavel, T.G. (1985). Literary narratives. In T. van Dijk (Ed.), *Discourse and literature.* Amsterdam: John Benjamins.

Pea, R.D. (1985). Beyond amplification: Using the computer to reorganize mental functioning. *Educational Psychologist, 20,* 167–182.

Peirce, C. (1935–66). *Collected papers.* (C. Hartshorne, P. Weiss & A.W. Burks (Eds.)). Cambridge, MA: Harvard University Press.

Penelope, J. (1990). *Speaking freely: Unlearning the lies of the father's tongues.* New York: Pergamon.

Petrides, M., & Milner, B. (1982). Deficits on subject ordered tasks after frontal and temporal lobe lesions in man. *Neuropsychologia, 20,* 249–262.

Piaget, J. (1932). *The moral judgement of the child* (M. Gabian, Trans.). London: Routledge and Kegan Paul.

Piaget, J. (1952). *The origin of intelligence in the child* (M. Cook, Trans.). London: Routledge and Kegan Paul.

Pine, J.M. (1995). Variation in vocabulary development as a function of birth-order. *Child Development, 66,* 272–281.

Pinker, S. (1984). *Language learnability and language development.* Cambridge: Harvard University Press.

Polan, H.J., & Ward, M.J. (1994). Role of the mothers' touch in failure-to-thrive: A preliminary investigation. *Journal of the American Academy of Child and Adolescent Psychiatry, 33,* 1098–1105.

Pollatsek, A., & Rayner, K. (1990). Eye movements and lexical access in reading. In D.A. Bolata, G.B Flores d'Arcias & K. Rayner (Eds.), *Comprehension processes in reading.* Hove: Lawrence Erlbaum Associates.

Pomerantz, J.R. (1981). *Perceptual organization.* Hillsdale, NJ: Lawrence Erlbaum Associates.

Posner, M.I., Peterson, S.E., Fox, P.T., & Raichle, M.E. (1988). Localization of cognitive operations in the human brain. *Science, 240,* 1627–1631.

Postman, L. (1961). The present status of interference theory. In C.N. Cofer (Ed.), *Verbal learning and verbal behavior.* New York: McGraw-Hill.

Potter, J. & Wetherell, M. (1987). *Discourse and social psychology: Beyond attitudes and behaviour.* London: Sage.

Propp, V. (1968). *Morphology of the Russian folk tale* (2nd ed.; L.A. Wagner, Trans. and revd.). Austin: University of Texas Press.

Rabbitt, P. (1992). Cognitive aging. *International Journal of Psychology, 27,* 8–9.

Rafaeli, S. (1988). Interactivity: From new media to communication. In R.P. Hawkins & J.P. Wiemann (Eds.), *Advancing communication science: Merging mass and interpersonal processes (Sage Annual Review of Communication Research,* Vol. 16).

Rasking, G. (1987, Sept.). *The hype in hypertext.* 'Hypertext '87' Proceedings, Chapel Hill, NC.

Rayner, K. (1978). Eye movements in reading and information processing. *Psychological Bulletin, 85,* 618–660.

Rayner, K., & Pollatsek, A. (1981). Eye movement control during reading: Evidence for direct control. *Quarterly Journal of Experimental Psychology, 33A,* 351–373.

Reason, D. (1984). *Generalisation from the particular case Study: Some foundational considerations.* Occasional Paper, Keynes College, University of Kent.

Reason, D., & Forrester, M.A. (1991, April). *Of mice and menus.* Proceedings of the IVth European Conference on the Effects of Information Technology on Children, Bulgarian Academy of Sciences, Varna.

Reichmanadar, R. (1984). Technical discourse: The present progressive tense, the deictic that and pronominalization. *Discourse Processes, 7,* 337–369.

Richards, J.C., & Schmidt, R.W. (Eds.). (1983). *Language and communication.* London: Longman.

Ricoeur, P. (1970). What is a text? Explanation and understanding. In John B. Thompson (Ed. and Trans.), *Hermeneutics and the human sciences.* Cambridge: Cambridge University Press.

Ricoeur, P. (1971). What is a text? Explanation and interpretation. In D. Rasmussen (Ed.), *Mythic-Symbolic Language and Philosophical Anthropology.* The Hague: Nijhoff.

Ricoeur, P. (1976). *Interpretation theory: Discourse and the surplus of meaning.* Fort Worth: Texas Christian University Press.

Ricoeur, P. (1977). Writing as a problem for literary criticism and philosophical hermeneutics. *Philosophic Exchange, 2*(3), 15.

Ricoeur, P. (1978). *The rule of metaphor: Multi-disciplinary studies of the creation of meaning in language.* London: Routledge and Kegan Paul.

Rips, L.J., Shoben, E.J., & Smith, E.E. (1973). Semantic distance and the verification of semantic relations. *Journal of Verbal Learning and Verbal Behaviour, 12,* 1–20.

Robinson, W.P. (1978). *Language management.* Sydney: Allen and Unwin.

Rogers, Y. (1989). Icons at the interface. *Interacting with Computers, 1,* 105–117.

Roland, P.E. (1984). Metabolic measurement of the working frontal cortex in man. *Trends in Neuroscience, 7,* 430–435.

Romaine, S. (1989). *Bilingualism.* Oxford: Basil Blackwell.

Rosch, E. (1975). Cognitive reference points. *Cognitive Psychology, 7,* 532–57.

Rosch, E., & Mervis, C.B. (1975). Family resemblances: Studies in the internal structure of categories. *Cognitive Psychology, 7,* 573–605.

Rose, N. (1990). Psychology as a 'social' science. In I. Parker & J. Shotter (Eds.), *Deconstructing social psychology.* London: Routledge.

Rumelhart, D.E. (1975). Notes on a schema for stories. In D.G. Bobrow & A.M. Collins (Eds.), *Representation and understanding: Studies in cognitive science.* New York: Academic Press.

Rumelhart, D.E. (1977). Toward an interactive model of reading. In S. Dornic (Ed.), *Attention and performance VI.* New York: Academic Press.

Russell, J.A. (1994). Is there universal recognition of emotion from facial expression? A review of the cross-cultural studies. *Psychological Bulletin, 115,* 102–141.

Rutter, D. (1987). *Communication by telephone.* New York: Pergamon Press.

Sacks, H. (1972). On the analyzability of stories by children. In J.J. Gumperz & D. Hymes (Eds.), *Directions in sociolinguistics: The ethnography of communication.* New York: Holt, Rinehart and Winston.

Sacks, H. (1980). Button, button, who's got the button? *Social Enquiry, 50,* 3–5.

Sacks, H., Schegloff, E., & Jefferson, G. (1974). A simplest systematics for the organization of turn-taking for conversation. *Language, 50,* 696–735.

Saper, B. (1995). Joking in the context of political correctness. *Humor: International Journal of Humor Research, 8,* 65–76.

Sapir, E. (1921). *Language: An introduction to the study of speech.* New York: Harcourt, Brace and World.

Saussure, F. de (1974). *A course in general linguistics* (W. Baskin, Trans.). London: Fontana.

Scardamalia, M. (1981). How children cope with the cognitive demands of writing. In C.H. Fredereksen & J.F. Dominic (Eds.), *Writing: The nature, development, and teaching of written communication* (Vol. 2). Hillsdale, NJ: Lawrence Erlbaum Associates.

Schank, R., & Abelson, R. (1977). *Scripts, plans, goals and understanding: An inquiry into human knowledge structures.* Hillsdale, NJ: Lawrence Erlbaum Associates.

Scheflen, A.E. (1964). The significance of posture in communication systems. *Psychiatry, 27,* 316–331.

Schegloff, E.A. (1988). Goffman and the analysis of conversation. In P. Drew & A. Wootton (Eds.), *Ervin Goffman: Exploring the interaction order.* Cambridge: Polity Press.

Schegloff, E.A., & Sacks, H. (1973). Opening up closings. *Semiotica, 8*(4), 289–327.

Scheifflein, B., & Ochs, E. (1981). *Language socialization across cultures.* Cambridge: Cambridge University Press.

Scheppele, K.I. (1994). Practices of truth finding in a court of law: The case of revised stories. In T.R. Sarbin & J.I. Kitsuse (Eds.), *Constructing the social.* London: Sage.

Schiffrin, D. (1992). Anaphoric then: Aspectual, textual, and epistemic meaning. *Linguistics, 30,* 753–792.

Schober, M.I., & Clark, H.H. (1989). Understanding by addressees and overhearers. *Cognitive Psychology, 21,* 211–232.

Scinto, L.M. (Ed.). (1986). *Written language and psychological development.* New York: Academic Press.

Scotton, C.M., & Ury, W. (1977). Bilingual strategies: The social functions of code switching. *Linguistics, 193,* 5–20.

Searle, J. (1969). *Speech acts.* Cambridge: Cambridge University Press.

Searle, J.R. (1976). The classification of illocutionary cuts. *Language in Society, 5,* 1–24.

Sebeok, T. (1983). Pandora's box: How and why to communicate 10,000 years into the future. In The Sign of Three: Dupin, Holmes and Pierce. In U. Eco & T. Sebeok (Eds.). Indiana: Indiana University Press.

Sebeok, T. (1994). *An introduction to semiotics.* London: Pinter.

Seidenberg, M.S., Plaut, D.C, Petersen, A.S., McClelland, J.L., & McKrae, K. (1994). Nonword pronunciation and models of word recognition. *Journal of Experimental Psychology: Human Perception and Performance, 20,* 1177–1196.

Selden, R. (1985). *A reader's guide to contemporary literary theory.* Hemel Hempstead: Harvester Press.

Shannon, C.E., & Weaver, W. (1949). *The mathematical theory of communication.* Urbana: University of Illinois Press.

Sharkey, N.E. (1990). A connectionist model of text comprehension. In D.A. Bolata, G.B Flores d'Arcias & K. Rayner (Eds.), *Comprehension processes in reading.* Hove: Lawrence Erlbaum Associates.

Sharples, M. (1993). *Computers and writing.* Dordrecht: Kluwer Academic Press.

Sinclair, J.McH., & Coulthard, R.M. (1975). *Towards an analysis of discourse: The English used by teachers and pupils.* London and New York: Oxford University Press.

Sinha, C. (1988). *Language and representation.* Hemel Hempstead: Harvester-Wheatsheaf.

Skinner, B.F. (1957). *Verbal behavior.* New York: Appleton-Century-Crofts.

Slomkowski, C.L., & Dunn, J. (1992). Arguments and relationships within the family: Differences in young children's disputes with mother and sibling. *Developmental Psychology, 28,* 919–924.

Smith, F. (1971). *Understanding reading.* New York: Holt, Rinehart and Winston.

Smith, F. (1973). *Psycholinguistics and reading.* New York: Holt, Rinehart and Winston.

Smith-Lovin, L., & Brody, C. (1989). Interruptions in group discussions: The effects on gender and group composition. *American Sociological Review, 54,* 424–435.

Snow, C., & Ferguson, C.A. (1977). *Talking to children.* Cambridge: Cambridge University Press.

Sperling, G. (1960). The information available in brief visual persentations. *Psychological Monographs, 74* (whole no.).

Stanovitch, K.E. (1980). Toward an interactive–compensatory model of individual differences in the development of reading fluency. *Reading Research Quarterly, 16,* 32–71.

Stern, D. (1974). Mother and father at play: The dyadic interaction involving facial, vocal and gaze behaviors. In M. Lewis & L. Rosenblaum (Eds.), *The effect of the infant on its caregiver.* New York: Wiley.

Stevenson, R.J. (1993). *Language, thought and representation.* London: Wiley.

Stillings, N., Feinstein, M. H., Garfield, J.L., Rissland, E.L., Rosenbaum, D.A., Weisler, S.E., and Ward, L.B. (1987). Linguistics and representation: Syntax. In *Cognitive science: An introduction*. Cambridge, MA, and London: MIT Press.

Stitch, S. (1983). *From folk psychology to cognitive science*. Cambridge, MA: MIT Press.

Stringer, P. (1990). Prefacing social psychology: A textbook example. In I. Parker & J. Shotter (Eds.), *Deconstructing social psychology*. London: Routledge.

Sturrock, J. (1986). *Structuralism*. London: Paladin.

Swearingem, C.J. (1990). The narration of dialogue and narration within dialogue: The transition from story to logic. In B.K. Britton & A.D. Pellegrini (Eds.), *Narrative thought and narrative language*. Hove: Lawrence Erlbaum Associates.

Tagg, J. (1988). *The burden of representation*. London: Macmillan.

Tang, C.S.K., Critelli, J.W., & Porter, J.F. (1995). Sexual aggression and victimization in dating relationships among Chinese college-students. *Archives of Sexual Behavior, 24*, 47–53.

Tanz, C. (1980). *Studies in the acquisition of deictic terms*. Cambridge: Cambridge University Press.

Taylor, I., & Taylor, M. (1990). *Psycholinguistics: Learning and using language*. Englewood, NJ: Prentice Hall.

Taylor, T.J., & Cameron, D. (1987). *Analysing conversation: Rules and units in the structure of talk* (Language and Communication Library, Vol. 9). Oxford: Pergamon Press.

ten Have, P. (1991). Talk and institution: A reconsideration of the 'Asymmetry' of doctor–patient interaction. In D. Boden & D.H. Zimmerman (Eds.), *Talk and social structure*. London/Cambridge: Polity Press.

Thibadeau, R., Just, M.A., & Carpenter, P.A. (1982). A model of the time course and content of reading. *Cognitive Science, 6*, 157–203.

Tiersma, P.M. (1993). Nonverbal communication and the freedom of speech. *Wisconsin Law Review, 6*, 1525–1589.

Todd, A.D. (1984). The prescription of contraception: Negotiating between doctors and patients. *Discourse Processes, 7*, 171–200.

Toolan, M. (1988). *Narrative: A critical linguistic introduction*. London: Routledge.

Trask, R.L. (1993). *A dictionary of grammatical terms in linguistics*. London: Routledge.

Trevarthen, C., & Hubley, P. (1978). Secondary intersubjectivity: Confidence, confiding and acts of meaning in the first year. In A. Lock (Ed.), *Action, gesture and symbol: The emergence of language*. London: Academic Press.

Underwood, G. (1985). Eye movements during the comprehension of written language. In A. Ellis (Ed.), *Psychology of language* (Vol. 1). London: Academic Press.

Underwood, G., & McConkie, G.W. (1981). *The span of letter recognition of good and poor readers* (Tech. Rep. No. 251). Urbana-Champaign: University of Illinois, Center for the Study of Reading.

Valdes, M.J. (1991). *A Ricoeur reader: Reflection and imagination*. Hemel Hempstead: Harvester Wheatsheaf.

van Dijk, T.A. (1976). Narrative micro-structures: Logical and cognitive foundations. *PTL: A Journal for Descriptive Poetics and Theory of Literature, 4*, 13–46.

Verjat, I. (1994). Confrontation of two approaches to spatial location. *Année Psychologique, 94*, 403–423.

Vygotsky, L.S. (1962). *Thought and language* (E. Haufmann & G. Vakar, Trans.). Cambridge, MA: MIT Press.

Vygotsky, L.S. (1978). Mind in society. In M. Cole, V. John-Steiner, S. Scriber & E. Souberman, (Eds.), *The development of higher psychological processes*. Cambridge, MA: Harvard University Press.

Vygotsky, L.S. (1981). The genesis of higher mental functions. In J. Wertsch (Ed.), *The concept of activity in Soviet psychology*. New York: M.E. Sharpe Inc.

Wales, R. (1983). Deixis. In P. Fletcher & M. Garman (Eds.), *Language acquisition*. 2nd ed. Cambridge: Cambridge University Press.

Watson, J., & Potter, R.J. (1962). An analytic unit for the study of interaction. *Human Relations, 15,* 245–264.

Welch, K.E. (1990). *The contemporary reception of classical rhetoric: Appropriations of ancient discourse.* Hove: Lawrence Erlbaum Associates.

Well, A.D. (1983). Perceptual factors in reading. In K. Rayner (Ed.), *Eye movements in reading.* New York: Academic Press.

West, C. (1990). Not just 'doctor's orders': Directive-response sequences in patients' visits to women and men physicians. *Discourse & Society, 1,* 85–112.

West, C. (1995). Women's competence in conversation. *Discourse & Society, 6,* 107–131.

West, C., & Frankel, R.M. (1991). Miscommunication in medicine. In N. Coupland, H. Giles & J. Wiemann (Eds.), *Miscommunication and problematic talk.* Newbury Park, CA: Sage.

West, C., & Zimmerman, D.H . (1985). Gender, language and discourse. In T.A. van Dijk (Ed.), *Handbook of discourse analysis. Vol. 4: Discourse analysis and society.* London: Academic Press.

White, H. (1980). Value of narrativity. In W.J.T. Mitchell (Ed.), *On narrative.* Chicago: University of Chicago Press.

Whitney, D.C., & Wartella, E. (1992). Media coverage of the political correctness debate. *Journal of Communication, 42,* 83–94.

Whorf, B. (1956). *Language, thought and reality.* Cambridge, MA: MIT Press.

Williams, J.N. (1993). Processing of anaphoric nouns in extended texts: The role of sentence information. *Language and Speech, 36,* 373–391.

Williams, M. (1989). Vygotsky's social theory of mind. *Harvard Educational Review, 59*(1), 108–126.

Williamson, J. (1978). *Decoding advertisements.* London: Marion Boyars.

Willis, F.N., & Rawdon, V.A. (1994). Gender and national differences in attitudes toward same-gender touch. *Perceptual and Motor Skills, 78,* 1027–1034.

Wing, L. (1988). The autistic continuum. In L. Wing (Ed.), *Aspects of autism: Biological research.* London: Gaskell.

Wittgenstein, L. (1953). *Philosophical investigations* (G.E.M. Anscombe, Trans.). Oxford: Basil Blackwell/New York: Macmillan.

Wootton, T. (forthcoming). *Early requesting and the sequential organisation of mind.* Cambridge: Cambridge University Press.

Wright, S. (1987). Now now not just now: The interpretation of temporal deictic expressions in South-African English. *African Studies, 46,* 163–178.

Yussen, S.R., Mathews, S.R., & Hiebert, E. (1982). Metacognitive aspects of reading. In W. Otto & S. White (Eds.), *Reading expository material.* London: Academic Press.

Zeevat, H., & Scah, R. (1992). Integrating pragmatics into update semantics. In A. Ortony, J. Slack & O. Stock (Eds.), *Communication from an artificial intelligence perspective.* Berlin: Springer-Verlag.

Zimmerman, D.H., & West, C. (1975). Sex roles, interruptions and silences in conversation. In B. Thorne & N. Henley (Eds.), *Language and sex: Difference and domninance.* Rowley, MA: Newbury House.

Index

Abelson, R. 45, 162, 207
Abkarian, G.G. 66, 197
Abrams, D.A. 192, 197
accountability 79, 80
acquisition of language 48,
    120
Adams, M.J. 156, 157, 158,
    160, 197, 203
adjacency pairs 98–99
    and greeting exchanges
        100
    first and second pair parts
        100–101
advertising 137, 139
affordances in conversation
    109–112
Agha, A. 71, 197
Allwood, J. 124, 197
Althusser, L. 164, 197
Andersen, P.B. 194, 197
Anderson, J.R. 180, 197
Anderson, R.C. 155, 159,
    197
Andersson, L.G. 124, 197
Appiganesi, R. 185, 197
appropriation 182
Argyle, M. 80, 81, 82,
    197
Aristotle 4, 10, 41
Armstrong, D.F. 83, 197
artificial intelligence 9, 44,
    78, 93
Atkinson, J.M. 99, 100,
    197
Atkinson, R.C. 152, 191,
    197
Austin, J.L. 52, 197
autoglottic inquiry
    167–168
autonomy principle 30

baby-talk 120
Baddeley, A. 11, 191, 192,
    197
Barbadian 116

Barthes, R. 10, 48, 87, 142,
    161, 197
Beattie, G. 78, 82, 84, 94,
    197
behaviourism 2, 7, 36
Bell, S. 194
Berger, J. 140, 198
Berger, P.L. 34, 197
Berninger, S. 111, 210
Bernstein, R. 128, 198
Billig, M. 190, 192, 198
Birdwhistell, E.L. 88, 197
Bissex, G. 170, 198
Bleich, D. 163, 198
Bloor, D. 45, 198
Bolata, D.A. 165, 198
Boulter, J. 176, 177, 198
Bowerman, M. 75, 199
Boyle, E. 61, 201
Brainwald, K.H. 119, 202
Bransford, J.D. 159, 164,
    198
Brener, R. 75, 198
Brody, C. 105, 119, 208
Brown, P. 47, 55, 60, 63, 66,
    71, 72, 119, 194, 198
Brown, P.J. 178, 198
Brown, R. 33, 35, 74, 198
Bruner, J. 32, 54, 200
Buhler, F. 168, 198
Burgin, V. 140, 198
Burgoon, J.K. 86, 198
Bush, V. 176, 198
Butterfield, E. 32, 204
Byatt, A.S. 174

Cameron, D. 80, 115, 116,
    209
Campbell, R. 126, 198
Carlson, T.B. 49, 109, 199
Carlson-Radvansky, L.A. 65,
    198
Carpenter, P.A. 152, 154,
    209
Carr, T.H. 160, 198

Carter, A.T. 61, 198
Cassell, J. 69, 205
Cattell, J.M. 165, 199
Charney, R. 75, 93, 198
Cheshire, J. 86, 202
Chiat, S. 75, 199
Choi, S. 75, 199
Chomsky, N. 4, 9, 24, 25, 36,
    37, 38, 58, 60, 130, 132,
    133, 156, 184, 199
Christie, D.F.M. 191, 199
Clark, E.V. 75, 199
Clark, H.H. 49, 55, 109, 160,
    199
Clark, N.F. 157, 202
code-switching 72–73
    bi-lingual 73
cognition and
    neurophysiology 31
cognitive 9, 28, 151, 158
    account of language 12,
        193
    psychology 9, 31, 55, 151,
        192
    representations of
        grammar 17, 128
    science 9, 28, 127
Collins, A. 172, 173, 199
Collins, A.M. 152, 199
Collins, R. 35, 99, 117,
    118
Collis, G. 75, 199
communication 2, 131, 194,
    196
    and facial expression
        89
    and intention 34, 50
    definition of 2, 131
    metaphors 43
    non-verbal 90
competence 14, 26, 119
computational linguistics
    4
computer 3, 4, 143,
connectionist 152, 192

conversational analysis 2, 14,
16, 55, 115
and interruption 119
and learning 107
and sex differences 105,
119
and topic change 105–106
background to 78–81
closing sequences 101
influence of 95
preference organisation
101
role of hearer in 108
conversational contexts 80,
111, 113, 115, 117
and affordances 111–112
and children's skills in 111
and participation 113
and power 115–117
immediacy of 80,
conversational implicature
52, 72,
co-operative maxims 51
co-operative principle 50–51
Coulthard, M.C. 188, 208
Covelli, L.H. 119, 205
Cox, C. 128, 199
Craig, H.K. 109, 199
Crawford, C.B. 86, 199
Critelli, J.W. 86, 209
critical analysis 3, 162,
critical theory 92, 161, 183,
196
Cromer, W. 157, 199
Crouch, I. 126, 200

D'Souza, D. 128, 129, 200
Dahl, O. 124, 197
Darwin, C. 88, 199
de Beaugrande, R. 156, 173,
199
de Villiers, G. 75, 199
de Villiers, P.A. 75, 199
DeBarnadi, J. 33, 48, 72, 199
deconstructionism 4, 10, 138,
deictic terms 55, 58,
deixis 2, 58
acquisition of 74–75
and conversation 76
and locatives 75
and perspective taking 75
and pronominals 63
and proximity 75
and reference 61
and story telling 68

and the deictic centre
61–62
discourse 68
in writing 61
place and space 64–65
time 66–68
Dennis, E.E. 128, 199
Derrida, J. 10, 92, 138, 161,
194, 199
Descartes, R. 26,
Descombes, A. 10, 188, 199
descriptive linguistics 2, 7
diachronic 8
Dillon, A. 182, 205
discourse 137
analysis 55, 188, 193
analysis in social
psychology 189
deixis 68
discursive 11, 15, 166, 191
psychology 191, 193
Doland, V.M. 178, 199
Donaldson, M. 74, 200
Dore, J. 34, 200
double-articulation 168
Drew, P. 99, 100, 105, 197
Dubois, B.L. 126, 200
Dunn, J. 109, 121, 200

Eco, U. 92, 139, 140, 161,
162, 200
Edwards, D. 11, 93, 188,
191, 192, 193, 200
Ehrlich, S. 126, 127, 199
Ekman, P. 88, 89, 200
Ellis, H.D. 191, 199
Enrico, J. 66, 200
entailment 52
epistemic subject 41, 48,
Ervin-Tripp, S. 54, 120, 200
ethnomethodology 11, 55,
78–79, 95, 115, 193
explanation and
understanding 124
eye–mind assumption 154

face 71–72
facial expression 88–90
biological view 88
cultural view 88–89
Feldman, C. 174, 200
Feldman, C.J. 32, 200
felicity conditions 53
feminist criticism 93, 116,
163

Ferguson, C.A. 120, 208
Fillmore, C.J. 70, 200
film theory 146
Finnegan, R. 167, 200
Fisher, I.E. 115, 200
Fisher, J.D. 86, 200
Fisher, S. 121, 209
Fiske, J. 140, 200
Fitzpatrick, M.A. 121, 200
Flores, d'Arcais, G.B. 165,
198
Flowers, L. 164, 172, 173,
178, 180, 194, 201
Fodor, J. 36, 201
Forrester, M.A. 54, 64, 75,
76, 109, 143, 201
Fortesque, M. 48, 201
Foucault, M. 48, 138, 161
Fox, D.S. 63, 201
frames and framing 117, 122
Frankel, R.M. 105, 210
Frawley, W. 38, 39, 41, 42,
44, 47, 48, 201
Frege, G. 49, 201
Freudenthal, D. 61, 201
Friesen, W.V. 88, 200
Frolich, D. 194, 204
functionalism 52

Gallaher, P.E. 82, 201
Garnham, A. 24, 201
Garret, C. 185, 197
Garrod, S. 61, 69, 160, 201
Garvey, C. 111, 210
gaze 85–86
Geerhardt, B. 73, 201
gender 117, 119, 126
Genette, G. 175, 201
Gentner, D. 172, 173, 199
Gergen, K.J. 186, 187, 201
Gibson, J.J. 110, 201
Giddens, A. 80, 201
Gilbert, G.N. 193, 194, 201
Giles, H. 34, 201
Gillman, A. 74, 201
Goffman, E. 35, 63, 80, 85,
108, 109, 116, 117, 118,
122, 123, 201
Goldberg, J. 104, 108, 120,
123, 201
Gollinkoff, R.M. 61, 83, 201
Goodell, E.W. 76, 201
Goodman, K.S. 156, 210
Goodwin, C. 111, 201
Goolasch, Y.M. 156, 210

Gough, P.B. 91, 155, 156, 201
Graddol, D. 86, 87, 88, 89, 94, 202
grammar 17
and ideology 127–128
competence 17, 127
definition of 19
universal 47, 60
Granger, J. 155, 203
graphical user interface (GUI) 143
Greasser, A.C. 157, 202
Greene, J. 12, 38, 202
Grice, H.P. 38, 51, 57, 202
Griffin, C. 193, 202
group-addressing speech 64
Gupta, M.A. 87, 202

Haida 66
Hall, E.T. 84, 202
Hall, J.A. 119, 202
Halle, M. 156, 199
Halliday, M.K. 56, 72, 160, 202
Halmari, H. 73, 202
Hampton, J.A. 47, 202
Haremustin, R.T. 121, 201
Harri-Augstein, T. 161, 202
Harris, R. 1, 167, 202
Harwood, P.J. 89, 204
Hasan, R. 160, 202
Haukiouja, T. 61, 202
Havelock, E. 174, 202
Haviland, S.E. 160, 199
Hayes, J.R. 172, 173, 202
Helsin, R. 86, 205
Heritage, J. 105, 200
Hesling, R. 86, 200
Hiebert, E. 160, 210
Himley, M. 170, 202
Hitch, G.J. 192, 202
Hodge, R. 11, 131, 132, 135, 136, 137, 171, 203
Hoffman, L.C. 157, 202
Hogg, M.A. 192, 197
Holenstein, E. 168, 169, 203
Hollos, M. 61, 74, 203
Holmes, J. 11, 54, 203
honorofication 71
Howe, C. 37, 203
Hubel, D. 30, 203
Hubley, P. 111, 209
Huey, E.B. 165, 203
Huggins, A.W. 160, 203

human–computer interaction 78
Humphrey-Jones, C. 108, 203
hypermedia(text) 4, 176–182, 183

ideological complexes 136
illocutionary force 53
immediacy assumption 154
implicature 50, 71
indirect meaning 42, 48
information processing 9, 32, 190
information technology 3, 166
interface design 42
interruption 119
intersubjectivity 79
Irwin, D.A. 65, 198

Jackendoff, R. 47, 203
Jacobs, A.M. 155, 203
Jakobson, R. 169, 203
Japanese 70, 183
conversational style 120
Jarvella, R.J. 93, 203
Jefferson, G. 94, 104, 107, 108, 114, 203
Johnson, D.M. 60, 63, 204
Johnson, M. 32, 47, 127, 204
Johnson, M.K. 159, 164, 198
Joula, J.F. 153, 203
Joyce, J. 2
Just, M.A. 152, 154, 209

Kalma, A. 85, 203
Kant, E. 26, 192
Karmiloff-Smith, A. 60, 62, 75, 203
Katsimaglis, G. 85, 203
Kearney, R. 162, 203
Kelley, G.A. 190, 203
Kelley, R.T. 172, 203
Kendon, A. 83, 85, 203
Kenner, A.N. 85, 203
King, R. 126, 127, 199
Kintsch, W. 155, 165, 174, 180, 204
Klein, W. 93, 203
Kopelman, M. 191, 204
Korean 70
Kress, G. 11, 131, 132, 135, 136, 137, 171, 204
Kristeva, J. 10, 204

Kuhn, T.S. 186, 204
Kvale, S. 32, 185, 186, 187, 204

Lacan, J. 34, 48, 146, 147, 204
Lachman, J. 32, 204
Lachman, R. 32, 204
Lain, L.B. 89, 204
Lakoff, G. 32, 40, 47, 127, 204
Landow, G. 177, 180, 182, 194, 204
Langer, M. 33, 204
language 1, 12, 26, 188
as social action 188
cognition dominant view of 26
cognitive account of 12, 35, 193
definition of 1
games 26, 45
language dominant view of 26, 32, 132, 188
structuralist account of 9, 132
langue 8, 14, 31, 37, 133, 169
Lanham, R. 176, 203
Lapsley, R. 146, 147, 148, 204
learning 55, 74, 107, 166, 170
and conversation 107
language 74
Lévi-Strauss, C. 10
Levinson, S. 46, 47, 50, 51, 52, 54, 56, 58, 60, 62, 63, 67, 68, 70, 71, 72, 76, 79, 100, 101, 119, 188, 194, 204
Levy, E.T. 69, 83, 204, 205
lexical processing 12, 156
lexicon 12, 154
Lindsay, P.H. 9, 204
linguistic anthropology 3
linguistics 5, 33, 42, 162, 183, 193
literary criticism 4, 42, 150
Livingston, M. 30, 204
Livingstone, S. 162, 204
local management system 96–97
locutionary act 53
logonomic rules 136
Luckman, T. 34, 197
Luff, P. 194, 196, 204

Luria, A.R. 31, 204
Lutz, C. 120, 204
Luyia 73
Lynn, M. 87, 204
Lyons, J. 64, 204
Lyotard, J. 147, 204

MacNamara, T. 153, 203
Makritsilipakou, M. 119, 204
Marr, D. 30, 204
Marschark, M. 83, 204
Marshall, C.R. 55, 199
Martlew, M. 171, 204
Mathew, S.R. 160, 210
Matsumoto, M. 88, 204
Maynard, D.W. 105, 106, 204
McAleese, R. 182, 205
McClelland, J.L. 152, 191, 207
McConkie, G.W. 152, 153, 154, 209
McGregor, G. 108, 205
McKnight, C. 182, 205
McKrae, K. 152, 207
McNeill, D. 61, 83, 205
meaning 14, 38–44, 86, 140
    and philosophy 40
    and photography 140
    and semiotics 39
    and words 38
    as discourse 14
    consensually recognised 86
    grammaticalised 44
    individualist view of 41
    semiotic definition of 40
    societal view of 41
    the concept of 38
memory and discourse 191–192
mental projection 42, 47
mentalism 7, 37
Merleau-Ponty, M. 33, 205
Mervis, C.B. 47, 207
metaphor 32, 47, 58, 128, 147, 190
    conduit 32, 43
    construction 95
    spatial purity 64
methodological solipsism 28–29, 31
methodology 25, 28, 91, 93

and language research 91–94
    and theory 25
    and solipsism 28
Middleton, D. 11, 192, 200, 205
Mills, J. 125, 126, 127, 205
Milner, B. 31, 205
Mishler, E. 121, 205
Mitchell-Kernan, C. 54, 120, 200
Model Reader 162
modernity 186
Montepare, J.M. 119, 121, 205
Mopan Maya 62
Morgan, J. 159, 205
Motley, M.T. 89, 205
Mulkay, N. 193, 201
Murata, K. 119, 205
Murray, S.O. 119, 205
Mynier, K. 87, 204

narrative 2, 147–148, 175–176,
    and conversation 105, 108,
    definitions of 147
Neisser, U. 191, 192, 205
Neuman, W.L. 91, 205
neuropsychology 4, 31
Newfield, C. 128, 205
Nguyen, M.L. 86, 205
Nguyen, T. 86, 205
Nickerson, R.S. 180, 206
Nofsinger, R.E. 101, 105, 205
non-verbal behaviour 81, 123
    and linguistic analysis 82
    communicative functions
        of 81–82, 90
    significance of 82–88
Norman, D.A. 9, 206
Nystrand, M. 170, 206

Ochs, E. 120, 208
Ortony, A. 45, 206
Oshima-Takane, Y. 16, 63, 75, 93, 206
overhearing 109
overlaps 103–104

parole 8, 14, 31, 37, 133, 134, 169
participant roles 63
Pathas, G. 99, 100, 102, 206

Pavel, T.G. 148, 175, 206
Pea, R.D. 176, 206
Pearson, P. 155, 159, 197
Peirce, C. 135, 138, 206
Penelope, J. 127, 206
perceptual affordances 110
perceptual span 153
performance 14
perlocutionary act 53
Petersen, A.S. 152, 207
Petrides, M. 31, 206
philosophy 9, 10, 33, 40, 93
    and meaning 40
    and psychological theory 93
    Contintental 10
    existential 33
Piaget, J. 74, 171, 206
Pine, J. 75, 206
Pinker, S. 60, 206
Plato 4, 10, 40, 41, 166
Plaut, D.C. 152, 207
Polan, H.J. 87, 206
politeness phenomena 71
political correctness 4, 128–129
Pollatsek, A. 153, 154, 160, 198, 206
Porter, J.F. 86, 209
Postman, L. 9, 206
postmodernism 4, 162, 186
    definition of 185
post-structuralism 4, 11, 142, 162, 164, 177, 196
postural congruence 87
Potter, J. 11, 55, 188, 191, 193, 199, 206
Potter, R.J. 105, 209
power relations in language 117–118, 123, 126–127, 186
    and text 125–129
    doctor–patient interaction 121–123
    interruption 119–120
    parent–child talk 120–121
pragmatics 14, 15, 54
    definitions of 54–55
    domain of 55
predicative assimilation 147
presupposition 45–46,
propositional attitudes 27, 57
Propp, V. 175, 206
proxemics 83–85
    and gender 85

psychoanalysis 34, 183
and language 34
psycholinguistics 4, 184
emergence of 4
punctual verbs 44

Quillian, M.R. 152, 199

Rabbit, P. 191, 206
Rafaeli, S. 113, 206
Rasking, G. 178, 206
Raynder, K. 165, 198
Rayner, K. 153, 154, 206
reading 149
and critical theory
161–164
and eye movements
152–154, 157
and hypertext 178
and memory models 152,
156
and writing 182
methods of investigating
152–153
models of 154–160
Reason, D. 46, 143, 207
Reichmanandar, R. 69, 207
recursion 17, 93
definition of 20–24
significance of 24
representation 27
response cries 80
rhetoric 189–190
Richards, J.C. 54, 207
Richardson, J. 182, 205
Ricoeur, P. 123, 124, 125,
147, 149, 180, 190, 207
Rips, L. 27, 207
Ritchie, L.D. 121, 200
Robinson, W. 34, 208
Rogers, Y. 142, 207
Roland, P.E. 31, 207
Romaine, S. 72, 207
Rosch, E. 27, 36, 47, 207
Rosenberg, B. 121, 205
Rumelhart, D.E. 155, 158,
159, 164, 191, 207
Russell, J.A. 89, 207
Rutter, D. 80, 111, 207
Rytinne, M. 86, 200

Sachs, J. 76, 201
Sacks, H. 46, 96, 99, 101,
102, 103, 105, 111, 112,
113, 114, 115, 124, 207

Sanford, A. 160, 201
Saper, B. 128, 207
Sapir, E. 33, 207
Saussure, F. 7, 38, 92, 131,
132, 146, 169, 207
Scah, R. 44, 210
Scardamalia, M. 171, 207
Schaefer, E.F. 109, 199
Scheflen, A.E. 87, 208
Schegloff, E.E. 82, 96, 99,
101, 102, 104, 111, 112,
113, 114, 117, 124, 208
Scheifflein, B. 120, 208
schema theory 158–159
Scheppele, K.I. 193, 208
Schiffrin, D. 69, 191, 208
Schmidt, R.W. 54, 207
Schoeber, M.I. 109, 208
Schork, N.J. 87, 202
Schram, P.J. 126, 198
Scinto, L.M. 169, 207
Scotton, C.M. 72, 208
Searle, J. 52, 53, 207
Sebeok, T. 131, 138, 139,
149, 207
Seidenberg, M.S. 152, 207
Selden, R. 10, 42, 125, 132,
146, 161, 162, 163, 207
Sellner, M. 159, 205
semantics 13, 93
truth-conditional 49, 52,
55, 56
semiotics 131–132
physical basis of 131
semiotic triangle 41–42
Sengel, E.J. 75, 199
sense 42
Shank, R. 45, 164, 207
Shannon, 32, 208
Sharkey, N.E. 155, 207
Sharples, M. 180, 207
Shiffrin, R.M. 152, 197
Shoben, E. 27, 207
Sinclair, J.McH. 188, 208
sign 8, 135, 138
and icons 135, 143,
Peirce's analysis of
138–139
types of sign 139
signification processes
134–136
signified 8–9, 139, 146
signifier 8, 139, 146
Sinha, C. 26, 27, 41, 143,
192, 208

Skinner, B.F. 7, 36, 208,
Slack, J. 45, 206
Slomkowski, C.L. 121, 208
Smith, E. 27, 207
Smith, F. 157, 208
Smith, P. 161, 202
Smith, W. 73, 202
Smith-Lovin, L. 105, 119,
208
Snow, C. 120, 208
social anthropology 3, 183
social constructionist 27, 32
social honorofics 58, 70
social psychology 3, 188,
feminist 12, 115, 126, 187
social semiotics 2, 11, 93, 132
and film 145–148
and ideology 136–138
and photography 140–141
definition of 11–12
sociolinguistics 55, 115, 183
sociology 3, 34, 55
Sorenson, E.R. 88, 200
speech 83, 167
and gesture 83
and language 167
speech act definitions 54
Sperling, G. 155, 208
Stanovitch, K.E. 155, 157,
158, 208, 209
Statz, M. 109, 200
Steinberg, J. 121, 205
Stevenson, R. 42, 208
Stillings, N. 30, 208
Stock, O. 45, 206
Stokoe, W.C. 83, 197
story grammars 159
structuralism 7, 177, 185
definition of 7
influence of 10
movement 7, 131
structuralist approach 8,
164
structuration 111, 113
structure 25
surface and deep 25
Sturrock, J. 7, 10, 16, 148,
209
Swahili 73
Swann, J. 86, 202
Swearingern, C.J. 174, 209
symbolic 4, 34
languages 4
order 34
synchronic 8

syntax 12–13, 20, 55, 92
    syntactic processing 13

Tagg, J. 140, 209
talk 2, 58,
    and body contact 86
    and conversation 109
    and gaze 85–86
    and gesture 82
    and posture 87
    and text 123–124, 167
    and thinking 61
    as social practice 116,
        127
Tamil 63
Tang, C.S.K. 86, 209
Tanz, C. 55, 60, 61, 75, 76,
    209
Taylor, I. 38, 209
Taylor, M. 38, 209
Taylor, T.J. 80, 115, 209
television 140
ten Have, P. 121, 209
text 2, 164, 196
    and discourse 128
    and talk 123
    and women 126–127
    open and closed 162–163
    world of 124
Thibadeau, R. 152, 209
thinking 2, 26
    and language 33, 58, 192
Thomas, L. 161, 202
Tiersma, P.M. 90, 209

Todd, A.D. 121, 209
Toolan, M. 175, 209
touching 86
    and intimacy 86–87
    deprivation 87
    privileges 86
transformational grammar
    22, 37, 184
transition-relevant place 96
Trask, R.L. 12, 209
Trevarthen, C. 111, 209
turn-taking 95–96, 115
    and interruption 103
    and pre-closings 103

Underwood, G. 153, 154,
    209
Ury, W. 72, 209

Valdes, M.J. 125, 182, 209
van Dijk, T.A. 165, 174, 175,
    211
Vega, C. 119, 205
Verjat, I. 64, 209
Vygotsky, L. 49, 166, 171,
    209

Wales, R. 75, 209
Ward, M.J. 87, 206
Ward, N. 153, 203
Wartella, E. 128, 210
Washington, J.A. 109, 199
Watson, J. 105, 209
Weatherell, M. 55, 206

Weaver, W. 32, 208
Welch, K.E. 190, 210
Well, A.D. 153, 210
West, C. 105, 115, 119, 122,
    123, 210
Westlake, M. 146, 147, 148,
    204
White, H. 147, 210
Whitney, D.C. 128, 210
Whorf, B. 33, 48, 210
Wilcox, S.E. 83, 197
Williams, J.N. 61, 69, 210
Williams, M. 25, 93, 210
Williamson, J. 137, 140, 210
Wilson, B. 191, 204
windows and menus 143–144
Wing, L. 82, 210
Wittgenstein, L. 26, 45, 48,
    186, 189, 193, 210
Wolverton, G.S. 154, 209
word recognition 154, 160,
    164–165
Wright, S. 67, 210
writing 166,
    and narrative 174–176
    development of 169–171
    electronic 178, 180

Yussen, S.R. 160, 210

Zeevat, H. 43, 210
Zimmerman, D.H. 105, 115,
    119, 210
Zola, D. 154, 209

DATE DUE

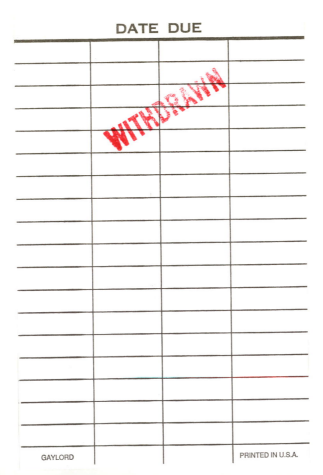